Praise for TEACH

"The attack on antiracist education is at our front [...] determined voice in this struggle than Jesse Hagopian's. Jesse is insightful, compassionate, and committed to building a better world. Each page in *Teach Truth* offers sharp and timely analysis that captures the urgency of our current moment, while also grounding us in the history that brought us here. This is a book that propels us forward." —**Bettina L. Love**, author of *Punished for Dreaming: How School Reform Harms Black Children*

"*Teach Truth* shows that the attack on critical race theory is part of a right-wing agenda involving voter suppression, antitrans laws, the erection of cop cities, criminalizing dissent, and privatizing education. And "color-blind" liberals who merely celebrate diversity without interrogating systems of power behind racial, gendered, class, and ableist hierarchies unwittingly aid and abet the war on truth. Writing from the trenches, Jesse Hagopian has given us a brilliant, incisive account of how we arrived here and a fearless field guide for how we fight back and reclaim education, truth, and democracy. They will ban this book; we must resist. There is more at stake than curriculum. We have a world to win." —**Robin D. G. Kelley**, author of *Freedom Dreams: The Black Radical Imagination*

"A scathing appraisal of the "mandatory illiteracy" legislation polluting our country, *Teach Truth* provides a road map for protecting truth and the freedom to learn in our classrooms. This work lives and breathes in the legacy of Howard Zinn, and Jesse's powerful words offer an empathic defense of history, justice, and our children's futures." —**Kimberlé Crenshaw**, coauthor of *#SayHerName: Black Women's Stories of Police Violence and Public Silence*

"Jesse Hagopian's *Teach Truth* is the book we need right now. It's the book we have always needed. It should not be controversial to tell teachers and legislators to teach truth. Yet in many states it is not only controversial; it is illegal. Hagopian clears away the cobweb of lies that have obscured our national history for generations of students." —**Diane Ravitch**, author of *Slaying Goliath: The Passionate Resistance to Privatization and the Fight to Save America's Public Schools*

"Memory is a terrain of struggle fought out in the archives, on the pages of history texts, and in the classroom. *Teach Truth* is a powerful call to action by an amazing teacher, historian, organizer, and movement intellectual. In it, Jesse Hagopian exposes the dangers of the current racist movement to silence and distort our collective history, labeling it "uncritical race theory." He also insists we cannot only complain and protest, but we must create, build, and change ourselves as we strive to change the world and seed a better future. A must-read for anyone concerned with education, justice, and our shared future. —**Barbara Ransby**, historian, professor, activist, and author of *Ella Baker and the Black Freedom Movement: A Radical Democratic Vision*

"A powerful and courageous call to action . . . audacious and essential. Ultimately, *Teach Truth* is more than just a book; it is a manifesto for those who dare to envision a just society. In a time when the integrity of our educational system is under siege, *Teach Truth* stands as an inspiring testament to the necessity of teaching and learning with honesty and courage." —**Jonathan Kozol**, author of *Savage Inequalities: Children in America's Schools*

"'Only truth and love govern us'—the mantra invoked by author Jesse Hagopian in an opening letter to his ancestors serves as both a searing rebuke and a call to action. In *Teach Truth*, Hagopian delivers a profoundly important critique of current efforts to erase history and make teaching the truth illegal. As teachers around the country face increasing consequences and intimidation for teaching the truth about a range of issues, from systemic racism to Palestine, this book presents a clear and defiant message: teaching the truth is nonnegotiable and is the starting point for creating the liberated world we imagine. —**Macklemore**, Grammy Award–winning artist, creator of "Hinds Hall" and "Hinds Hall 2"

"*Teach Truth* is a mighty stream flowing against the tide of a world fractured by falsehoods. It's a call to prioritize humanity, to embrace radical honesty, and to forge pathways toward a democratic future. This work channels the voices of those on the front lines of education, amplifying the shared humanity at the heart of learning. In a world where truth is often broken, this book invites us to reimagine the educational landscape as a space for healing, transformation, and the pursuit of justice." —**Michael Bennett**, Super Bowl winner and author of *Things That Make White People Uncomfortable*

"Given the current iteration of the educational colonization project, we must arm ourselves with the resources needed to resist, disrupt, dismantle, and rebuild. This book is an excellent resource for understanding the connections between truth suppression, colonization, racism, and neoliberal privatization. Furthermore, it lays the groundwork for healing from this ongoing assault on our right to teach truth. I look forward to using this book with the future students I challenge to embrace teaching truth in pursuit of education justice for all." —**Denisha Jones**, PhD, J.D., executive director of Defending the Early Years, Steering Committee of Black Lives Matter at School

TEACH TRUTH

The Struggle for Antiracist Education

JESSE HAGOPIAN

Haymarket Books
Chicago, Illinois

Published in 2025 by
Haymarket Books
P.O. Box 180165
Chicago, IL 60618
www.haymarketbooks.org

ISBN: 9798888902516

Distributed to the trade in the US through Consortium Book Sales and
Distribution (www.cbsd.com) and internationally through Ingram Publisher Services International (www.ingramcontent.com).

This book was published with the generous support of Lannan Foundation,
Wallace Action Fund, and Marguerite Casey Foundation.

Special discounts are available for bulk purchases by organizations and
institutions. Please email info@haymarketbooks.org for more information.

Cover and text design by Rachel Cohen.

Printed in Canada by union labor.

Library of Congress Cataloging-in-Publication data is available.

2 4 6 8 10 9 7 5 3 1

For my ancestors:
Writing this book has allowed me to delve into
the portal of history and draw nearer to you.
I am grateful to be closer to you now than ever before
and grateful for all you have taught me.
No one has the right to tear us apart by erasing your legacy.
My supreme aspiration is to guard your memory and make you proud.

I believe unconditionally in the ability of people to respond when they are told the truth. We need to be taught to study rather than believe, to inquire rather than to affirm.

—**Septima Clark**

CONTENTS

A Promise to My Ancestors

As I began writing this book during the summer of 2021, my dad, Gerald Lenoir, made a stunning discovery: he unearthed the long-buried knowledge of the location of the plantation where our family had been enslaved.

Through meticulous genealogical research, he found out my great-great-grandfather, Thomas H. Lenoir, was born into slavery on the Lenoir Plantation in Morgantown, Marion County, Mississippi, in March 1844. He also found evidence of Thomas's mother, Tempi, having been enslaved and leased out to another Lenoir plantation in Lawrence Country, Mississippi. After the Civil War, Thomas married my formerly enslaved great-great-grandmother, Laura Ratcliff (who then took his last name), and together they had fifteen children. My dad also found a source suggesting that the French Lenoir enslavers who imposed their name on our family got their name, which means "the black," from Moorish people who intermarried with Europeans. The white Lenoirs traveled from France to New York, then to the Carolinas, before settling in Morgantown, where they established a cotton and tobacco plantation.

We immediately felt called to travel to Morgantown, and to Lawrence County, to see the land where our people had toiled. As we made preparations for the journey, my dad made another stunning revelation: the legendary blues artist J. B. Lenoir's ancestors were likely enslaved on the same plantation as ours. As a blues artist myself, this connection resonated for me like a blue note plucked on a National guitar. J. B. is one of the most incisive social commentary blues musicians of all time, with songs about police violence, lynching, the Vietnam War, and civil rights activism, and he even put the blame for poverty on the president in his "Eisenhower Blues" song that the record company refused to release. In the days following my dad's revelation, I took a stage name by adopting his last name and using my initials to go by "J. D. Lenoir" for the Blue Tide—the blues band I play harmonica for with Daniel Rapport. I then wrote the lyrics for the song we recorded titled "Where I Got My Name (Down in Mississippi)." In the song I sing the lines, "My family fled / now I'm headed on back / I got to find the place where white owned Black." Those lyrics were my plan, anyway.

However, just as we were preparing to leave, the Delta variant of COVID-19 surged, forcing us to cancel the trip. When COVID-19 case rates dipped, we started to plan our trip again, but then my dad had a stroke that left him incapacitated with vertigo for months (and still dramatically reduces his energy), and we had to cancel the trip again. My brother, Jamana Lenoir, had also wanted to travel with us, but he had a severe phobia of flying. Then, on top of all that, I contracted COVID-19, which developed into a particularly debilitating form of long COVID—leaving me dizzy and fatigued—and we had to cancel the trip yet again.

During these months, expectations built as we longed for connection with our ancestors. Yet during this dizzying time we were simultaneously witnessing, with increasing distress, a multitude of legislative attempts to require educators to lie to students about the history of structural racism in the United States. Whether it was learning of educators who were pushed out of the classroom for teaching the truth about the cruelty of slavery, or it was our ancestors urging us on from the other side, my dad, brother, and I all came to the realization that despite the obstacles each one of us faced, we could no longer delay our journey to learn the truth about our family's history.

On June 1, 2023, the three of us, along with my dad's friend John Jernegan, traveled to Marion County, Mississippi, to find the Lenoir Plantation. As we neared our destination, a stop at a gas station outside of Morgantown brought a sobering reminder of the past's lingering shadows. My brother approached a Black woman there to inquire what she knew about our destination. She replied, "I don't know anything about Morgantown, except that it's not a place for us to go." These ominous words, coupled with the knowledge that during Jim Crow, Morgantown had been a "sundown town" (an all-white municipality that required Black people to be gone by sunset), stirred apprehension among our party as we loaded back up in the car and began the final approach to the very ground where our people had been held captive. As I stared out the window at the old oak trees, their branches draped with Spanish moss, a recognition began to creep over me that this journey was not only one of historical inquiry but also a confrontation with ghosts still haunting the corridors of America's collective memory.

In the weeks leading up to this moment, my dad connected with a man named Louis Morgan, whose lineage traced back to James Morgan—the very namesake of Morgantown. We didn't know what to expect when we met him, but shortly after arriving in Morgantown, Louis greeted us warmly and soon eased our nerves with his wholehearted embrace of our pilgrimage. He regaled us with the area's history and then led us to a barbed-wire fence that separated us by several hundred yards from the land where our ancestors had toiled and carved out their existence. Louis informed us that the man who owned the land didn't live there now, and it was doubtful we would get to set foot on the exact location of the plantation. I was deeply disappointed that we had come all this way and now were unable to feel the earth that my ances-tors had worked. As if reading my mind, Louis wisely warned us that we had better not consider going on someone's land without their permission. As we filmed, snapped pictures, and strained the shadows of our ancestors, mirac-ulously, the white man who now owns the land appeared and approached us from the other side of the fence. To be honest, I was uneasy about what his reaction to our presence—and our purpose for being there—might be.

He began by asking us what we were doing and where we were from. My dad, with a steadiness that belied the gravity of his words, declared, "I have traveled from California with my sons to show them the land where our kin were enslaved." In that moment, I marveled at his courage to hand this white man the heavy truth of our history. However, I wasn't sure that the truth would unlock the gate to his property and allow us to gain entrance to the land we had come so far to see. Remarkably, however, the landowner was moved by my dad's story and invited us to come around to the other side of the fence. When he opened the gate, it felt as if he was not just opening an entrance to his property but granting us passage back through time and beyond the barbed wire that surrounds so much of American history. He then led us back to a clearing that he told us was the location of a cemetery where the enslaved people buried their loved ones. Upon reaching the grave-yard, we saw that only one weathered headstone remained.

We requested, and were granted, some time as a family at the graveyard to pay our respects and hold a ceremony to honor our enslaved ancestors who lay beneath us, and whose experience during slavery has profoundly shaped our lives; I count these moments among the most precious of my life. We began our ceremony with each of us placing valued items in a box, which bore the symbol of the tree of life, as an offering to our ancestors. We decided that before burying the box, I would read aloud a letter I had written to our ancestors on behalf of our family. Under the unforgiving glare of the midday sun, sweat trickling down my brow, I felt the weight of the past pressing on me. As I prepared to read, I stole a glance at my father and brother. Their presence was a source of strength, yet also a reminder of the heaviness of the responsibility to represent my family to our ancestors. My heart began to pound in my chest, a drumbeat echoing the pulse of generations past. I took a breath, wiped my brow, cleared my throat, and then began reading these words:

Beloved ancestors,

Many obstacles have been placed in the way of us returning to the land where you were enslaved, abused, and forced to work to enrich the white Lenoir enslavers. The pandemic, a stroke, a fear of flying, and long COVID delayed our journey here. Before that, the education system withheld any knowledge of where you came from, the cruelty you endured, or the creativity and beautiful resistance you contributed to the world. The system of white supremacy used many tactics to deceive us and prevent our family from making this pilgrimage to where you were held captive and denied manumission.

Despite the many obstacles and the plots to hide this place from us— and deny us knowledge of this land and your existence here—we have found it! Your family has returned to claim you!

We have returned to the forced enslaved labor camp that was politely referred to as the Lenoir Plantation. We have returned to the place where you no doubt spent endless hours picking cotton and tobacco, with the promise of the lash if you slowed down or refused. We have returned to the site of unspeakable horrors.

But we have also returned to the place where you all dared to live. A place where you all had the incredible courage to love—despite knowing that falling in love could inflict a terrible pain when your beloved was sold away or worked to death. We are here! We are at the very place where you found ways to guard your humanity from those who thought it was possible to steal. We are here where you sang together, granted forgiveness to a friend who hurt your feelings, dressed the wounds of those who were injured, and held those in need of comfort.

We are here to experience a truth deeper than any that can be understood intellectually. We are here to make a promise to you, to this land, and to each other: you will not be forgotten.

It doesn't matter if they pass laws that make it illegal to speak of you, teach about you, or learn about you, because those laws don't govern us. Only truth and love govern us, and so we will pass on the knowledge of this land and your existence here to our posterity and to all who we encounter.

We send to you our deepest gratitude for gifting us the will to survive and the spirit of resistance that you passed to us through your blood and through your stories.

With eternal love,

Jesse, Jamana, & Gerald

After reading the letter, we knelt on the ground to be closer to our ancestors who lay beneath, and I felt their love being returned in a wave of light and healing that washed over us. That moment will sustain me until my last breath in pursuing and teaching the truth about both my enslaved ancestors and the yet uncompensated and unrecognized role their labor played in the establishment of this country. I offer this book as a confirmation of the vow I made that day to my ancestors to set their story free and teach truth, regardless of the consequences.

Truthcrime and Uncritical Race Theory versus the Beloved Classroom Community

If we teach that the founding of the United States of America was somehow flawed—it was corrupt, it was racist—that's really dangerous. It strikes at the very foundations of our country.

—**Mike Pompeo,** former CIA director and secretary of state

We've never been a racist country.
—**Nikki Haley,** Republican presidential candidate

With sufficient general agreement and determination among the dominant classes, the truth of history may be utterly distorted and contradicted and changed to any convenient fairy tale that the masters of men wish.

—**W. E. B. Du Bois**

1

It was a warm night in the Dallas-Fort Worth area on June 3, 2020, and Colleyville Heritage High School principal James Whitfield could not sleep.

It wasn't the heat that tormented him, however. Like countless Black souls wracked by the recent murder of George Floyd, Whitfield found himself entangled in a maelstrom of emotions and knew he had to address the tumultuous times with his school community. Whitfield, a seasoned educator of two decades, had served in the Dallas, Texas, area as a classroom teacher, assistant principal, and principal at the middle and high school levels. When I spoke with Whitfield in September 2023, he confided that his journey into education was a quest born of necessity from his experience growing up around Midland, Texas. "I went through my elementary school education feeling rather invisible," he shared. "And then everything changed for me in the seventh grade because of a man by the name of Kevin Carmona. He was my seventh-grade basketball coach. I couldn't play basketball. I was terrible. I was not athletic. I was nappy headed and scrawny.... But this was the first time in my school experience that I saw somebody that looked like me at school."[1] Whitfield also had another coach who helped guide him through two pivotal moments in his adolescence, his mother's leukemia diagnosis during his sophomore year and when he became a father at the age of seventeen in the spring of his senior year. "Coach Stephenson wrapped his arms around me, he didn't allow me to wallow in self-pity—he loved me and continued to encourage me."[2] Whitfield resolved to become the beacon he had once sought, an educator who could be a shining light to those in need, much as his coaches had done for him in his youth.

At 4:30 a.m., Whitfield decided he couldn't wait any longer to act on his convictions and sent an email to his school community to address injustices he saw, declaring systemic racism was "alive and well" and that everyone needed to work together to reach "conciliation for our nation." He went on to say, "Education is the key to stomping out ignorance, hate, and systemic racism. It's a necessary conduit to get 'liberty and justice for all.'"[3]

"I felt a duty being the first African American principal in this school's history to speak out on that and to send a note to the community," Whitfield told me. "It was a note of encouragement. . . .We know it's going to be hard, but we can do this together." Initially, the responses to his message were "overwhelmingly positive." But a few months later, after President Donald Trump launched a war on critical race theory (CRT), implacable right-wing groups began the attack. Whitfield didn't believe much would come from the criticism he received, but then a raucous school board meeting in July 2021 proved him wrong.

The call for Whitfield to be fired was led by a man named Stetson Clark. Clark's credentials to comment on Whitfield's performance as a principal include being an alumnus of the notorious Goldman Sachs investment bank (which participated in sabotaging the global economy that triggered the 2008 Great Recession), running an unsuccessful campaign for school board, and being a father of children who did not attend Colleyville Heritage High. At the board meeting, Clark spun the fairy tale that Whitfield was there to indoctrinate kids and destroy the school district—as evidenced by Whitfield's recommendation on Twitter of Richard Rothstein's best-selling book, *The Color of Law*, which explains how federal policy and banking practice worked to segregate neighborhoods. Reflecting on this attack, Whitfield told *The Guardian*, "What's interesting is far-right opponents are saying they want the curriculum to say America is not inherently racist, that America did all things perfectly and everything is rosy and good and slavery was just a minor footnote. But they've already got that."[4]

"How 'bout you fire him!" one angry voice rang out in the meeting hall that evening. "The revolution will not be televised," Clark shouted, feeling stifled by the directive not to mention Whitfield by name.[5] Clark was clearly oblivious of the irony (which he may have appreciated more if he'd learned Black history in school) that he was quoting the words of one of the most radically creative voices of the Black freedom struggle, poet and musician Gil Scott-Heron.

"The people that got up and did all the hooting and hollering and calling for my termination largely didn't even have kids in the district," Whitfield recalled. "While it was a tough time, I was encouraged because the students and parents that I actually served were being very specific about who they knew me to be. They were speaking the truth."

The truth, however, was immaterial to those determined to rid themselves of a Black principal who had the temerity to speak his mind; a few weeks later the district issued Whitfield a disciplinary letter suspending his employment. Then on September 20, 2021, the Grapevine Colleyville Independent School District voted unanimously to not renew Whitfield's contract.[6]

After months of attacks, and with no clear path to getting his job back, Whitfield finally succumbed to the pressure and agreed to part ways with the school district. Just like that, Whitfield was ripped away from his life's pursuit of empowering young people through education because he dared to acknowledge systemic racism.

Unfortunately, as disturbing as this attack on Whitfield is, it is not a unique experience among educators in the United States today. As of June 2022, *The Washington Post* identified at least 160 educators who lost their jobs or had to resign because they taught about race or LGBTQ+ issues.[7] This count was undoubtably very low, as it couldn't have tallied the many educators who didn't want to go public with their story—and many more have been pushed out of their classrooms since the report. As National Public Radio reported about the vitriol from those who oppose antiracist education in the schools, "Mobs are yelling obscenities and throwing objects. In one district, a protester brandished a flagpole against a school board official. Other cases have included a protester yelling a Nazi salute, arrests for aggravated battery and disorderly conduct, and numerous death threats against public officials."[8] Many of those public officials were school board members who believed students had a right to learn about systemic racism, and in 2021 alone, at least six educators across the country resigned after receiving death threats.[9]

The intensity of the attacks on antiracist education compel me, before going any further, to issue a warning to the reader: This book contains illegal history and contraband ideas. If you share the historical lessons and concepts in this book with children, you could face severe penalties, including harassment, termination of employment, fines, physical attacks, and even imprisonment.

These illicit lessons have been designated "critical race theory," but you needn't have ever taken the graduate-level legal studies course on systemic racism and jurisprudence, or even know anything about the theory, to be found culpable of using it to corrupt the minds of youth. Once apprehended in today's CRT dragnet, harsh punishments are meted out for those who promulgate antiracist ideas or expose kids to parts of US history that reflect poorly on the national character. Educators who dare teach honestly about race, whether their lessons have any connection to CRT or not, risk being maligned by billionaire-funded organizations that seek to deny America's history of oppression and charge those who refuse to conceal this history with a nefarious plot to teach kids to hate white people.

Astoundingly, almost half of all public school children across the country today are subjected to laws that forbid honest education about the history of racism.[10] But the force of these laws is much more extensive than even this statistic suggests. The fear of retribution for teaching the truth has created a chilling effect so cold that an incredible two out of every three US teachers report self-censoring discussions on race, gender identity, and sexuality in their classrooms.[11]

Although large majorities oppose book banning and curriculum banning, billionaires are using their wealth to manipulate political and educational systems and swell the number of students who are prohibited from engaging with texts containing an analysis of racism and oppression. Even as book bans increased by 33 percent in 2022, The EveryLibrary Institute found 75 percent of voters expressed "preventing book banning" was important to them when voting, and 43 percent said it was "very important." Only a minuscule 8 percent of respondents thought there are "many books that are inappropriate and should be banned."[12] Additionally, in a 2023 nationally representative survey, over 80 percent of registered voters conveyed to the Black Education Research Center that it is essential for public school students to be educated on both the history of racism and slavery in the United States and its contemporary impacts on students and communities.[13]

It is precisely this broad opposition to the most overt attacks on educating young people honestly about racism and US history that has produced such intense vitriol against CRT from a small minority of people who wield immense power and wealth; they are using their influence to impose laws and policies that rewrite history so as to suggest to students that the troubled world they see around them is the best that can be achieved and that inequality is natural and inescapable.

What Is Critical Race Theory?

The tragicomedy of the political situation we find ourselves in today is that members of the GOP who are pushing anti-CRT bills, along with white parents who have been persuaded by these politicians, as well as the vast majority of educators who are being accused of teaching CRT, all have little idea of what CRT is. One of the most compelling pieces of evidence that CRT, antiracist pedagogy, and Black history are, in fact, absent from many classes was a February 2022 poll that revealed only "27 percent of Americans say the American History they were taught in school reflected a full and accurate account of the role of African Americans in the United States."[14] If CRT is the omnipresent force in school that its detractors claim it is, a significantly larger proportion of people nationwide would have reported being taught a robust account of Black history.

Given that CRT has been repackaged and weaponized against antiracist educators, it's important to understand the theory beyond the mischaracterizations by the right-wing and the superficial or patronizing accounts common in the mainstream media. Kimberlé Crenshaw, credited with coining the term, describes CRT as "a way of seeing, attending to, accounting for, tracing and analyzing the ways that race is produced . . . the ways that racial inequality is facilitated, and the ways that our history has created these inequalities that now can be almost effortlessly reproduced unless we attend to the existence of these inequalities."[15] CRT is a field that emerged from legal scholars, lawyers, and activists in the 1970s and early 1980s as a way to make sense of the victories and defeats of the Black freedom movement from the mid-1950s through the mid-1970s. These social examiners wanted to understand how the Civil Rights Movement could have achieved important legal victories—such as the *Brown v. Board of Education* decision, the Civil Rights Act of 1964, and the Voting Rights Act of 1965—and yet Black people were still oppressed, lacking political and economic power.

CRT cohered around several important insights, among them that (1) race is a social construction, not a biological reality; (2) racism is structurally embedded in the law, oftentimes even when the law appears to be race neutral; (3) advancements in challenging aspects of systemic racism occur when it serves the interests not only of Black people agitating for their rights, but also of the white power structure (convergence theory); (4) various social identities—such as race, gender, class, and sexuality—intersect and overlap and are impacted by interconnected systems of oppression and privilege (intersectionality); (5) whiteness functions as a valuable asset within society, granting access to resources, opportunities, and societal advantages (whiteness as form of property); (6) advancements toward racial equity often trigger a reactionary response from the white power structure aimed at maintaining the status quo and preserving white privilege; and (7) storytelling is one of the most effective tools for combating systemic racism, allowing for the expression of counternarratives to oppose dominant and oppressive ideologies.[16]

The irony is that the attack on CRT, in many ways, confirms its core principles. For example, the assertion racism can be embedded in the law, even when it appears race neutral, is borne out by legislation passed around the country that bans any discussion of history that causes feelings of "discomfort"—laws that don't explicitly say that Black history is banned and yet have that effect because discussions of slavery, segregation, and mass incarceration often make white people uncomfortable. In addition, the CRT tenant asserting that movements that achieve progress for racial justice are met with a white backlash is exemplified in the laws banning discussions of systemic racism in the wake of the 2020 uprising for Black lives (as I describe in more detail later in this chapter).

Although the vast majority of educators have not studied CRT and are not teaching this legal framework in schools, social justice teachers of many different traditions share an analysis with critical race theorists on many issues, including that race is a social construction (in congruence with the scientific consensus) and that racism is a structural problem that fuels injustice in the criminal legal system, the school system, housing systems, and beyond.

Uncritical Race Theory

In the cacophony of today's political discourse, debates about CRT are ubiquitous, but what's not discussed, and what I believe must be studied, is uncritical race theory. "Uncritical race theory" is the term I am developing here to define systems of belief that unquestioningly subscribe to prevailing views on race that reinforce existing racial power relations. Uncritical race theory denies that racism exists at all, or maintains that racism primarily victimizes white people, or rejects any systemic or institutional analysis in favor of an interpersonal explanation that understands racism as only sporadic and merely the product of individual bias.

Uncritical race theorists position themselves as neutral and objective, unencumbered by ideology or a theory of race—when in fact they have a highly developed theory of race, even if they are unaware of the origins or the full dimensions of this theory. To be clear, uncritical race theorists would never refer to themselves as such because it would divulge that their opposition to CRT (and every other antiracist framework) is not anchored by research and historical inquiry, but rather is the result of unsubstantiated and unmoored theories that sink under the most cursory of examinations. When educators analyze race in their lessons, uncritical race theorists accuse them of politicizing the curriculum—a claim that approaches reason only if you believe that teaching children that the uncritical acceptance of the current racist structures and institutions is not political.

Consider the Civic Alliance's "American Birthright" curriculum, established by a handful of extremely wealthy right-wing patrons trying to replace state standards, influence textbook authors, and infuse teacher training programs with uncritical race theory. In 2023, the Woodland Park school district in Colorado became the first in the nation to fully adopt the American Birthright social studies standards.[17] Facts be damned, the ninth-, tenth-, and eleventh-grade modules of the curriculum teach students that European imperialism "improved life expectancy . . . among colonized peoples."[18] The truth is that during the height of British colonization of India from 1872 to 1921, Indian life expectancy dropped by an startling 20 percent, and during the seventy years since independence, Indian life expectancy has increased by approximately 66 percent, or twenty-seven years.[19] Colonial administrators sponsored by Belgian king Leopold II in the Congo kidnapped children and transported them to child colonies to work or train as soldiers, with estimates suggesting more than half died there. The brutality of Belgian colonialism caused the deaths of an estimated ten million Congolese.[20] In the Americas, Europeans killed some fifty-six million Indigenous people, so many people that scientist have determined the genocide actually led to planetary cooling.[21]

American Birthright provides a textbook case of how uncritical race theorists attempt to camouflage their theory of race by dressing up their advocacy for the current relations of power in society not as a political position, but as natural facts. *American Birthright: The Civics Alliance's Model K–12 Social Studies Standards* states, "Some educators are so caught up in pedagogical 'theory' that they have forgotten that facts come first. Some activists in our schools, public and private alike, are so antagonistic toward our culture, without recognizing what they owe to it, that they seek to erase our worthy history of liberty from the curriculum."[22] Uncritical race theorists have been coached to see their unquestioning belief in America's "worthy history of liberty" as the only natural and objective way to view history, and critiques of racism as "political" or only a "theory."

Describing people who accept status quo beliefs about race as "uncritical race theorists" is important because it helps underscore that people opposing antiracist education aren't actually rejecting "theory" about race altogether—they are merely trading one theory for another and trying to hide their theory of race behind a smokescreen. They have a highly developed theory of race, but they would prefer that the underpinnings and origins of their theory go unexamined. Uncritical race theorists demand an anodyne telling of history where the United States was delivered by the stork—and they would rather not look any further into how the country was made, lest it offend delicate sensibilities. They tell themselves America doesn't fornicate, cuss, drink, brawl, abuse, exploit, lie, cheat, or steal. But as James Baldwin reminded us, "People who shut their eyes to reality simply invite their own destruction, and anyone who insists on remaining in a state of innocence long after that innocence is dead turns himself into a monster."[23]

It's important to understand that uncritical race theory is used by liberals and conservatives, who both often advance narratives of color blindness, or postracialism, in their meager attempt to explain how race functions in society. In this way, the term is useful for pointing out the overlap between liberal and conservative ideas when they both dismiss structural racism as a salient axis of power in our society. This overlap between liberal and conservative views on race became pronounced in the wake of Barack Obama's election as president. The conservative radio host Lou Dobbs, for example, said in November 2009, "We are now in a 21st-century post-partisan, post-racial society."[24] Only two months later, the liberal MSNBC host Chris Matthews said of President Obama, "He is post-racial by all appearances. You know, I forgot he was Black tonight for an hour."[25] Both these pundits were about as insightful on race as Stephen Colbert's satirical remark (when he anchored the *Colbert Report* impersonating a conservative talk show host), "Now, I don't see race. People tell me I'm white and I believe them."[26]

With liberal politicians and media often legitimizing the color-blind approaches to race, conservatives have seized on it as their primary strategy for banning conversations about structural racism in the schools (as I explain in chapter 3). One of the ways they attempt to bolster their color-blind attack on CRT is to misuse the words of Martin Luther King Jr.—as if King dreamed of a day when little Black boys and girls could hold hands with little white boys and girls on their way to a school that would outlaw their ability to learn about the Civil Rights Movement, Black history, and the legacy of structural racism. Republican senator Kevin McCarthy, for example, tweeted, "Critical Race Theory goes against everything Martin Luther King Jr. taught us—to not judge others by the color of their skin."[27]

The cynical irony of uncritical race theorists who use the words of King to promote bills to restrict teaching about racism is that if King were alive today, they would spare no invective as they charged him with being one of the most subversive of the critical race theorists. Imagine for a moment the uproar from uncritical race theorists that would ensue if King were alive today and students assembled in the auditorium to hear him talk about the "unspeakable horrors of police brutality," as he put it in his "I Have a Dream" speech.[28] In many states and school districts today, a teacher quoting this section of King's speech and explaining what those horrors were risks being punished for politicizing the classroom. Or consider King's pronouncement in 1967 that "the doctrine of white supremacy was embedded in every textbook and preached in practically every pulpit" and was entrenched as "a structural part of the culture."[29] King's radical understanding of structural racism and white supremacy put him in direct confrontation with the uncritical race theorists of his time, even if they attempt to co-opt his message today.

Uncritical race theory has adapted over the generations to meet the needs of white supremacy in various eras, but a persistent (and pitiful) core tenant of its analysis is the decoupling of racism from the systems and institutions that produce it. Uncritical race theory during the seventeenth, eighteenth, and nineteenth centuries was dominated by the mainstream discourse that God created the white master race to rule the others. In 1701, for example, Massachusetts judge John Saffin argued: "God has set in the world, who ordained different degrees and orders of men, some to be high and honorable, some to be low and despicable; yea, some to be born slaves.... Otherwise there would be a mere parity among men." This kind of thinking informed Roger B. Taney, chief justice of the US Supreme Court, to declare in the 1857 *Dred Scott* decision that Black people "had no rights which the white man was bound to respect; and that the negro might justly and lawfully be reduced to slavery for his benefit."[30] At the beginning of the twentieth century uncritical race theory shifted its primary justification for racism to the bogus ideology of eugenics—the pseudoscience that posited that different races of human beings evolved separately and the white race is the most advanced.

The predicament for contemporary uncritical race theorists is that the previous ideological foundations of racism—that it was ordained by God or proven by science—were jackhammered by slavery abolitionists, civil rights activists, and scientists, and these outdated explanations no longer provide adequate shelter for their dilapidated racial views. As mass social movements (such as the abolitionist movement, Reconstruction, or the Civil Rights Movement) imploded those explanations of race, new impoverished schools of thought emerged to justify racial oppression—yet they lacked the explanatory power of earlier systems of racial thinking that, although utterly false, at least attempted to explain the origin of race. Today's uncritical race theorists have their go-to justifications for their racist beliefs: Black people are lazy and want government handouts, they suffer because of their own deficient culture of poverty, and other such drivel. Yet they haven't developed a way to explain what race is or where the concept came from, as their predecessors did. Uncritical race theorists content themselves by simply proclaiming they don't see race or attacking antiracist views without offering their own thoroughgoing analysis of the origins of the concept of race. After all, how could they analyze this history? If they acknowledged that the concept of race was invented in a specific era by rich, white, male property owners to enforce the divisions needed for the wealthiest 1 percent to maintain their power, it would expose how similar dynamics are still at play today and threaten to upend the racist status quo in society.

Antiracist analytic traditions—such as CRT, ethnic studies, cultural studies, or Black studies—are very clear about what race is: a socially constructed categorizing system of humans, with no basis in biology, reflecting the prevailing power relations dating to the transatlantic slave trade, which was used to justify the enslavement of African people and divide and conquer the laboring class of people from all origins. The decision by European colonizers in the Americas to invent and enforce the concept of race was hastened by Bacon's Rebellion, a multiracial uprising of white indentured servants and enslaved Black people in colonial Jamestown, Virginia, in 1676. The rebels captured Jamestown from the British Crown and, astonishingly, held it for some eight months before the British army could subdue the insurgency. Before the rebellion, little distinction was made between laborers from African and European origins—both were seen as a common, unfree class, haplessly below the station of property-owning aristocrats. In the aftermath of Bacon's Rebellion, as legal scholar Michelle Alexander explains, "deliberately and strategically, the planter class extended special privileges to poor whites in an effort to drive a wedge between them and black slaves."[31]

Some of the first laws pertaining to the newly invented categories of race were written in the wake of Bacon's Rebellion and "as the status of people of African descent in the British colonies was challenged and attacked, and as white indentured servants were given new rights and status, the word *white* continued to be more widely used in public documents and private papers to describe the European colonists." Alexander writes of the poor white people at the time: "Their own plight had not improved by much, but at least they were not slaves. Once the planter elite split the labor force, poor whites responded to the logic of their situation and sought ways to expand their racially privileged position."[32] Or as the legendary abolitionist Frederick Douglass put it, "They divided both to conquer each."[33] The elites were able to keep the vast majority of white people in poverty by granting them just enough privileges to get them to separate from enslaved Black people and work against them. To this day, uncritical race theorists replicate this strategy by thwarting unity between the white and Black working classes, preventing the development of the solidarity that would be required to build a struggle strong enough to improve wages, health care benefits, and other essential resources that both groups urgently require.

Gloria Ladson-Billings, one of the leading educators who brought CRT into educational scholarship, explains: "Biologists, geneticists, anthropologists, and sociologists all agree that race is not a scientific reality. . . . As members of the same species, human beings are biologically quite similar. . . . However, humans have constructed social categories and organization that rely heavily on arbitrary genetic differences like skin color, hair texture, eye shape, and lip size. They have used these differences as a mechanism for creating hierarchy and an ideology of White supremacy."[34] There is only one human race, and because racial categorization is not a genetic reality (but rather a power arrangement instituted by those who hold the power in society), racial categories have changed over time and are applied differently in various societies. Cultural studies theorist Stuart Hall describes race as a "floating signifier" because its meaning has shifted over time according to power relations, emphasizing that "racialized behavior and difference should be understood as discursive constructs rather than genetic or biological facts."[35]

The history of uncritical race theorists' efforts to enforce disremembering in education is vast and requires examination by those who believe students have the right to learn the truth about the nation's past. Some precursors of today's antihistory laws include the mandatory illiteracy laws imposed on enslaved Black people; the Reconstruction-era attempts by white missionaries to implement assimilationist instruction to teach newly emancipated Black people to accept white supremacy; the removal of hundreds of thousands of Native American children from their homes—including forcibly removing kids as young as four—and their placement in physically and emotionally abusive boarding schools designed to strip them of their culture; the late 1800s and early 1900s schooling in Hawai'i that taught Native Hawaiian and Asian immigrants to accept colonization and to "disidentify with Hawai'i and Asian countries of origin while embracing dominant American world views and values";[36] the McCarthy-era attacks that resulted in the firing of thousands of antiracist and left-wing teachers; the "Americanization classes" instituted by the War Relocation Authority in the Japanese internment/incarceration camps for "indoctrinating the younger generation of Japanese Americans with 'American values'" even as they suffered human rights violations by the US government;[37] the curricular campaigns by groups like the Daughters of the Confederacy that resulted in the valorization of the Confederacy in textbooks during the Jim Crow era and beyond; and the attacks on ethnic studies programs, including the outlawing of the Mexican American Studies program in Tucson, Arizona, in 2012 (as I detail in chapter 1).

The current hostility to CRT is indicative of a broader assault on critical thinking. Consider that the Texas GOP adopted a resolution to its party platform that openly opposed allowing students to develop critical thinking, stating, "We oppose the teaching of Higher Order Thinking Skills (HOTS) (values clarification), critical thinking skills and similar programs."[38] This plank received widespread ridicule; the rebuke was so resounding, the Texas GOP communications director claimed it was all a big mistake, yet said it would be difficult to remove because the platform had been approved by a party convention. Having learned their lesson from this debacle, instead of directly attacking critical thinking, uncritical race theorists landed on the term "critical race theory" as a better target for their attack on any questioning of how power is distributed in society.

Today's uncritical race theorists, in the same breath they use to decry cancel culture and without even blushing, will call for the canceling of any book or educator that diverges from the orthodoxy of American exceptionalism. Perhaps I don't need to persuade you that something is profoundly wrong with a society so terrified of its past that it endeavors to strangle history, dump its corpse in a casket, bury it beneath the earth, and not even leave an epitaph that would allow young people to recognize it had ever existed or be able to appreciate its heritage.

The Backlash Blues

The 2020 uprising for Black lives, ignited by the police killings of George Floyd, Breonna Taylor, and others, propelled antiracist literature to the top of national best-seller lists and thrust discussions of systemic racism, long marginalized, into the mainstream. Described by *The Washington Post* as the "broadest in U.S. history," the protests spanned every state, with various polls estimating between fifteen and twenty-two million people marching for Black lives that summer.[39] In many instances, youth helped to organize and lead these demonstrations and often developed demands for Black studies and antiracist curriculum. As eighteen-year-old Omaha high school student activist Vanessa Amoah told *The Washington Post* in August 2020, "George Floyd, Philando Castile—none of it would have happened if this country worked on proactively teaching anti-racist values."[40]

This movement significantly influenced curriculum, prompting many educators to integrate discussions of systemic racism into their lessons. Although only a few cities even temporarily decreased their police budgets as a result of the protests, perhaps the most significant policy outcome of the uprising was the removal of police, or defunding of police, from more than fifty school districts nationwide—demonstrating the power of students and educators in the struggles for racial justice and the importance of education as a site of struggle for the broader social movements.[41] Amidst these shifts, uncritical race theorists expressed panic over the growing racial justice consciousness among young people.

As a counter to the uprising, in the fall of 2020, Christopher Rufo, now a senior fellow at the conservative Manhattan Institute, ignited the attack on truthful teaching when he captured President Trump's attention with the concocted threat of CRT (as described in more detail in chapter 3). During his final few months in office, Trump fueled a firestorm against antiracist pedagogy, from kindergarten classrooms to government trainings. On Constitution Day, September 17, 2020, Trump announced his new "1776 Commission" to "promote patriotic education" and attack CRT, as a response to the 1619 Project—the initiative begun by Nikole Hannah-Jones and other writers from *The New York Times*, which "aims to reframe the country's history by placing the consequences of slavery and the contributions of Black Americans at the very center of the United States' national narrative."[42]

Trump mendaciously blustered in his speech that day, "Our mission is to defend the legacy of America's founding, the virtue of America's heroes, and the nobility of the American character. We must clear away the twisted web of lies in our schools and classrooms and teach our children the magnificent truth about our country. We want our sons and daughters to know that they are the citizens of the most exceptional nation in the history of the world."[43] Trump acting as the arbiter of historical truth—a man documented to have told an incredible 30,573 lies during his time in office—wrapped the entire affair in absurdity.[44] Trump and his supporters made their educational agenda clear from the beginning: replace inquiry with allegiance; replace critical thinking with obedience. Enough with investigating the past, evaluating multiple perspectives, questioning the validity of different sources, or asking whose viewpoints may have been ignored altogether. Any facts that contradicted the so-called "magnificent truth about our country" were declared verboten by the president in favor of a curriculum that promoted strict adherence to American exceptionalism.

Suddenly, educators who had never heard the term "critical race theory" were attacked as CRT indoctrinators simply for teaching the truth about Black history. With the bit firmly in their mouths, the braying jackasses who carry water for the billionaires funding the attack on antiracist teaching branded the various methods for supporting diverse communities of students or teaching about race—such as Black studies, ethnic studies, critical pedagogy, culturally responsive pedagogy, cultural studies, social and emotional learning, or DEI (diversity, equity, and inclusion)—all as CRT. The distinctions between these pedagogical methodologies made no difference to politicians who were searching for a way to improve their political fortunes at the expense of educators who were trying to help their students make sense of the uprising for Black lives of 2020 and a deeply unequal society.

Truthcrime and Educational Closeting

We are bearing witness to an era in which teachers who allow students to learn about racial disparities stemming from the legacy of slavery and segregation can be charged with what I will call a "truthcrime." A truthcrime is any act of honest pedagogy in a jurisdiction where truthful teaching has been outlawed. Truthcrime is enforced disremembering. A truthcrime law, then, is one that makes lying to children obligatory and effectively renders honest educators as truthcriminals. The goal for the enforcers of truthcrime, in the end, is to make committing a truthcrime literally impossible because there will be no one left who learned honest history, and therefore no one left to teach it. This requires rewriting the past so that it appears to justify the dramatic inequality that exists today and so that it impedes the ability of those who have learned the revisionist history to imagine a future without oppression.

That the concept of truthcrime would be vital to understanding contemporary society in the United States may at first seem hyperbolic. Yet consider that in a growing number of states and school districts, politicians have imposed truthcrime legislation to coerce educators to lie to their students about aspects of US history—especially with regard to structural racism, sexism, and heterosexism—that powerful people would prefer went unexamined.

Since 2020, more than two hundred bills have been introduced at federal and state levels to prevent students from examining the history of structural racism in the United States.[45] These bills can be divided into several categories of truthcrime laws:

1. Bans on "divisive concepts"

2. Bans on lessons that cause "discomfort"

3. Bans on CRT

4. Bans on specific antiracist curriculums

5. Bans on civic engagement

Many truthcrime laws—such as in Iowa and West Virginia—forbid teaching so-called divisive concepts, including outlawing any teaching that their state, or the United States, "is fundamentally racist or sexist." Consider that according to the *Merriam-Webster Dictionary*, the word "fundamental" means "serving as an original or generating source." Given that the original source of our country was the genocide of Native people and the enslavement of African people, it isn't possible to teach the truth about the founding of the country without talking about how racism is fundamental to the establishment of the United States. Additionally, it is also impossible to talk about America's birth without understanding how sexism was systemically enforced by wealthy white men who consolidated their power by disenfranchising all women, while owning and often sexually abusing Black women.

Some truthcrime laws—such as in Oklahoma and Florida—prohibit pedagogy that might make students "feel discomfort" because of their race or sex. The goal here is quite transparently to ease white male student comfort. The discomfort felt by Black students who are made to endure lessons that conceal the contributions and struggles of Black people from the curriculum quite clearly isn't a concern for those who fret about student discomfort. In fact, a 2024 Pew study found Black teens are nearly twice as likely as white teens to be made uncomfortable when the subject of racial inequality comes up in class (33 percent of Black youth reported discomfort compared with only 19 percent of white youth).[46] Yet when charlatans like Christopher Rufo attack critical race theory for making white students feel uncomfortable, they fail to acknowledge the routine discomfort Black students experience in school because of racist incidents, textbooks that often erase the contributions of African Americans, or lessons that cast Black people only as victims of enslavement, without highlighting their resistance (discussed further in chapter 1).

Some truthcrime laws—such as in Texas and Idaho—specifically exclude the teaching of what they understand to be "critical race theory," a term they have broadly defined so it can apply to any legitimate learning about the history of racism. North Dakota's ban of CRT, for example, defines it as "the theory that racism is not merely the product of learned individual bias or prejudice, but rather that racism is systemically embedded in American society and the American legal system to facilitate racial inequality."[47] The implications of this legal stipulation are profound: it compels educators to assert that racism can only be defined as individual bias. Consequently, when teaching about the history of slavery, educators would be required to lie to students and teach that slavery resulted solely from the racial prejudice of individual enslavers, rather than acknowledging its reinforcement by a system of laws that legalized slavery (such as the Three-fifths compromise of the Constitution or the Fugitive Slave Act) or the system of profit-driven enterprises that benefit from it (such as the textile industry).

Other laws—like the one from the Florida State Board of Education and a proposed bill in Missouri—outlaw specific curricula from organizations such as *The New York Time's* 1619 Project, the Zinn Education Project, Black Lives Matter at School, Teaching for Change, or Learning for Justice. In addition, some of the bans are directed at "action civics" that help students understand how they can intervene around a social issue they care about. The law in Texas reads, "[A] teacher may not require, make part of a course, or award a grade or course credit . . . for a student's . . . efforts to persuade members of the legislative or executive branch at the federal, state, or local level to take specific actions by direct communication." Maybe you can sympathize with the poor politicians who resorted to passing laws like this? Try to imagine the horror of receiving letters from students about what matters to them and actually having to listen to the people you're supposed to represent. After all, why face criticism when you can just revel in your own sense of infallibility and ignore the voices of those who will be most affected by your decisions? These kinds of laws seek to extract any democratic impulse from schools and replace it with obedience to authority. As the Zinn Education Project explains, "Igniting young people's desire to take action to transform society—whether through writing a legislator, testifying at a school board meeting, participating in a protest, or organizing a social media campaign—is one mark of truly democratic schooling. This is what the Right seeks to suffocate."[48]

Still others of these truthcrime laws are an admixture of several of these antidemocratic provisions. Although the verbiage may vary from bill to bill, the intent remains consistent: to mandate educators deceive children about history and ideas they find embarrassing, uncomfortable, or potentially destabilizing to the racial power hierarchy. *Rethinking Schools* explained the fraudulence of these "divisive concept" bills when the journal editorialized:

> These laws peddle in bait-and-switch tactics, using the language of anti-discrimination to mask their perpetuation of a discriminatory and unjust status quo. Louisiana's "divisive concepts" law lists "That one race or sex is inherently superior or inferior to another race or sex" as its very first banned concept. No disagreement there. But further down the "divisive concepts" list we find "That either the United States of America or the state of Louisiana is fundamentally, institutionally, or systemically racist or sexist." Using the bait of anti-racism and anti-sexism, the law switches to demand educators repudiate the very existence of racism or sexism at all. This in a state where Black women face the worst pay gap in the country,

earning a median $26,488 a year in wages, compared with $55,386 in median annual wages earned by white men there. By banning educators from teaching about these realities, lawmakers seek to deny young people the right to understand—and so effectively act upon—the world they've been bequeathed. These bills are an attack on democracy itself.[49]

As well, laws banning DEI have gained momentum (as I write about in chapter 2), especially since the US Supreme Court's ruling in June 2023 that banned affirmative action in college admissions. In the first few months of 2024, GOP lawmakers in at least seventeen states introduced at least three dozen bills to restrict or require public disclosure of DEI initiatives. Although primarily targeting higher education institutions, these laws also extend their reach to K–12 schools and districts. For example, in January 2024, Utah governor Spencer Cox signed a law primarily directed at public colleges and universities but with implications for other state institutions, including public schools. This law prohibits districts from providing training to staff or students on discriminatory practices and forbids the establishment of offices or positions within districts dedicated to coordinating such activities.[50]

Additionally, truthcrime laws have been used to ban thousands of books in districts around the country—a great deal of them written by Black, Brown, or lesbian, gay, bisexual, transgender, queer/questioning, plus others (LGBTQ+) authors. One school in Florida, mindful of the truthcrime laws and book-banning efforts in the state, went so far as to send home a permission slip with students to ask for their parents' consent to "participate & listen to a book written by an African-American."[51] Yes, you read that correctly: students had to get permission to read a book by a Black author—and this didn't happen in 1824, or 1924, but in 2024. Laws have been written to threaten librarians with extensive jail time for distributing books that provide accurate information about gender and sexuality, and police have even interrogated school librarians about their book collections (as I explain in chapter 2). The hysteria has gotten so bad in the last couple of years that school board members have threatened to burn books and at least one large public book burning has occurred in the country since these truthcrime laws were passed (further explained in chapter 1).

You might have once thought that a dystopian story you shuddered at was fantastical; "firemen" who burn books in *Fahrenheit 451*; a state that declares "Ignorance is Strength" in *1984*; the "Sameness" social engineering attained in part by allowing only one person to remember the past in

The Giver. But consider those tales alongside the chilling story of post-truth schooling in present-day America.

The state of Florida's official curriculum declares slavery to have been of "personal benefit" to Black people.[52] For real. Not in the Ku Klux Klan (KKK) youth handbook, but in the mandated education standards of a state. As well, Florida banned the Advanced Placement (AP) African American studies class and passed a law to prosecute teachers who are caught allowing students to access banned books that deal with issues of race, gender, or sexuality with "up to five years in prison and a $5,000 fine for displaying a forbidden book, which is a third-degree felony."[53] A bill was proposed in Arkansas to ban the teaching of solidarity.[54] A legislator in Oklahoma suggested that students be taught that the Tulsa Race Massacre—the 1921 attack where white people rioted and killed some three hundred Black people and burned their thriving neighborhood to the ground—was not racially motivated.[55] In proposals to impose Big Brother–style surveillance in the classroom, uncritical race theorists have attempted to mandate teachers wear body cameras so as to catch transgressors teaching illegal ideas.[56] Entire school districts have had their accreditation downgraded because permissive educators allowed discussions in the classroom about such subversive topics as "discrimination."[57]

Many states and school districts have coupled the attack on antiracist teaching with what I will call "educational closeting"—schooling that seeks to deny the history and humanity of LGBTQ+ people. In March 2022, Florida governor Ron DeSantis signed into law the Parental Rights in Education bill, better known as the "Don't Say Gay" bill by its opponents—which prohibits classroom instruction related to gay, lesbian, or transgender issues or sexuality or gender identity more broadly. This prompted the Miami-Dade School Board to refuse to recognize October as "LGBTQ History Month" out of concern that it would violate the law.[58] Florida is one of fifteen states that censor discussions of LGBTQ+ people or issues in school,[59] and one of twenty-five states that ban transgender students from participating in sports consistent with their gender identity.[60]

The hysteria has reached such a frenzy that educators who insist on truthful discussions of US history have been doxed, have had threats made against their lives, and have even been physically attacked (as I discuss in chapter 2). Nearly 70 percent of high school principals reported in a November 2022 survey "substantial political conflict" in their school around issues such as "race, LGBTQ students' rights, access to books in libraries, and social-emotional learning."[61]

Research from the UCLA Law School's CRT Forward Tracking Project reveals that measures to stop the honest education about racism and oppression have been passed at either state or local levels in every state except Delaware and Vermont.[62] The same study found that in 2021 and 2022, government officials introduced 563 measures aimed at restricting teaching about race and racism and that 241 of those measures (43 percent) were passed. Moreover, the adopted measures—90 percent of which target K–12 education—reach "over 22 million public school children, almost half of the country's 50.8 million public school students."[63]

A January 2022 study revealed 84 of these antihistory bills target K–12 schools, 38 targeted higher education, and 48 included a mandatory punishment for educators found in violation of the law.[64] Yet the problem isn't just the statewide bans. Even in states where truthful teaching about racism and oppression has not yet been forbidden, individual school districts have nonetheless enacted history bans; further, it's important to recognize that truthful teaching about racism isn't being ambushed only in the South or only in so-called red states. In California, for example, seven of the eleven truthcrime bills introduced in local school districts were passed, affecting approximately 110,000 students statewide.[65] In addition to the state and local bans, significant efforts are being made for a federal ban on antiracist teaching.

In the boundless satire that is the United States of America, Juneteenth—the oldest commemoration of the ending of slavery—became a federal holiday at the same time legislators were making it a truthcrime to teach about the origins of the commemoration in many states, including in Texas, where the holiday originates. "Land of the free" continues to take on new and intricate shades of mockery as many educators have been fired or pushed out for teaching about racism since the attack on CRT began. Right-wing groups have published the names of educators who teach about race, making them public targets and exposing them to harassment and even death threats (described further in chapter 2).

The attack on antiracist educators has created such an intense war on truth that one in four teachers report being pressured by school officials or district leaders to limit their classroom conversations about race and racism.[66] Committing a truthcrime in the classroom is dangerous under any circumstances, but even more so if committed when "teaching while Black." Black educators, especially Black women and women of color (who have also been the target of overlapping racist and sexist attacks long before the current anti-CRT frenzy), have endured some of the worst abuse.

A revival of some of the worst authoritarian, racist, sexist, and homophobic policies of the Cold War era is currently underway. This includes reemploying the tactics of the Red Scare, which were used to persecute anyone who was labeled a communist—often those in movements for racial, economic, and social justice—and had an especially devastating impact on teachers. Additionally, today's educational closeters are reviving the tactics of the Lavender Scare from that same era, which were used to persecute anyone who was labeled homosexual, leading to the firing of thousands of federal employees and educators across the country.

Uncritical race theorists use the terms "critical race theory," "woke," and "gender ideology" to stoke fear, just as the labels "communist" and "homosexual" were weaponized during the Cold War in the late 1940s and 1950s by Wisconsin senator Joseph McCarthy (and many other politicians and power brokers on both sides of the aisle) to attack anyone who believed in creating a more equitable society (a history I describe further in chapter 2).

Refusing to capitulate to this fear are those I call "honest educators" and "truth teachers"—terms I have developed to refer to educators who teach truthfully about history, structural racism, and other forms of oppression, while organizing against the criminalization of honest accounts of history (more fully described in chapter 5).

What Is Truth? How Can It Be Taught?

"The blues is truth," legendary African American blues bassist and songwriter Willie Dixon once said.[67] Anyone who has fully immersed themselves in Billie Holiday's soulful cry, John Lee Hooker's hypnotic boogie, J. B. Lenoir's keening wail, Big Mama Thornton's resonant roar, Taj Mahal's gravelly groan, Buffalo Nichols's urgent growl, or Shemekia Copeland's evocative ring knows the veracity of this insight. Black composer W. C. Handy, dubbed the "Father of the Blues," remarked, "In its origin, modern blues music is the expression of the emotional life of a race."[68] Blues piano player and writer "Barrelhouse" Bonni McKeown further elaborated, "Blues is the opposite of exploitation, subjugation and separation of people by rule of fear."[69] Author and dancer Monique Couvson (formerly Monique Morris) described the importance employing the blues as a framework for education, writing, "The blues is about bearing witness to contradictions and then working through them to bring about critical, intellectually responsible thinking and action."[70] Taken together, these explanations illuminate the profound truth that is found by transcending societal constraints to tell one's own story—and to do it with style.

But not everyone would agree.

Jonathan Sumption, a former Supreme Court justice of the United Kingdom, spoke for many uncritical race theorists when he asserted, "A number of intolerant ideologies have swept through the worlds of learning, literature and the visual and performing arts over the past two decades. I am concerned with one of them. Its essential feature is the diversion of academic disciplines to a task for which they are usually ill-suited, namely the reform of modern society so as to redress perceived inequalities, notably of race.... Objectivity and truth have been the main casualties."[71] I'm going to hazard a guess Sumption can't play the blues, and if you handed him a harmonica, he would blow into the wrong side of it. In Sumption's telling, teaching designed to help young people understand how inequality and racism have impacted their lives is a rejection of objectivity and truth. In fact, as I explain further later, the reality is quite the opposite: education that encourages young people to tell their own stories—and doesn't ask them to censor the ways racism and inequality have shaped their experience—helps them critically analyze oppression and allows them to arrive at the truth.

A true understanding of history arises from critically engaging with contradictions that arise in society and analyzing the struggle between competing political forces that shape knowledge.

Here the concepts of "standpoint theory," "strong objectivity," and "curriculum standpoint" are eminently useful for those genuinely concerned with teaching truth and not simply maintaining existing inequitable power relations. Standpoint theory, for example, helps explain the vast discrepancy between Mildred Lewis Rutherford's description of slavery and Harriet Tubman's. Rutherford, the historian general of the United Daughters of the Confederacy, wrote a book in 1920 titled *Truths of History: A Fair, Unbiased, Impartial, Unprejudiced and Conscientious Study of History* to argue for a more sympathetic rendering of the Confederate South and slavery in children's textbooks. She titled section five of the book "Slaves Were Not Ill-Treated in the South. The North Was Largely Responsible for Their Presence in the South." In this lesson Rutherford writes, "The servants were very happy in their life upon the old plantations.

William Makepeace Thackery, on a lecture tour in America, visited a southern plantation. In 'Roundabout Papers' he gives this impression of the slaves: 'How they sang! How they danced! How they laughed! How they shouted! How they bowed and scraped and complimented! So free, so happy!'"[72]

Rutherford's *Truths of History* might well have been the inspiration for Bob Dylan's line from his song *Things Have Changed*: "Gonna get low-down, gonna fly high / All the truth in the world adds up to one big lie." Her description of slavery is a prime example of what ethnic studies educators call a "master narrative" as it reinforces existing inequitable power relations. Compare her description of slavery to Harriet Tubman's "counternarrative": "I think slavery is the next thing to hell."[73] Both of these women claimed to be telling the truth about slavery, so how do you know who to believe? Feminist scholar Sandra Harding's articulation of standpoint theory helps explain the vast contradiction between Rutherford's description of slavery and Tubman's and aids the inquiry into which is true by pointing out that power and knowledge are inextricably linked—"They co-constitute and co-maintain each other," as she puts it. The point is, our understanding of history changes dramatically when we include other voices besides only the wealthy and white. Whereas uncritical race theorists make claims to truth without analyzing how their relationship to money and power influences their views (a topic explored in chapter 3, "The Political Economy of Truth-crime"), honest educators help students understand how systems of power shape our understanding of society by examining the contradictions inherent in these systems. Through discussions, critical inquiry, and reflective practices, students can learn to resolve these contradictions by synthesizing diverse perspectives that are often excluded in corporate textbooks.

Recognizing that power and wealth shape the institutions that produce knowledge helps explain why Rutherford's description of slavery as a benevolent institution was long the predominant view in America—and in some warped minds, persists to this day—despite it being simply not true. The contradiction between the lived experiences of the enslaved and the narratives produced by the enslavers underscores the importance of analyzing the material conditions and social relations that produce knowledge. The enslavement of African people in the Americas is an objective fact, one both the enslaver and the enslaved would agree occurred. However, the slave system is viewed differently depending on one's position relative to enslavement. The enslavers, like the *Truths of History* textbook quoted previously, often described slavery as beneficial for the development of enslaved Africans and denied the brutality of it all since they viewed Black people as mere property or animals.

Including the analysis of slavery from the position of the enslaved is the only way to seek the truth because it doesn't require justifying the existing social relations and instead allows for a genuine inquiry into the system of slavery, revealing what it was: a brutal system of oppression, sexual exploitation, and genocide that enriched white enslavers. In this way, standpoint theory helps us see that if we want to understand the reality of slavery and racism, we will gain a more accurate understanding by considering the perspective of Black enslaved people—rather than that of white enslavers—because the latter are fundamentally concerned with maintaining unequal power relations, rather than describing reality.

The social location of oppressed people is a more useful starting point for investigating society because it's a perspective that is not invested in constructing knowledge to defend the existing social order or omitting realities that don't validate the rule of those in power.

This doesn't mean, however, that only enslaved people could acknowledge the harsh realities of slavery—some white people sought to understand the reality of the slave system and struggle against it, rather than justify it. Additionally, there were Black people who sought to curry favor from enslavers and obtain benefits from the white slaveocracy by justifying the slave system, rather than challenging it. This clearly negates any notion that one's identity alone either permits or denies access to truth. But what it does demonstrate is that the goals of telling the truth while seeking to justify the inequalities of the social order are stubbornly impossible to do simultaneously.

Of course, that doesn't stop uncritical race theorists from trying. As scholar, activist, and truth teacher Wayne Au explains,

> [T]hose with more power can exert stronger influence on our common-sense understandings of the world, even if such commonsense understanding fundamentally operates as distorted conceptions of material reality. . . . [R]ather than a call for a form of relativism, a standpoint is perhaps better conceived as a tool that allows, following [Nancy] Hartsock, for "the creation of better (more objective, more liberatory) accounts of the world."[74]

To arrive at a more accurate telling of history, Harding suggests we employ a "strong objectivity" that requires "the subject of knowledge be

placed on the same critical, causal plane as the objects of knowledge"[75]—
meaning that the process of learning, the people producing knowledge,
and their relationship to power must be investigated alongside the particular subject matter. Strong objectivity contrasts with traditional views of
objectivity—or "weak objectivity"—which attempts to position historical
inquiry as neutral and unbiased rather than admitting that everyone conducting research has a social location, a set of values, and a political perspective that influences the conclusions one reaches.

This has important conclusions for education. Flowing from standpoint
theory and "strong objectivity," Au has developed the concept of "curriculum standpoint," which maintains that

> curriculum is an extension and expression of material and social rela-
> tions. Textbook companies, non-profit organizations, parents, business
> groups, school boards, state and federal education committees, politi-
> cians, school principals, school departments, and individual teachers
> all have differing levels of interests in, and control over, curriculum.
> This means that whatever knowledge is taught in schools is fraught with
> every aspect of power and politics we see in society. In this same sense,
> those with more resources and power are positioned to try and influence
> what curriculum is taught in schools. Curriculum standpoint embraces
> this reality, understanding that curriculum itself is imbued with the
> social locations of its authors, designer, or sponsors (e.g., major corpora-
> tions), and as such curriculum creates potentialities for understanding
> the world more clearly or in more obscurity relative to such locations.[76]

Curriculum standpoint suggests that teaching the truth requires educators to critically analyze their own identities in relationship to the subject
they are teaching and to reveal the relationship of the texts used in the class
to systems of power vis-à-vis such categories as class position, race, gender,
sexuality, ability, and more. The honest historian Howard Zinn made a similar argument when he said, "Historians should say what their values are,
what they care about, what their background is, and let you know what is
important to them so that young people and everybody who reads history
are warned in advance that they should never count on any one source, but
should go to many sources."[77]

Of course, truth teaching is complicated by the fact that once one encoun-
ters empirical evidence, the interpretation of that evidence is influenced by

people's various experiences, worldviews, and biases. Even deciding which facts to include in a text or in a curriculum is a subjective process. As critical pedagogue Ira Shor put it, "No curriculum can be neutral. . . . The contents included and excluded in curriculum are political choices."[78]

It should be noted, however, that even as educators select different facts to emphasize or interpret historical events differently, they are not negating the reality of past events; just because people interpret past events differently doesn't change the truth that they occurred as they did. The past is the past, and it does not change because of one's biases. However, history—the collection of stories we tell about the past—does reflect the experiences and values of the person telling it, hence the necessity to be forthcoming with students about whose view is being expressed. With this in mind, in the following section (as well as in the preface, chapter 5, and in the conclusion) I reveal some of my experiences and aspects of my identity that shape who I am and how I view the world. In this way, I utilize the conceptual frameworks of standpoint theory and strong objectivity to show how my life of teaching about and organizing against oppression, far from disqualifying me to teach the truth, enhances my ability to provide an honest education.

The bedrock of truth that forms the foundation of this book is the plain fact—supported by the overwhelming preponderance of historical evidence as well as family stories passed down from my ancestors—that the United States was founded on the genocide of Native Americans and the enslavement of African people to work the stolen land. Those foundational injustices were compounded by the exploitation of immigrant labor from all over the world—especially the hyperexploitation of Asian labor and the labor of those from Latin America, but also from many European countries. In addition, this book is rooted in the truth that Indigenous people, Black people, people of color, and working-class people of every origin have built resistance to the expropriation of life and land.

It's important to understand that educators can't engage in truth teaching by compelling students to memorize a list of facts that the educator believes to be true. The practice of truth teaching requires a process of engaging students in a dialogue about historical evidence from multiple perspectives and sources, and analyzing the sources to understand the biases of those sources before drawing conclusions about the validity of the information. As George Carlin, the great comedian and truth teller put it, "Don't just teach your children to read. . . . Teach them to question what they read. Teach them to question everything."[79] The Student Nonviolent Coordinating Committee (SNCC), the organization that created the Freedom Schools during the Freedom Summer campaign of 1964, perceptively described truth teaching this way:

> You see, to ask questions really means to try and find truth, which really means to ask more questions. To ask more questions means to make more challenges, which really means to do things *you* think are important to you. That's dangerous, too, and usually isn't allowed by the same people who keep us from knowing about us.[80]

Truth teaching requires supporting students to develop critical thinking skills and to learn to investigate the perspectives and assumptions that are embedded in every text they encounter. An honest education helps students identify the ideology that underpins every text and every argument they encounter—including those being made by their own teacher—and helps them learn to identify narratives that challenge the status quo and those that reinforce existing power relations.

"The way to right wrongs is to turn the light of truth upon them," remarked Black truth teacher, journalist, and antilynching crusader Ida B. Wells-Barnett—one of the figures who induce night sweats from uncritical race theorists because of how she shattered fairy tales told to students of the infallibility of America, holding up a mirror to the country that didn't always say "fairest of them all." Light has long been a metaphor for the freeing power of truth, one especially invoked by the Black freedom struggle. In *Freedom Dreams*, Robin D. G. Kelley writes, "We absolutely *need* light: the light of social movements ('I've got the light of freedom'), the light of hope ('facing a rising sun/of a new day begun'), the light of spirit ('this little light of mine/I'm gonna let it shine')."[81]

Truth is that light, illuminating what was previously concealed in shade; or it can be that mirror allowing for self-reflection; or it can be a blues song, telling it like it is. But truth is something else, as well. Truth is a fire alarm; it will disrupt whatever you are doing, and it can even become quite irritating to many if it rings long enough. People in a society such as ours who have been habituated to accepting lies often find the truth as grating as the piercing decibels of a school fire drill. Sometimes people just want to climb up a ladder, disconnect the fire alarm from the ceiling, take the batteries out of it, and silence it—even though it may have been trying to communicate something important, even lifesaving.

But the truth resembles an alarm in another way; if you don't ignore it, it can make you move with urgency, look for the emergency, and take action. Educators, students, and parents around the country have pulled the truth alarm, and this is not a drill; educational arsonists have lit fires across the nation to incinerate antiracist ideas. Those lighting the fires are also blowing smoke—acrid plumes of lies threatening to envelop the American classroom, which, when inhaled by students, can cause a loss of (critical) consciousness. Moreover, as you will learn in chapter 1, educational arson isn't only an important metaphor, but also an accurate description of the extremist uncritical race theorists throughout history who burn books and schools.

My Confessions and Intentions

Before going any further, I must make this confession: I am not a dispassionate observer of the war on antiracist curriculum occurring in this country. I have a stake in this struggle as a Black educator, a parent of two kids in the public schools, and a lifelong antiracist activist and organizer. I have been a teacher for more than twenty years in the public schools, teaching at the elementary, middle, and high school levels. I should be honest about something else: I have deliberately taught children what is now, in numerous places, illegal history, and I have distributed these illicit lessons to educators and children in states where they are contraband. I have knowingly and repeatedly written lessons and taught them to children—in elementary schools, middle schools, and high schools around the country—that reveal structures of racism, white supremacy, xenophobia, sexism, homophobia, transphobia, ableism, and imperialism. I have even gone as far as making students uncomfortable by sharing my family's history of enslavement and teaching truths about America's legacy of maintaining structural racism and exploiting working-class labor of all racial backgrounds. I have advocated that teachers in states where it is illegal to teach honest accounts of the history of racism and sexism break the law—and even advocated that they do so collectively in an act of civil disobedience.

Not only have I taught antiracist lessons, but I have also published some on the Zinn Education Project website, making them widely available for educators around the country. For example, I wrote a lesson about Rosa Parks that is designed to help students engage with the documentary *The Rebellious Life of Mrs. Rosa Parks*—and the book of the same name by Jeanne Theoharis—and help them understand the reality that Mrs. Parks was an advocate for the Black Power movement and a supporter of groups like the Black Panther Party. I also cocreated a lesson with my friend Adam Sanchez to teach students about the Black Panther Party and their approach to fighting structural racism that is used by teachers around the country, including where there are prohibitions on such teaching.

I should also come clean about my criminal history. The truth is, I once was arrested. It happened inside the chambers of the Washington State Legislature when I attempted a citizen's arrest of the lawmakers who were voting to cut the education budget—despite the declaration in our state constitution that education is the state's "paramount duty." Further, my arrest stirred my social studies students—to whom I had taught the history of movements for racial and social justice—to organize a mass walkout at our high school and march to city hall where they demanded full funding for the schools.

Of course, uncritical race theorists will assert that any commitment to antiracist pedagogy and activism disqualifies me as an effective educator. However, a clear way to see that uncritical race theorists aren't actually interested in improving education or defending kids is that they don't address any of the real crises facing our children and schools. As parents in Uvalde (Texas), Nashville (Tennessee), Parkland (Florida), Sandy Hook (Connecticut), and all over the country can tell you, gun violence has become the leading cause of death for kids in America, with 3,597 children having died by gunfire in 2021.[82] Further, kids are being poisoned by the lead in drinking water at an alarming number of schools—documented in at least 350 schools and day care centers for a total of about 470 times around the country[83]—and the dire condition of tens of thousands of school buildings across the United States represents "a threat to the well-being of future generations," according to the National Council on School Facilities and a coalition of other top school facilities officials. Meanwhile, the Green New Deal for Public Schools, which would invest $1.4 trillion in school modernization over the next decade, has languished.[84] So I confess; I have been working to counter the contrived panic around CRT while prioritizing these real crises in education.

What This Book Is About

This book is an interrogation of the curricular violence being enacted in states and school districts around the country and a study of the Teach Truth movement that is being organized to defend antiracist, social justice education. But it's more than that. This book is also about whether truth is deemed a goal worthy of pursuit, or if deception will become the expressed ethos of educational institutions. It's about whether young people are allowed to consider honest accounts of America's history or if such inquiry will be designated a truthcrime. It's about what methods for analyzing power—if any—will be permitted by the government. It's about the movement for the right to access liberatory epistemologies that can aid social movements in ridding the world of the economic, political, educational, and social systems of harm. It's about whether the pursuit of a multiracial democracy is a goal that is legal to discuss and organize around. Most importantly, this book is about the process of collective healing that is possible through collective remembering and organizing.

In this book I make several arguments about the driving forces behind both the advocacy for truthcrime legislation and the struggle for honest education. First, to effectively counter the imposition of truthcrime laws and curricular violence by uncritical race theorists, it's crucial to grasp their strategy for perpetuating inequality and systemic racism, as I illustrate throughout this book. I will argue that the importance of analyzing truthcrime laws extends beyond understanding education debates or curriculum theory and is fundamental to understanding US politics and social movements.

Second, as I elaborate in chapter 3, truthcrime laws—as immediate reactions to the fear the right wing experienced during the 2020 uprising for Black lives—are part of an electoral strategy designed by billionaires and their Republican Party operatives to frighten white families and rally their base to the polls. These strategists have also determined that if they don't implement harsh measures to regulate what is legal to learn, their long-term electoral prospects, especially among young voters, are bleak. It's also important to understand that they have coupled this suppression of learning with voter suppression tactics, ranging from voter ID requirements and purges of voter rolls to gerrymandering and the closure of polling places. These measures disproportionately disenfranchise Black, Brown, poor, young, elderly, and disabled voters.

Although the mainstream media frames the policies designed to limit teaching and learning about systemic racism entirely in terms of elections, there are much deeper motivations at work. A third argument advanced in this book (also found in chapter 3) is that truthcrime legislation is an essential component of a strategy to advance neoliberal privatization. Uncritical race theorists hope to further the transfer of wealth from taxpayers to private institutions by persuading white families that because their children are being shamed by antiracist education, they should leave the public schools and seek voucher programs and charter schools.

A fourth argument (developed in chapter 1) is that the most fundamental impetus for outlawing honest education is the drive of settler colonial societies, like the United States, to mislead their populace regarding their nation's origins, which are deeply entrenched in dispossession and genocide. It is here I examine how today's truthcrime laws are part of a long continuum of curricular violence, miseducation, and the suppression of history tracing back to the European colonization of the Americas.

Finally, above all else, this book is a celebration of the resistance to what professor Henry Giroux has called the "violence of organized forgetting" (a concept detailed in chapter 1) and the healing power of honest history. I examine the Teach Truth movement (in chapter 4) and then consider its contribution to what I propose calling the "radical healing of organized remembering" (in chapter 5)—a pedagogical and organizational strategy for resisting and recovering from the violence of truthcrime laws. Here I suggest that individual memories are too easily manipulated by well-funded uncritical race theorists who use their resources to distort the historical record. Yet acts of collective resistance—both inside the classroom and in broader social movements—are capable of transmitting historical lessons vital to the restoration of healthy people and healthy struggles for racial and social justice.

In this book you will meet educators who have been harassed or fired for deciding to teach honest accounts of history, assigning books with Black characters, or suggesting that the legacy of slavery and segregation cause ongoing harm in our society. You will meet librarians who have had books taken out of their collections because they present the realities of the lives of Black people or are about LGBTQ+ people. You will encounter stories of educators who received death threats because they supported what has become a subversive principle of affirming diversity in schools. You will discover students who endured racial slurs, hate speech, and threats to their lives—and then were chastised for espousing "critical race theory" when they demanded their school districts take action to stop racist attacks. You will learn of Black schools and universities that received bomb threats for nurturing the lives of their African American students. Also in these pages, you will encounter brave educators who assiduously maintain a tradition of truth teaching and liberation pedagogy, empowering students to decipher the motivations, goals, and methods of the attack on CRT and supporting them in interpreting the history of structural racism.

Although uncritical race theorists' banning of curriculum and books may seem like displays of authoritarian strength, they betray a deep insecurity. The very act of censorship indicates a fear of the ideas and knowledge contained within. After all, if these ideas held no sway, there would be no need to suppress them. The fact is, uncritical race theorists are attacking antiracist education precisely because so many people are demanding it be taught. Furthermore, by banning CRT and Black studies, they invite curiosity about the lessons those disciplines hold. This risky gambit threatens to motivate students to wonder what uncritical race theorists don't want them to know. Ever tried telling a young person to mind their own business and to keep out of something? Maybe it didn't end up like you had hoped. Once young people decide they will no longer allow anyone to hide history from them, they will seek the truth about social movements that toppled slavery and Jim Crow segregation and effectively challenged many systems of oppression. When this happens, students' quest for these historical lessons will no longer be just about earning a grade, but about changing the world.

The Beloved Classroom Community

The criminalization of literacy for enslaved people couldn't suppress their struggle to learn; they engaged in clandestine educational practices regardless of the law. Jim Crow segregation didn't stop the movement for Black education; Black educators organized unions and built Citizenship Schools. McCarthyism and the Red Scare didn't end the movement for antiracist curriculum; courageous educators taught these lessons covertly, and then the Civil Rights Movement finally galvanized masses of people who abandoned their fear of being labeled a "red" and made education a central site of struggle. The bombing of Freedom Schools during the Civil Rights Movement didn't obliterate curiosity or the striving for liberatory education—and neither will today's truthcrime laws. As students, educators, and parents rise against truthcrime, they will implement ethnic studies pedagogies that ensure every student's heritage is included in the curriculum and every student has the analytical tools to challenge racism and oppression. This movement will be the prerequisite for a longer struggle to extend Martin Luther King Jr.'s concept of the "beloved community" to the schoolhouse to create the beloved classroom community.

James Baldwin wrote in *Nothing Personal* that lying about our past produces an "unspeakable loneliness," which he believed contributed to creating "a loveless nation."[85] Centering love in the classroom, then, is vital to fostering the connection, repair, and freedom our society so desperately needs. The beloved classroom community is animated by a deep and enduring love for every child. One of the leading theorists and practitioners of critical pedagogy, bell hooks, explained it like this: "The loving classroom is one in which students are taught, both by the presence and practice of the teacher, that critical exchange can take place without diminishing anyone's spirit, that conflict can be resolved constructively. . . . Love in the classroom prepares teachers and students to open our minds and hearts. It is the foundation on which every learning community can be created. Love will always move us away from domination in all its forms. Love will always challenge and change us."[86]

Former Colleyville Heritage High School principal James Whitfield (whom we met at the beginning of this introduction) provided insight on the power of a deeply connected and loving classroom during his May 19, 2022, testimony to the House Subcommittee on Civil Rights and Civil Liberties. He was invited to testify at the "Curriculum Sabotage and Classroom Censorship" congressional hearing addressing the ongoing initiatives aimed at restricting discourse on American history, race, and LGBTQ+ issues in public K–12 classrooms, as well as the punitive measures targeting educators who teach truthfully about these subjects. Whitfield took Congress to school, conducting a master class at the hearing on the need to defend honest education. Whitfield told me his nerves got to him when he first entered the imposing congressional chamber as he contemplated the weighty task of defending public education. However, when he heard the testimony of courageous youth who spoke before him to defend their right to learn honest history, it steeled his resolve and alleviated his anxiety.

Seated before the committee, a placard reading "Dr. Whitfield" before him, he taught a lesson from the heart in a way that cut through all the trappings of congressional formality. Leaning into his microphone, he began his advanced congressional course on defending the freedom to learn by saying,

> My name is James Whitfield—I'm a husband, and a father of three amazing children. Most recently, I served as a high school principal in Northeast Tarrant County, Texas, a suburb of Dallas. I'm here today to tell you there is reason for concern. . . . Every kid deserves . . . someone who believes in them, inspires them, empowers them, holds them accountable, and, above all, loves them.[87]

Whitfield's is a vision for a beloved classroom community that's possible when positive relationships are forged on a basis of truth and solidarity.

When educators love their students enough to teach them the truth—and when it's a hard truth, they are there to nurture them through the lesson with tenderness—transcendent experiences are possible that empower young people to heal from the traumas they have endured and create the healthy and thriving futures they envision. Tiffany Mitchell Patterson, a Black truth teacher from West Virginia, explained the path we must walk to get there when she signed the Zinn Education Project's public pledge to teach the truth and left these remarks:

> The road to freedom hinges on the youth knowing the raw and rugged truth about the systemic ills of this country. Through truth our young people can imagine and fight for a new world where we are ALL free.[88]

Part I

Disremembering

CHAPTER 1

Educational Arson, Epistemicide, and Organized Forgetting

Our Freedom School had been burned down by some white people who didn't want the negro to get an education or to ever be free.
—**Thirteen-year-old boy** from Mississippi, summer 1964

Children are organically predisposed to be critical thinkers. . . . Sadly, children's passion for thinking often ends when they encounter a world that seeks to educate them for conformity and obedience only. Most children are taught early on that thinking is dangerous.
—**bell hooks,** *Teaching Critical Thinking: Practical Wisdom*

"They have an agenda," James Whitfield (the former teacher and principal of Colleyville Heritage High School in Texas whom we met in the introduction) told his "class" of congresspeople in the House Subcommittee on Civil Rights and Civil Liberties. "And your mere existence threatens that— so they come after you . . . educators continue to be asked to do more, with less, all while navigating the complexities of their role and enduring baseless attacks by individuals with political agendas."

This political agenda was on display during three days in the middle of June 2022, when the Faith & Freedom Coalition held its thirteenth annual "Road to Majority Policy Conference" in Nashville, Tennessee. On the final day of the conference, senator Ted Cruz, the Republican from Whitfield's home state of Texas, ascended the stage, stepped in front of the podium and a giant screen with his image projected on it, gripped a wireless microphone, and addressed more than two thousand true believers who had assembled to build momentum for the GOP ahead of the 2022 midterm elections.

Rousing the faithful, Cruz bellowed, "Let me tell you right now, critical race theory is bigoted, it is a lie, and it is *every bit as racist as the Klansmen in white sheets.*"[1] Cruz's sermon on history and morality was met with a stirring ovation from the congregants. I invite you to sit with Cruz's quote for a moment and really consider its implications. Cruz wants you to associate *an actual terrorist organization that tortured and killed thousands* with schoolteachers who engage students in discussions about structural racism. He wants you to associate the KKK with, for example, educators who explore how the racial violence that the KKK inflicted on Black people during Reconstruction and the Jim Crow era continues to have reverberations in white supremacist attacks today. The irony here is profound; while Cruz compares those who teach CRT to the KKK, his own attack on antiracist education aligns with one of the Klan's primary objectives: thwarting Black education and antiracist pedagogy—which they have done ferociously throughout US history.

Cruz's admirers that day did not question his lie that CRT and the KKK were synonyms because they had been taught uncritical race theory from a young age. This ideology trained them to accept dominant discourses about race, such as the absurd "color-blind" notion that any acknowledgment of race—whether from white supremacist terrorists or antiracist educators—is itself racist.

The Violence of Organized Forgetting

At the founding rally of the Organization of Afro-American Unity on June 28, 1964, Malcolm X delivered these words in a speech that describes the predicament Black children still face in school today: "When we send our children to school in this country they learn nothing about us other than that we used to be cotton pickers. Every little child going to school thinks his grandfather was a cotton picker. Why, your grandfather was Nat Turner; your grandfather was Toussaint L'Ouverture; your grandfather was Hannibal."[2]

We can add that Black children also don't learn that their grandmothers were Sojourner Truth, Harriet Tubman, or Ida B. Wells-Barnett. Critical pedagogue Henry Giroux has called the intentional disremembering of history inflicted by ruling elites the "violence of organized forgetting" in his insightful book bearing the same title.[3] Giroux describes the violence of organized forgetting as an effort by those in power to hide vital lessons of the past that could empower social movements such as "the historical legacies of resistance to racism, militarism, privatization and panoptical surveillance [which] have long been forgotten and made invisible in the current assumption that Americans now live in a democratic, post-racial society."[4] The violence of organized forgetting is an essential concept for grasping the intellectual brutality that students of color are subjected to when the contributions and struggles of their ancestors are cut out of the curriculum with truthcrime laws. As Ekene Okolo, a seventeen-year-old senior at Westview High School in San Diego, observed, "The banning of CRT makes it seem like POC (people of color) identities aren't worthy enough of being shared or talked about. It keeps the white narrative at the forefront of our education system."[5]

Clarence Lusane highlights some of the many manifestations of the violence of organized forgetting, writing, "Confederate flags and monuments, statues of enslavers, buildings and schools named after white supremacists, sports teams with racist names, bigoted historical markers and textbook accounts of history—and omission of the true extent of the suffering and resistance of people of color—have all contributed to the normalization of racial hierarchy in the United States."[6] As of 2022, there were 723 confederate monuments and over 2,000 schools across the country that used Native Americans as mascots (often coupled with racist imagery, slogans, or songs).[7]

In addition to the overtly violent attacks on history and antiracist education, organized forgetting can be achieved more discreetly through what is known as the "hidden curriculum"—the implicit lessons, values, and social norms that are conveyed to students through the various components of the educational system. The hidden curriculum operates as a mechanism for transmitting and perpetuating hegemonic ideologies and social hierarchies. Messages about race, gender, and sexuality are woven into the fabric of this hidden curriculum, reinforcing stereotypes, biases, and dominant narratives. When the hidden curriculum is applied to teaching about the past, I call it the "gentrification of history" because of how wealthy white people's stories are moved into textbooks and lesson plans that push out the histories of Black, Indigenous, and people of color (BIPOC). When the histories of BIPOC are redlined out of the curriculum, it perpetuates a narrative of BIPOC inferiority without ever having to explicitly affirm white supremacy.

Often, elites prefer to exert hegemony by gentrifying history and teaching with the hidden curriculum, but when that curriculum is exposed—as it was on a wide scale during the 2020 uprising for Black lives—they are perfectly comfortable resorting to criminalizing ideas or history that challenge their authority. Defending students from the violence of organized forgetting requires a critical examination of both the explicit truthcrime laws that overtly ban honest education and of the gentrification of history that has long functioned to disempower BIPOC, LGBTQ+, and working-class people.

It's worth spending some time taking a close look at some of the most pernicious examples of the violence of organized forgetting in schools today. The institutionalization of organized forgetting was revealed when Florida's State Academic Standards were approved in 2023, declaring slavery was of "personal benefit" to enslaved Black people. Florida governor Ron DeSantis defended the overtly racist standards, saying, "They're probably going to show that some of the folks that eventually parlayed, you know, being a blacksmith into doing things later in life."[8] The description of American slavery—a system that institutionalized the rape of Black women, routine torture, and forced labor from childhood to death—as a job training program that was advantageous for African Americans reveals the moral bankruptcy of the uncritical race theorists' attack on antiracist education and CRT.

Yet be sure this gratuitous curricular violence is not confined to the state of Florida. The textbook mega company Prentice Hall inflicted the violence of organized forgetting in its widely used *History of the United States*, which insisted that not all slaveowners were harsh because "a few [enslaved people] never felt the lash." It even attempted to teach children that slavery could be a cheery affair, stating, "Many [of the enslaved] may not have even been terribly unhappy with their lot, for they knew no other."[9] This wasn't a textbook from the Reconstruction era—I found a copy of this book in my own school's book room a few years ago.

The Connecticut Adventure textbook, published in 2001, taught fourth graders for fifteen years that enslaved people in the state were "cared for like members of the family"—until families told the truth about the brutality of slavery and were able to get the book removed in 2016.[10] A textbook from the industry titan McGraw-Hill contained a map of the United States with a caption that said the Atlantic slave trade brought "millions of workers from Africa to the southern United States to work on agricultural plantations."[11] These are just a few examples of textbooks that have been used by thousands of students all over the United States that confirm the assertion of C. L. R. James's that "the only place where Negroes did not revolt is in the pages of capitalist historians."[12]

As dishonest as the mainstream textbooks are, some uncritical race theory organizations believe they don't do enough to inflict the violence of organized forgetting. Consider the example of PragerU, a right-wing propaganda group that produces slick videos and cartoons to teach uncritical race theory to children. PragerU has a budget of some $60 million a year and a hundred-person staff who have produced videos that have now been viewed over one billion times—and its content has even been adopted in six states: Arizona, Florida, Louisiana, New Hampshire, Montana, and Oklahoma.[13] To fully appreciate PragerU's dedication to dishonesty, you would need to see their video titled *Frederick Douglass: The Outspoken Abolitionist*, which depicts a cartoon Frederick Douglass explaining to two white children (who have traveled back in time to the year 1852 to see him) why slavery was "a compromise to achieve something great." In PragerU's memory hole historical account, they force deceitful dialogue into the mouth of Frederick Douglass, portraying him saying, "Children, our founding fathers knew that slavery was evil and wrong . . . they wanted it to end . . . There was no real movement anywhere in the world to abolish slavery before the American founding . . . Our system is wonderful."[14] PragerU actually portrays Frederick Douglass saying "our system is wonderful"—and not just in any year, but in the year 1852. That was the year he gave one of the most powerful speeches in history, titled "What to the Slave

Is the Fourth of July?" where he absolutely eviscerates the US government:

> What, to the American slave, is your Fourth of July? I answer: a day that
> reveals to him, more than all other days in the year, the gross injustice
> and cruelty to which he is the constant victim. . . . There is not a nation
> on the earth guilty of practices, more shocking and bloody, than are
> the people of these United States, at this very hour. Go where you may,
> search where you will, roam through all the monarchies and despotisms
> of the old world, travel through South America, search out every abuse,
> and when you have found the last, lay your facts by the side of the every-
> day practices of this nation, and you will say with me, that, for revolting
> barbarity and shameless hypocrisy, America reigns without a rival.[15]

But, of course, the uncritical race theorists at PragerU are quite at ease
with lying about Douglass to hide his radical condemnation of slavery and
the American government that perpetuated it. The assault on Americans'
understanding of the history of slavery has been so vicious that over half
the population today believe the white supremacist lie that the Civil War
was not fought over slavery.[16] In Oklahoma, one lawmaker proposed insti-
tutionalizing the violence of organized forgetting by "prohibiting teaching
certain concepts pertaining to America and slavery" including "that one
race is the unique oppressor in the institution of slavery"; that "another race
is the unique victim in the institution of slavery"; and that "America, in general, had slavery more extensively and for a later period of time than other
nations."[17] Given that white people in the United States enslaved Black people, and that slavery lasted longer in the United States than all but two other
nations in the Americas, this bill was clearly aimed at criminalizing the truth
and imposing the violence of organized forgetting. The American Historical
Association (the largest membership association of professional historians
in the world) explained the impact of this bill, stating, "The practical effect
of this policy would discourage instructors from teaching students that the
US Constitution prohibited Congress from abolishing US participation in
the international slave trade for two decades" and that "the overwhelming
majority of slave holders in the US identified as white; and slavery was abolished three decades later in the United States than in most of the British
Empire."[18] In other words, this bill would mandate lying to kids.

The lies by omission about Black history are also harmful. The gentrification of history is rampant in corporate textbooks, which often reduce

Black history to enslavement and fail to teach the truth about the incredible contributions African Americans have given the world in science, art, music, mathematics, literature, struggles for democracy, and beyond. As one teacher explained to Learning for Justice in their "Hard History" report, "When students see themselves or their Black classmates only represented as slaves in textbooks, that affects their sense of self and how other students view them."[19] Teaching truth requires educators to engage in efforts to oppose historical gentrification by helping their students critically examine textbooks to develop an understanding of the ways they often exclude or misrepresent Black people. Yet anti-Blackness isn't the only problem with the curriculum.

LGBTQ+ stories and women's voices are also often silenced in the curriculum. According to a national GLSEN survey, only one in five queer students "were taught positive representations of LGBTQ people, history, or events in their schools." Additionally, over half of these students indicated that such information was unavailable in their school libraries.[20] An honest account of history must also center the everyday lives and struggles of women, yet as Rethinking Schools editorialized, "If you go by most U.S. history texts, the only piece of women's history worth space in the curriculum is the fight for suffrage. But women defining and fighting for freedom for themselves and their communities has been at the center of American history from the beginning."[21] Micaela Wells was a high school senior in 2021 when she wrote about the sexism she encountered in the curriculum. "Although my textbook—branded AMSCO and published by a company called Perfection Learning—isn't endorsed by AP or the College Board, it closely follows the official AP U.S. History curriculum," she wrote. She continued,

> In this advanced text is a 20-page chapter on World War II. As I read about President Franklin D. Roosevelt, the Pan-American conferences and the war's impact on society, I came across a paragraph creatively titled "Women." Merely a hundred words later, "women" were abandoned. I was bothered that the writers had deemed 100 words sufficient for teaching students everything important about women during that era. What bothered me even more was my own lack of surprise.[22]

Indigenous voices are muted as well. In one study of Native Americans in textbooks, a researcher concluded, "The readers were not encouraged to take the perspective of Indigenous Americans but instead were provided with explanations and justifications for the destruction of Indigenous peoples by the United States."[23] The violence of organized forgetting was on display in the 2017 Richmond Hill Canadian textbook for elementary school students that attempted to erase colonization and genocide by writing, "When the European settlers arrived, they needed land to live on. The First Nations people agreed to move to different areas to make room for the new settlements."[24] A US history textbook titled *The Making of a Superpower: USA 1865–1975* that was published in 2015 had a picture of two balanced scales, with a caption on one side that read, "Criticisms of treatment of Native Americans" and the other side, "Defense of the treatment of Native Americans." The question posed below the image asked, "To what extent do you believe the treatment of Native Americans has been exaggerated?"[25]—asserting to students that it's acceptable to deny the genocide of Native people.

The textbook portrayal of Asian Americans has also been abysmal. "Researchers have found that when Asian Americans were included in the textbooks, they were either primarily depicted as victims with little to no agency or as new immigrants who have made no contribution to the country," remarked Erika Lee, a professor of history and Asian American studies at the University of Minnesota. "The consequences of this invisibility, this erasure has laid the foundations for ignorance, for hate, and for violence."[26] From the sugarcoating of the brutal working conditions of Chinese laborers who built the transcontinental railroads, to the whitewashing of US imperialism in the Philippines during the Spanish American War, to the obscuring impact of the mass incarceration of Japanese Americans during World War II, textbooks have largely been dishonest with students about the extent of anti-Asian racism in the United States.

Citing a 2023 study by the Johns Hopkins Institute for Education Policy and UnidosUS, Sarah Schwartz wrote, "[T]extbooks generally reference Latinos in the context of foreign policy, and often portray Latinos as passive recipients of U.S. government action rather than as actors themselves."[27] A previous study of school textbooks by Elizabeth Martínez reveals similar erasure and dehumanization for Mexican Americans. Martínez describes a sixty-page unit called "Settling the Land" in the textbook *From Sea to Shining Sea*, writing, "Mexican Americans appear only as farmworkers, and even then their historic role in producing vast agricultural wealth is not recognized (nor is that of Filipinos). A single photo shows an orchard with a rain of almonds being shaken out of some trees—by machine, not people. . . . Nowhere does the text say that agriculture was made possible in the Southwest by an art that

Mexicans and Indians taught to Anglos: irrigation." She points out that in the fourth-grade textbook *Oh California*, "Nowhere can we find the lower-class Mexicans, nowhere the many Mexicans who were violently repressed and driven off the land, often even lynched, from the Gold Rush days to the 1930s, nowhere the massive strikes by Mexican workers in the 1930s or the deportation of thousands who were actually citizens."[28] Just as with other people of color, corporate textbooks have made the true histories of Mexican Americans, and other Latine people, invisible in the curriculum.

It is also essential to understand that there is a connection between curricular violence, truthcrime laws, and physical violence. In May 2023, the NAACP issued a travel advisory in response to what the organization described as governor Ron DeSantis's "aggressive attempts to erase Black history and to restrict diversity, equity, and inclusion programs in Florida schools." The travel advisory stated, "Florida is openly hostile toward African Americans, people of color and LGBTQ+ individuals."[29]

DeSantis fired back, "Claiming that Florida is unsafe is a total farce," in a conversation he had with Elon Musk.[30] Then, only three months later, on August 26, 2023, 21-year-old white male Ryan Christopher Palmeter entered the Dollar General store in Jacksonville, Florida, armed with a rifle with swastikas painted on it and fatally shot three Black people: Angela Michelle Carr, 52; Jerrald Gallion, 29; and Anolt Joseph Laguerre Jr., 19. Palmeter left behind a twenty-seven-page diatribe riddled with abhorrent racism, homophobia, transphobia, and antisemitism.

The GOP's "war on woke" had escalated into a literal battleground with deadly consequences. "What Gov. DeSantis has done is created an atmosphere for such tragedies to take place," NAACP president Derrick Johnson said. "This is exactly why we issued the travel advisory."[31]

Over the weekend before the fatal shootings had taken place, the gunman had driven to a parking lot at Edward Waters University—Florida's first historically Black college—and began putting on tactical gear. When students reported him, campus security approached, and he sped off.

This incident and the subsequent killings brought up painful memories for Nat Glover. Glover, as a 17-year-old, was the victim of the infamous racist attack almost sixty years earlier known as "Ax Handle Saturday," when a mob of Ku Klux Klan members beat him with ax handles after he left his part-time job washing dishes at a local diner. "We are just in an environment now that is toxic as it relates to race," Glover stressed, as he reflected on the Jacksonville shooting, "This notion of us against them, Black versus white, is being promoted."[32] These are the stakes in the struggle for teaching honest history. Truth teachers know that if school isn't honest with students about the United States' history of racial violence—and the organized resistance to it—the violence of organized forgetting can contribute to physical acts of racial violence.

Educational Arson

What is fire? It's a mystery. Scientists give us gobbledegook about friction and molecules. But they don't really know. Its real beauty is that it destroys responsibility and consequences. A problem gets too burdensome, then into the furnace with it.

—**Ray Bradbury**, *Fahrenheit 451*

On May 10, 1933, biblioclast Nazi Brownshirt storm troopers and university students across Germany threw twenty-five thousand books onto bonfires while giving the Hitler salute and singing Nazi anthems. In Berlin, forty thousand people gathered to hear the German minister of Public Enlightenment and Propaganda, Joseph Goebbels, give a vile antisemitic speech in which he declared,

> The era of extreme Jewish intellectualism is now at an end. . . . The future German man will not just be a man of books, but a man of character. It is to this end that we want to educate you. As a young person, to already have the courage to face the pitiless glare, to overcome the fear of death, and to regain respect for death—this is the task of this young generation. And thus you do well in this midnight hour to commit to the flames the evil spirit of the past.[33]

Goebbels's antisemitism, and assertion that the past was an "evil spirit" that must be burned, explains how the kerosene of fascism is used by those I call "educational arsonists"; they are the fire team shock troops of a social order built on lies. Yet, to be clear, educational arsonists haven't only inflamed Nazi Germany. Uncritical race theorists throughout history have blown a lot of smoke to cloud the truth—and where there's smoke, there's fire. A subset of uncritical race theorists have literally lit fires to burn knowledge.

Those in power have used many strategies to enforce the violence of organized forgetting and eradicate systems of thought that challenge their power. The destruction of ways of knowing and understanding the world is a practice that Boaventura de Sousa Santos has called "epistemicide." Epistemicide is the erasure of ways of knowing that do not conform to dominant colonial paradigms, and it is a form of intellectual violence that marginalizes alternative knowledge systems and perpetuates inequalities in the production and dissemination of knowledge. Recognizing and valuing epistemic diversity is essential for building more equitable societies. Epistemicidal maniacs have long sought to destroy cultural knowledge, antiracist ideas, and discussions of sexuality and gender that challenge patriarchy and heteronormativity. Yet educational arsonists seek more than the destruction of the knowledge; they also desire a public spectacle designed to terrorize people into suppressing their curiosity and quelling critical thinking. Although educational arsonists certainly are uncritical race theorists, they are more than just those who refuse to critically analyze dominant explanations of race. Educational arsonists use the threat of the flame along with actual flammable liquids, matches, torches, dynamite, and bombs in an attempt to cremate bodies of knowledge that support antiracist and social justice struggles.

The *Fahrenheit 451* firefighters only appear as fantasy to those unaware of the reality of the way the flame has been set upon Black and Indigenous people's pursuit of education. Except real-life educational arsonists don't limit their pyromania to books, as they also enjoy the burning of schools and even teachers. As Heinrich Heine's explained, "Those who burn books will in the end burn people."[34] Consider the white mob that lynched David Wyatt, a Black teacher in Brooklyn, Illinois, hanging him from a telephone pole in the public square in 1903 and then setting his body on fire. Educational arsonists are enchanted by the power of the flame, not dissimilar to characters in Octavia Butler's prophetic dystopian novel *Parable of the Sower*, who use the drug called "pyro" because "[i]t makes watching the leaping, changing patterns of fire a better, more intense, longer-lasting high than sex."[35]

Who are the actual educational arsonists addicted to raising the temperature to 451 degrees Fahrenheit (the temperature at which paper

burns)? Meet Spanish bishop Diego de Landa. When de Landa came
into contact with the Mayan people in 1562, he encountered a more than
2,000-year-old culture that had produced some of the most significant
advancements in astronomy, mathematics, agriculture, architecture, and
linguistics of any people on earth. The Mayan people built elaborate cities,
devised the most accurate calendar of any civilization, and created one of
the world's first written languages. They wrote codices (books) made out
of huun (paper) from the inner bark of a fig tree—a more durable writing
surface than the papyrus used in Europe at the time. The Mayan books
were the written records of their civilization, including religious, scientific,
mathematic, and historical texts. On July 12, 1562, Spanish educational
arsonists, also known as conquistadors, burned almost every Mayan text
in existence in a giant conflagration of ignorance and craven power. Diego
de Landa described why he ordered the epistemicide: "We found a large
number of books in these characters and, as they contained nothing in
which were not to be seen as superstition and lies of the devil, we burned
them all, which they regretted to an amazing degree, and which caused
them much affliction."[36]

Today, only four Mayan books have survived the educational arson of
the colonizers. The Spanish Crown's eradication of Mayan texts validates
de Sousa Santos's statement that "in the most extreme cases, such as that
of European expansion, epistemicide was one of the conditions of genocide."[37] Of course, these educational arsonists also massacred many thousands of Indigenous people, including burning people alive.

Who, then, are the educational arsonists in the United States? During
the Reconstruction era (after the Civil War), well over six hundred schools
were burned down by the KKK and other white supremacists in an effort to
throw Black education on the bonfire. During the era, the New York Society for the Suppression of Vice embossed an image of a book burning on its
official seal to promote its creed of educational arson. Anthony Comstock,
the founder of the society, would have delighted in today's truthcrime and
educational closeting policies seeking to eliminate any discussions of sexuality in schools. He was so disgusted by what he judged were sexually inde-
cent texts that he championed a series of state and federal laws that banned
"obscenity," which came to be known as the Comstock laws. Comstock's
notion of the obscene included Walt Whitman's poetry collection *Leaves
of Grass*, anatomy textbooks for medical students, and anything providing

women with information about contraception. In 1935, Comstock's society oversaw the destruction of an estimated fifteen tons of literature[38]—476 books, 11,450 magazines, and about 100,000 pamphlets—including fifteen copies of the book *The Man in the Monkey Suit* because it presented policemen in "an unfavorable light."[39]

During the McCarthy era of the mid-1940s and 1950s, educational arsonists burned books they labeled subversive, socialistic, or obscene. Notable examples include the Catholic Church burning ten thousand comic books in 1948 due to fears they were contributing to juvenile delinquency, and the US government burning three thousand copies of *Scientific American* in March 1950, based on the specious claim that their article on the atomic bomb contained a "secret" to bomb making.[40]

During the Civil Rights Movement many Black schools and churches were bombed and burned—along with schools that took steps to integrate. In August 1956, Clinton High School in Tennessee was ordered to admit Black students, making it one of the first public schools in the South to be desegregated under court order. On October 5, 1958, educational arsonists struck Clinton High School with approximately one hundred sticks of dynamite that turned the redbrick to dust, leaving only a pile of rubble. In August 1964, educational arsonists threw an incendiary at a Freedom School in Gluckstadt, Mississippi, and reduced the building to its brick foundation. The Freedom School educators asked the students to write reflections about the attack and a thirteen-year-old boy explained,

> I think it was a great disaster to come and find that on August 10, our Freedom School had been burned down by some white people who didn't want the negro to get an education or to ever be free.
>
> I think it's a shame how all the good books get burned, how the pencils and tables got burned, how the church piano and all the good church benches were burned to ashes.[41]

Educational arsonists attacked these adolescent Black children because they were learning how to get free. Charlie Cobb, a member of the SNCC, was the one who proposed the idea for the Freedom Schools during the organization's 1964 Mississippi Freedom Summer campaign. I spoke with Cobb in August 2022, and he explained the pedagogical philosophy of the Freedom Schools and how they differed from traditional schools:

Black people, young Black people in Mississippi were taught not to think. They were taught to believe in their own inferiority. They were taught to believe in the necessity of white supremacy. That's what the schools taught. I mean, in 1962, when I came to Mississippi, the chapter on the Civil War in the Mississippi school books was the war of Northern aggression against the South. This, we recognized as a huge problem, but we didn't know how to tackle it right away. We knew it was necessary. We were influenced by people like Septima Clark and Ella Baker, and there were . . . people that were encouraging us not only to think about ourselves differently, but to think about ways to facilitate other young people our age and younger to think, and that's what the schools were largely about. Aside from the remedial stuff, reading, writing, and arithmetic, the Freedom Schools were created to teach people that there was a different way to think about themselves in the world.[42]

Educational arsonists struck again in West Virginia in 1974 when the Kanawha County School Board voted to adopt new multicultural textbooks. Because students would now be able to learn more about Black history, educational arsonists firebombed one elementary school, dynamited another, and attacked a third school with Molotov cocktails.[43] In addition, they detonated fifteen sticks of dynamite near a gas meter at the board of education office just after a meeting had adjourned. Thankfully, no injuries resulted from these attacks, but the violence and destruction shook the community.[44] The Heritage Foundation—one of the organizations leading the call for truthcrime laws today—got its start by providing legal support for those in West Virginia who were attacking multicultural books.[45]

Arsonist attacks on Black institutions persisted beyond the decline of the social movements of the 1960s and 1970s. Between 1996 and 2005, some two thousand Black churches were burned down.[46] PBS News reported that "[i]n 1996, over 160 black churches burned across the nation. Many of them were in poor, rural areas. This was particularly devastating, as rural black churches also serve as centers of community and provide a wide range of social services."[47] One of those social services is very often education, whether it be K–12 education, tutoring, or Sunday school; and the Black church has long been seen as a threat by educational arsonists who fear its potential for collective learning, organizing, and uplift. "The church building in Cerro Gordo, set afire May 23, was attached to the church and used as a school," said a 1996 article in the *Los Angeles Times*.[48]

Threats from educational arsonists, also frightened of empowered Black children, persist in contemporary society. In 2016, the Black Lives Matter at School movement was sparked when a white supremacist made a bomb threat at John Muir Elementary School in Seattle. The threat arose due to a planned event organized by faculty, parents, and a group called Black Men United to Change the Narrative, led by DeShawn Jackson, to celebrate their Black students. The event featured shirts designed by art teacher Julie Trout that read "Black Lives Matter, We Stand Together." In 2021—amidst the GOP's nationwide attack on teaching the truth about race, gender, and sexuality—the Fredericksburg-based *Free Lance-Star* newspaper reported that two members of the Spotsylvania County School Board in Virginia advocated for burning certain books, with director Kirk Twigg exclaiming he wanted to "see the books before we burn them so we can identify within our community that we are eradicating this bad stuff."[49] As generous as his offer was to at least look at the books before he destroyed them, Twigg's comment was dry kindling for the flame of ignorant white rage. The increasingly incendiary rhetoric from uncritical race theory extremists even resulted in educational arsonists igniting terror during Black History Month, 2022, with a series of bomb threats against several historically Black colleges and universities across the United States.[50]

On February 2, 2022, educational arsonist and far-right Tennessee pastor Greg Locke organized a large gathering of his followers to participate in a group book burning—not long after the McMinn County School Board in Tennessee voted unanimously to ban the Pulitzer Prize–winning graphic novel *Maus* (which depicts the author Art Spiegelman interviewing his father about his experiences as a Polish Jew and Holocaust survivor). Locke live streamed his act of educational arson as the sizable crowd threw books into a bonfire that he hissed had "demonic influences."

Tennessee state representative Jerry Sexton became the torchbearer for educational arson when he exclaimed that he would burn books deemed inappropriate by the government. "Let's say you take these books out of the library, what are you going to do with them?" Representative John Ray Clemmons asked Sexton. "I don't have a clue, but I would burn them," Sexton replied.[51] Although Sexton's threat was despicable, he at least spoke the truth when he acknowledged that he "didn't have a clue."

In September 2023, a video went viral of Missouri state senator Bill Eigel, who was campaigning for governor, using a flamethrower to torch a stack of boxes at a fundraising event. "In the video, I am taking a flame thrower to cardboard boxes representing what I am going to do to the leftist policies and RINO [Republican in name only] corruption of the Jeff City swamp," Eigel explained to the media. "But let's be clear, you bring those woke pornographic books to Missouri schools to try to brainwash our kids, and I'll burn those too—on the front lawn of the governor's mansion."[52] This kind of increasingly unhinged declaration that "woke" books are pornographic and should be burned—invoking the policies of the most repressive eras of American and German history—is an alarming escalation in the attack on honest education. This dangerous rhetoric contributed to libraries in suburban Chicago experiencing a series of bomb threats over several weeks in 2023, mirroring similar threats reported in other states, including a wave of educational arsonist threats targeting public libraries in Minnesota in 2024.[53]

For hundreds of years educational arsonists have used the flame in an attempt to scorch ways of knowing that foster community, unity, and resistance; the flame has proven an effective method for inflicting intellectual violence on students. However, as Ralph Waldo Emerson said, "Every burned book or house enlightens the world; every suppressed or expunged word reverberates through the earth from side to side."[54] Educational arsonists are tremendously destructive, and yet the terror they perpetrate is also their weakness because every page consumed by the flame illuminates their cowardice and contemptibility. The first step in combating educational arsonist must be to sound the truth alarm.

Black Education "Makes Tyrants Quake and Tremble"

As truth teacher and Black public intellectual Cornel West wrote in *Race Matters*, "No other people have been taught systemically to hate themselves—psychic violence—reinforced by the power of state and civic coercion—physical violence—for the primary purpose of controlling their minds and exploiting their labor for nearly four hundred years."[55] West's assessment of the attack on Black education is an important explanation of the goals of uncritical race theorists. As West suggests, they are at ease with using physical violence to control Black people who rebel against white supremacy, but they would prefer a more stable situation where oppressed people are taught to internalize inferiority and learn to accept there is little that can be done to challenge inequity. As sixteen-year-old Kerry Santa Cruz explained to NBC News about the struggle to stop legislation that bans honest discussions of structural racism, "It's important for kids, especially Black kids, to learn about race so they can understand who they are. So they don't end up hating themselves for being Black. Education is good."[56]

Because education has the potential for this kind of empowerment of Black people, it has been under attack since African people were first kidnapped and brought to the Americas. Enslavers attempted to erase any memory of collective resistance to slavery and of their African heritage— including their foundational contributions to science, literature, history, art, music, and every other human endeavor. As the French colonial governor of Martinique wrote to a French minister in Haiti in the late 1700s, "The safety of the whites demands that we keep the Negroes in the most profound ignorance. I have reached the stage of believing firmly that one must treat the Negroes as one treats beasts."[57]

Just as today's attack on antiracist education was a direct response to the 2020 uprising for Black lives, the first antiliteracy laws banning Black people from reading or writing in the American colonies were a direct response to the Stono Rebellion of enslaved African people. On Sunday, September 9, 1739, Jemmy, an enslaved African man likely from Angola, gathered with around twenty-two other rebels near the Stono River, twenty miles southwest of Charleston, South Carolina. Jemmy, who is also referred to as "Cato" by some sources, was the acknowledged leader of the group—and he was literate. Jemmy was not the only enslaved person in the colony who could read and write, and it's important to recognize that a significant number of West Africans were literate in Arabic and came from rich scholarly traditions of higher education, especially in Timbuktu, Mali, where some of the first universities in the world were ever opened.

As Jemmy and the other Africans assembled at the Stono River, they hoisted a banner that simply read "Liberty!" So began the largest revolt of enslaved people in South Carolina's history, and the largest uprising in a British colony before the American Revolution. They continued by marching down the roadway chanting "liberty." These freedom fighters managed to gather dozens of other African people from nearby plantations, killing the slave owners as they went, swelling their ranks to between sixty and one hundred. Before the rebellion was put down, they had killed twenty-three white people, with the South Carolinian militia ultimately killing around forty-four Africans.

As a direct response to the Stono Rebellion, South Carolina passed the "Negro Act" of 1740, which "did more than any single piece of legislation in the colony's history to curtail de facto personal liberties, which slaves had been able to cling to against formidable odds during the first three generations of settlement."[58] The law explicitly legalized the killing of African people, stating, "And it shall be further enacted by the authority aforesaid . . . if any such slave shall assault and stricke [sic] such white person, such slave may be lawfully killed." Other restrictions on Black freedom included halting enslaved people's ability to travel freely, assemble, grow their own food, earn money, carry firearms, or learn how to read or write. The provision in the law forbidding literacy was a consequence of the belief of the enslaving class that the Africans had communicated their plan for the Stono Rebellion through the written word.[59]

South Carolina's prohibition of Black literacy would spread throughout the Southern colonies. Black education was certainly a threat to enslavers in the antebellum American South whose cotton industry was wholly reliant on enslaved African labor and who feared that Black literacy would imperil their power. As well, Black education was a threat to Northern white industrialists, who maintained their supremacy through segregation and control of low-wage labor—and who had an insatiable lust for cheap cotton, produced by enslaved Black people, that fed their mechanized looms. This was, in the words of Massachusetts senator Charles Sumner, an "unhallowed alliance between the lords of the lash" in the South and "the lords of the loom" in the North.[60]

The great Black abolitionist David Walker observed in his 1829 classic text *Walker's Appeal to the Colored Citizens of the World*, "For colored people to acquire learning in this country, makes tyrants quake and tremble on their sandy foundation. Why, what is the matter? Why, they know that their infernal deeds of cruelty will be made known to the world."[61] On December 11, 1829, the Savannah, Georgia, police department seized sixty copies of the *Appeal*. Ten days after the confiscation, the legislature—in addition to the ban on teaching any "slave, negro or free person of colour" to read—passed a truthcrime law requiring the punishment of Black people, or anyone else, who brought into Georgia "any printed or written pamphlet, paper of circular, for the purposes of exciting to insurrection, conspiracy or resistance among the slaves, negros, or free persons of color."[62]

The written word—as Walker and the Georgia authorities both knew—could be a great weapon for Black people in the battle against white supremacy. As *Harpers Weekly* put it in 1867, "The alphabet is abolitionist."[63] Enslaved literate people could forge traveling passes that could allow them increased mobility as they struck out on their quest to run away. Writing could help pass messages about how to escape and where to go or to rally enslaved people together in a common uprising. Books could inspire literate Black people to revolt against slavery, as was the case with Nat Turner, who cited the Bible as inspiration for launching his 1831 uprising. As the scholar and truth teacher Brian Jones wrote on the struggle for Black education, "In the South, Black parents—free and slave, and often risking death—pursued every opportunity to educate their children. Meanwhile in the 'enlightened' northern states, Black parents had to wage a determined struggle to secure equal access to the schools their tax dollars were building for white children."[64]

Because acquiring literacy was overwhelmingly a clandestine activity for enslaved people, "the very act of learning to read and write subverted the master-slave relationship and created a private life for those who were owned by others."[65] White enslavers knew this and "made every attempt to control their captives' thoughts and imaginations, indeed their hearts and minds."[66] As Jarvis Givens explained in his indispensable work *Fugitive Pedagogy: Carter G. Woodson and the Art of Black Teaching*, "Black education was a fugitive project from its inception—outlawed and defined as a criminal act regarding the slave population in the southern states and, at times, too, an object of suspicion and violent resistance in the North." He goes on to explain,

> Black achievement and criminality were closely linked transgressions in an antiblack world. The criminality of Black learning was a psychosocial reality. According to Frederick Douglass's master: a slave having learned to read and write was a slave "running away with himself": stealing oneself, not just stealing away to the North or stealing away to Jesus but stealing away to one's own imagination, seeking respite in independent thought.[67]

The punishments for enslaved people caught reading or writing were severe. An enslaved African named Scipio was killed for teaching a Black child how to read and write, and the slave master had the child beaten severely to make him "forget what he had learned."[68] Tom Hawkins was an enslaved carriage driver who had learned to read and write while taking his enslavers' children to school. When the white owners discovered Hawkins could read, they cut off his thumb and got another enslaved person to drive the carriage. Former enslaved person William Henry Heard recalled of his time as an enslaved laborer: "We did not learn to read nor write, as it was against the law for any person to teach any slave to read; and any slave caught writing suffered the penalty of having his forefinger cut from his right hand; yet there were some who could read and write."[69] This incredible statement summarizes so much of the viciousness of white supremacy and so much of the determination of Black people to obtain education.

After the Civil War, while many white elites opposed education for Black people altogether, others saw the importance of a kind of schooling that would be necessary for maintaining white supremacy. E. S. Richardson of Webster Parish, Louisiana, explained the usefulness of racist miseducation, theorizing that if African Americans could learn that "their only true friends are in the South, we need have no fear for white supremacy." Georgia governor Allen D. Candler espoused the intellectual inferiority of Black people and advocated limiting their education, writing in 1901, "I do not believe in the higher education of the darky. He should be taught the trades, but when he is taught the fine arts he gets educated above his caste which makes him unhappy."[70]

The National Association for the Advancement of Colored People (NAACP) published a pamphlet in 1939 entitled *Anti-Negro Propaganda in School Textbooks*, which read:

> We have seen a rising tide of resentment among our young people, a resentment that springs from the knowledge that they have been misled, misguided, miseducated deliberately by some of those who write their textbooks. . . . A full phase of this fight must be directed against those who would deny to the Negro citizens of America their rightful heritage, a place of sturdy dignity among the pioneers who have laid the condition and helped develop our country. Each year this malicious and poisonous propaganda is spread more subtly though the textbooks of our schools, where its demoralizing action paralyzes the mental health of our young people.[71]

This kind of racist curriculum prompted the NAACP to launch a nationwide campaign in 1946 to combat racist caricatures in schoolchildren's textbooks.

Although activist campaigns, often led by Black teachers, in some cases were able to expand the teaching of Black history and antiracist curriculum, the violence of organized forgetting was still largely maintained in the US school system. Huey Newton, cofounder of the Black Panther Party, grew up attending schools in North Oakland in the late 1940s and early 1950s and recalled with resentment that "during those long years in the Oakland public schools, I did not have one teacher who taught me anything relevant to my own life or experience."[72]

The Civil Rights and Black Power movements helped launch an era of curricular struggle, winning ethnic studies programs and greatly expanding education about the histories of Black, Indigenous, and people of color. But the decline of the social movements during the late 1970s precipitated a decline of the experiments in liberatory education. As the mass rebellions of the 1960s and 1970s receded, so too did many people's hopes for fully uprooting institutional racism in schools. Increasingly, this resulted in efforts for Black education to begin accommodating to the dictates of a white supremacist system. The 1990s saw a particularly concerted ambush of honest education that sought to expand the historical record to include BIPOC. "While multicultural education had been the subject of occasional conservative critiques since its inception," wrote Francesca López and Christine Sleeter, "the early 1990s saw a barrage of coordinated and somewhat repetitive critiques, written primarily for a popular audience. They first emerged in the form of conservative articulations of what children should be taught in school, then quickly escalated into a broad attack on multicultural curricula write large. Their substance was similar to today's critiques of critical race theory."[73] Uncritical race theorists, attempting to capture the curriculum, have built on those attacks ever since.

The Origin of Modern Truthcrime Laws

Organized Forgetting and Attacks on Tucson's Mexican American Studies Program

One of the most important contemporary examples of the violence of organized forgetting occurred when the Mexican American Studies (MAS) program was attacked in Tucson, Arizona, beginning during the 2010 school year. The MAS program was extraordinarily popular and was shown to significantly boost graduation rates. Despite this success, Arizona's superintendent of public instruction, Tom Horne, helped author House Bill (HB) 2281 in 2010 to attack the MAS program.

This legislation outlawed any course designed to "advocate ethnic solidarity" or "promote resentment toward a race or class of people" (namely white people)—a template for mischaracterizing and villainizing antiracist pedagogy that has been replicated with today's truthcrime bills. Sooth students and truth teachers in Tucson organized a beautiful resistance to defend the MAS program that included rallies, teach-ins, and walkouts. The national Teacher Activist Groups network launched a campaign called "No History Is Illegal: A Campaign to Save Our Stories" that included a website to share curriculum from the MAS program with educators around the world.

Despite the movement, with the threat of losing a significant amount of state funding because of HB 2281, the Tucson School Board terminated the MAS program on January 10, 2012. "I wore black that day to school. I was all suited up and my students said, 'What's up?,'" Tucson MAS program truth teacher Curtis Acosta told me in an interview I conducted in August 2022, "I said, 'Well, this is how you dress when you go to a funeral,' and that's what that board meeting was that night.'" The editors of *Rethinking Schools* explained why Tucson buried the MAS program's beautiful body of work: "This kind of education is a threat to those who would prefer Mexican Americans as quiet and compliant workers." Mayra Feliciano, a cofounder of the Tucson student activist group UNIDOS (United Non-Discriminatory Individuals Demanding Our Studies) and an alumna of the MAS program, explained, "As long as people like Superintendent John Huppenthal and TUSD board members are afraid of well-educated Latinos, they will try to take away our successful courses and studies."[74] One of the things the uncritical race theorists were certainly scared of—as evidenced by HB 2281's banning of teaching about solidarity—were the words from the poem by Luis Valdez called "Pensamiento Serpentino" that Acosta's students recited at the beginning of class:

> In Lak'ech
> I Am You or You Are Me
> Tú eres mi otro yo.
> You are my other me.
> Si te hago daño a ti.
> If I do harm to you.
> Me hago daño a mí mismo.

I do harm to myself.
Si te amo y respeto,
If I love and respect you,
Me amo y respeto yo.
I love and respect myself.[75]

Afraid of love and respect, superintendent of public instruction John Huppenthal banned this poem from being recited in the Tucson schools.[76] In an open letter written by Acosta after the MAS program was ended, he spoke to the pain that was caused by Tucson Unified School District's violence of organized forgetting:

> I do not feel safe teaching *The Tempest* or "Beyond Vietnam" by Dr. King as I normally have for years, since it is clear that the district wants us to not only abandon the history and culture of Mexican Americans, but also the curriculum and pedagogy developed by Mexican American teachers. The only safe route appears for us to flee from any history or voices of color, authors that echo the themes that we had used in the past, and embrace curriculum that does not venture down those pathways.[77]

Just as with the current attack on CRT, the uncritical race theorists in Arizona coupled their curricular attack with banning books that discussed the history of oppression and exploitation in the United States and Latin America. In at least one incident, the authorities entered the room in the middle of class and confiscated the contraband books in front of the students. Some of the books banned in Tucson included Paulo Freire's *Pedagogy of the Oppressed*, Rodolfo Acuña's *Occupied America*, Elizabeth Martínez's *500 Años del Pueblo Chicano/500 Years of Chicano History in Pictures*, and *Rethinking Columbus*, edited by Bill Bigelow and Bob Peterson.

The students and educators built a beautiful resistance to the attack on their education, and as a result of a lawsuit they filed, a Ninth Circuit judge overturned the outlawing of the MAS program in 2017, ruling its banning was "motivated by racial animus."[78] Yet even though a federal judge found the banning of the MAS program illegal, the template created by the illegal banning of the program has spread around the country.

"We kicked their ass," Acosta told me of the Ninth Circuit ruling. "We won in federal court. We proved that all their attacks on us came from racial animus and malice towards our young ones of Mexican American descent. So you can imagine my shock that now those original talking points are being used again nationally." As the Zinn Education Project wrote of the comparison between the attack on the MAS program and the recently proposed truthcrime bill in Arkansas, "Both pieces of legislation ban teaching the overthrow of the US government, but what the right-wing legislators pushing these laws really aim to do is eliminate teaching about racial injustice or any curriculum that would promote 'solidarity.' Race, gender, social class? All are banned as categories of analysis in the curriculum."[79]

The Organized Forgetting of Slavery

During the debate on his bill banning so-called divisive concepts in the Louisiana state legislature, representative Ray Garofalo Jr. muttered he didn't "want to say anything I shouldn't say," signaling that he was going to be choosing his words carefully when questioned about the bill. Moments later, Garofalo showed off his wide-ranging skill set when he effortlessly transitioned from a politician into a master pedagogue and provided an example to the world of what he considered a delicate touch in the classroom when it comes to sensitive historical issues. "If you are having a discussion on whatever the case may be, on slavery, then you can talk about everything dealing with slavery: the good, the bad, the ugly," Garofalo illuminated.[80]

One state senator, having the nerve to correct the master pedagogue in the midst of his lesson on antebellum America, interjected, "There's no good to slavery, though"—to which Garofalo Jr. deftly retorted, "Whatever the case may be." Nervous guffaws escaped from the lawmakers' lips in the chamber. Some were laughing from the embarrassment of hearing the quiet part out loud, and some at the absurdity of someone trying to ban CRT who could clearly benefit from brushing up on some key antiracist lessons so as to fully grasp that there were no virtuous aspects of the genocide, torture, family separation, sexual assault, and forced labor that was American slavery. After Garofalo Jr. was pressed, he did backtrack his comment. But the truth is, teaching that there were positive aspects of slavery isn't just a gaff committed by one politician; rather, it has been a typical narrative of American corporate textbooks (in some cases even up to contemporary times) and something that has been regularly taught to millions of students across the country throughout US history.

The introduction of truthcrime laws has intensified the offensive against an honest understanding of the horrors of slavery and the foundational role it played in the creation of the United States. Take the example of Greg Wickenkamp. Wickenkamp grew up in Cedar Rapids, Iowa, and was called to teaching after his first career in nonprofit organizations, "because I enjoy working with young people, but also because education has really broadened who I am and how I see the world and helped me get past some of the prejudices which I was socialized into," he told me when I spoke to him in April 2023. When Iowa's truthcrime bill, House File 802, passed in June 2021, Wickenkamp was teaching eighth grade social studies in Fairfield, Iowa, and he wrote an op-ed to the *Iowa Informer* stating,

> As historian Michel-Rolph Trouillot wrote decades ago, it is the ongoing systemic power relations, biases, and silences which we must address if we want history to serve as a pathway to critical thinking and towards the creation of a more just world. "To condemn slavery alone is the easy way out," he wrote, adding that "what needs to be denounced here to restore authenticity is much less slavery than the racist present within which representations of slavery are produced." HF 802 restricts educators' ability to heed Trouillot's call.[81]

But, as Wickenkamp's experience would eventually prove, even condemning slavery became too much for the Hawkeye State. Not long after Iowa's truthcrime bill was passed, a Des Moines law firm named Ahlers Cooney, which represents over 250 of Iowa's school districts, held a webinar to aid districts navigating teaching about race. At this online session, someone from their firm described the antebellum and Jim Crow eras in the United States as "things that may have occurred such as slavery and segregation, that may be viewed to some as being racist."[82] Besides suggesting a moral ambiguity of slavery—and potentially even questioning whether it occurred—the law firm also explained that broader discussions of systemic racism were prohibited. During the webinar a question was asked about how to teach about redlining—the practice of denying loans to BIPOC in neighborhoods designated for white people—without violating Iowa's truthcrime law that stipulates it is illegal to teach that the "U.S. or state of Iowa is fundamentally or systemically racist or sexist." The *Gazette* summed up the law firm's answer: "Did redlining exist? Yes. Was redlining a system of exclusion that relegated Black Americans to a lower quality of life? Yes. Did Iowa communities engage in the practice of redlining? Absolutely. Has Iowa then engaged in systemic racism? Now that's a bridge too far."[83] This is the breathtaking logic of uncritical race theory; Ahlers Cooney precisely described the practices that constitute systemic racism, and affirmed that they had occurred in Iowa's history, but then denied that systemic racism had occurred. These are the blatantly illogical tenants of uncritical race theory—the kind of doublethink that Orwell described in *1984*.

"In the fall after the legislation passed it was sort of disturbing to hear colleagues that I respected say, 'I'm, just not going to touch on race or class or gender in my classroom. I don't want to be scrutinized,'" Wickenkamp told me. "Others kept on teaching the truth, but I had friends in the state who received death threats. And I know a teacher right now who's going back and forth about whether to leave the profession." Wickenkamp himself came under attack from a local right-wing politician charging that he was teaching his students to hate America and to hate white people because he was teaching the award-winning book by Jason Reynolds and Ibram X. Kendi, *Stamped: Racism, Antiracism, and You.* These kinds of experiences led Wickenkamp to request a meeting with the superintendent of his school district to clarify what he was prohibited from teaching. "I really wanted to make it clear that I was going to teach that slavery was wrong," Wickenkamp explained to me. "And I wanted the district to have my back. I was hopeful, maybe overly optimistic, that they would say, 'Of course, we have your back, this is going to be okay.'"

On February 8, 2022, after months of attempting to get an explanation on what, specifically, he was banned from teaching, Wickenkamp finally scored a meeting on Zoom with superintendent Laurie Noll (a recording of which is available online).[84] "I was so flustered in that meeting. My emotions were very high," he told me. Speaking to the Zoom box on his computer that framed Noll in her office, Wickenkamp asked, "Knowing that I should stick to the facts . . . is it acceptable for me to teach students that slavery was wrong?"

Instead of giving the only morally acceptable answer—"Yes! Slavery was wrong!"—Noll instead elucidated uncritical race theory with her reply: "We had people that were slaves within our state. We're not supposed to say to [students], 'How does that make you feel?' We can't—or, 'Does that make you feel bad?' We're not to do that part of it."[85]

Upon hearing this answer, Wickenkamp's eyes widened, and then, after a beat, he thrust his shoulders back before leaning back in to the computer to say, "Wow . . . I understand the level of support I'll be provided from here on out."[86]

As morally reprehensible as Superintendent Noll's answer about slavery was, it was embraced by leading uncritical race theorists such as *The Federalist*, which published an article arguing, "Sure, the superintendent could've communicated this better, but it should've been easy enough to understand. Wickenkamp's job is to teach history, not morality."[87] In the dystopic hellscape of a future longed for by *The Federalist*, the condemnation of slavery is contraband from the classroom and the humanity is driven out of education.

Not long after his meeting with Superintendent Noll, Wickenkamp went on leave. "It became a health issue," he told me. "My therapist at the time advised that I take FMLA [Family Medical Leave Act] because I wasn't sleeping. I was not feeling as though I was as present as I could be for my students." Still suffering from being attacked by politicians for teaching about slavery and systemic racism, as well as the failure of his school district to support him doing so, Wickenkamp made the difficult decision to not come back from his leave and he quit teaching. In his resignation letter, Wickenkamp wrote,

> I am leaving because the district as a whole was unwilling to offer any meaningful support for diversity, equity, and inclusion (DEI). Wanting to avoid the death threats colleagues in the state received, I emailed the school board in the summer of 2021 with several simple action items that could be taken to support students and teachers in light of HF802. These included ones as straightforward as issuing public statements acknowledging the district's commitment to DEI and in support of teachers' professionalism. No meaningful proactive actions were taken. I am leaving because local politicians scapegoated and slandered my curriculum, and the district acquiesced to these politicians rather than offering any support. . . . I have enjoyed working with students, the community, and many of my colleagues. Sadly, a culture of unprofessionalism, poor communication, and a lack of support for teachers and students, particularly around issues of DEI, has driven me out.
>
> The above examples are but a few of many.
>
> Regards,
>
> Greg Wickenkamp, M.Ed

"I want to go back to the classroom," Wickenkamp concluded our conversation by telling me. "But I don't know if I can do that in Iowa. Now we even have policies saying we need to misgender students and other really harmful things. So I'll see what the future holds, but I'd like to return to the classroom."

Conclusion

"Evil Must Be Forgotten"

Class was in session when Whitfield continued his instruction to Congress. "I've witnessed how toxic things can get," he proclaimed, "when people with nefarious agendas come to town. The lies. The bigotry. The intolerance. The racism."[88] Whitfield's truth teaching shed light on the destructive nature of those working to enforce organized forgetting in schools across the country.

This cognitive violence was exhibited by a parent identified as Cal from Bellevue, Washington, when he explained to a right-wing media outlet, "Frankly, I don't want to have to, every night, unpack what the district poured into my son's head and have to then reteach proper US history." He continued, "I want my son to know that George Washington was an amazing leader and did some amazing things . . . I don't want my son learning George Washington . . . had slaves, period. Full stop."[89]

And there you have it—the clearest, most distilled, expression of uncritical race theory and the philosophy of those who oppose antiracist education and advocate for the violence of organized forgetting. Cal, like others who have been persuaded by the propaganda of billionaire-funded think tanks, believes that "proper" history includes lying about racism, slavery, and the founding of our country; the truth is an aggravating fire alarm, and Cal is at the top of the ladder removing the batteries.

The cotton-picking truth is that George Washington owned 123 enslaved Black people, and the total number of enslaved people on his Mount Vernon chattel labor complex (politely referred to as his planation) increased to 317 when he joined Martha in holy matrimony, with the addition of another 153 of her own that she had inherited from her ex-husband.[90] Washington owned Black people until his last breath and bequeathed his human property to his wife when he died. If only Cal's high school history teacher had introduced him to the writings of the Black public intellectual W. E. B. Du Bois, he might have come to understand the truth about George Washington and the white supremacist impulse to lie about the nation's history. As

Du Bois wrote in the concluding chapter to *Black Reconstruction*, titled "The Propaganda of History,"

> One is astonished in the study of history at the recurrence of the idea that evil must be forgotten, distorted, skimmed over. We must not remember that Daniel Webster got drunk but only remember that he was a splendid constitutional lawyer. We must forget that George Washington was a slave owner, or that Thomas Jefferson had mulatto children, or that Alexander Hamilton had Negro blood, and simply remember the things we regard as creditable and inspiring. The difficulty, of course, with this philosophy is that history loses its value as an incentive and example; it paints perfect men and noble nations, but it does not tell the truth.[91]

The issues Du Bois raised still echo in today's truthcrime laws that seek to ensure evil is forgotten.

The persistent withholding of this information from schoolchildren has produced centuries of social and racial illiteracy. Honest historian Keeanga-Yamahtta Taylor astutely summarized the refusal to remember American history and slavery:

> In the United States, we like to discuss the distortions of the nation's history as amnesia, when it is more appropriate to understand our affliction as selective memory clotted with omissions intended to obscure the raw truth about our society. From the local to the national, our history of slavery has been recast as part of our narrative of forward progress. Where slavery is depicted as our founding "national sin," it is as quickly dispatched as having been exorcized through the carnage of the Civil War, setting the United States upon its essential course toward a more perfect union. Slavery's essential role in building the most powerful nation on earth has been minimized, if not wholly ignored—as have been the roots of slavery to the nation's enduring crisis of racism and its attendant impacts within the lives of Black people thereafter.[92]

Here Taylor asks us to consider that the founding of the United States on the brutal system of slavery has not been merely forgotten, like an item on a grocery list, but instead has been intentionally disremembered and then replaced with a narrative that valorizes those in power. Moreover, when uncritical race theorists do admit to any wrongdoing that may blight America's otherwise pristine record, they cast it as the tale of linear progress in an unrelenting march toward freedom. This discursive framework erases the many zig-zags and lurches the nation has taken, both toward and away from democracy. For example, advances for racial justice during Reconstruction were suddenly shut down with the imposition of Jim Crow, but then, after generations, the Civil Rights Movement helped restore some of the vital rights that had been taken away. The truth is, the United States has moved in the direction of democracy when Black people, and other oppressed and exploited people, have collectively organized to demand their rights. Yet when honest educators allow their students to consider this perspective, uncritical race theorists enforce organized forgetting with truthcrime laws, and sometimes even with the educational arsonist's flame.

Uncritical race theorists today may not be able to hear themselves in the 1830 Louisianan law that criminalized "whosoever shall write, print, publish or distribute any thing having a tendency to produce discontent among the free colored population of the state, or insubordination among the slaves therein."[93] Yet if you listen to this statement published by the right-wing Heritage Foundation, you can hear the echo from the antebellum Louisiana legislature: "CRT scholarship on teaching methods is also used to advocate activism. . . . Curricular content for action civics range from encouraging students to volunteer in their community to suggesting that teachers assign students, even elementary-age students, material that advocates for unionizing workers and protesting against 'gentrification,' complex subjects even for adults to consider."[94] You can hear the uncritical race theorists' fear, in both statements, that learning could lead to dissatisfaction with the existing conditions, which could, in turn, lead to antiracist action.

The following chapter examines specific attacks on antiracist education around the country, which, when put together, reveal the methods of today's uncritical race theorists to impose the violence of organized forgetting.

CHAPTER 2

"We're Going to Hunt You Down"

The Attack on Students, Educators, and Books

*Better get out of town before people show up to your class
room [sic] to make you leave this town.*
　　—Threat from an **unnamed man** in Richland, Washing-
　　　ton, against elementary school teacher Kirsten Sierra

*An admin of the district recently told the media specialist
that if you're teaching slavery, make sure you're teaching the
positive sides of it as well.*
　　—**Chris Guerrieri,** twenty-two-year veteran teacher
　　　　　　　　　　　　from Duval County, Florida

"The past several months have been traumatic for my family and I, to say the least," James Whitfield continued, as he taught his class of US representatives at the hearing in May 2022. "I've witnessed firsthand what an environment can become when the most extreme, vile, hate-filled elements take grip of a community."[1] This kind of hatred is coiling around communities across the country, injecting a particularly toxic poison into the lives of educators and students.

"I first heard about it through a friend," Nevaeh Wharton, then an eleventh grader, from Traverse City, Michigan, told me when I spoke with her and her mother, Jala Sue, in November 2021. "It was at night, I was getting ready for bed, and she texted me saying that her friends created this really bad group chat that she was part of, but she just didn't give me much details on it," Wharton continued, her rising emotions evident.

"I didn't know what was going on. So, I just went to bed. When I woke up the next morning, I was getting ready for online school. Then my friend texted back to say, 'You were in it.' I asked, 'What is it? Is it really bad?' She said, 'They're selling people of color around the area.'"

On that spring night in 2021, Wharton told me that her heart pounded as she learned white students at her high school and another local high school were conducting a mock slave auction on the social media app Snapchat, purchasing their Black peers. Nevaeh—who is biracial with a Black father—asked her friend about who had bought her and how much she was sold for, and her friend replied, "In the end, you went to me for free." That someone she thought was a friend had been part of this was shocking. Despite her role as buyer, Nevaeh's classmate sent eight screenshots with the messages exchanged during the auction. "They said such terrible things about me and other students," she told me.

As Nevaeh's dark brown eyes scanned the messages, she identified acquaintances who were both auctioneers and buyers—and then saw the name of one of her close friends who was making bids. Wharton went on an emotional journey after this betrayal that ranged from disgust, to hurt, to deep sadness, all of which "turned to anger." Wharton showed her mom the screenshots. "My stomach and heart just dropped," Sue told me. "I was scared for her life because of the verbiage; when you read something that says, 'Let's kill all the blacks,' it's truly terrifying. This is my kid, you know, and they're talking about 'let's start another holocaust.'"

Wharton continued by explaining how they talked about how one Black student would be good for cotton picking and how they intertwined homophobia and ableism with their racism, attacking LGBTQ+ students and offering a 50 percent discount for a Black student with autism. These students' open call for slavery and genocide revealed the cruelty of a society that uses its school system to disremember the contributions and struggles of Black people, thereby facilitating their dehumanization.

"I Was Really Nervous to Speak"

As abhorrent as the racist hate Wharton endured was, unfortunately, it is not unique.

Donald Trump's presidency normalized open displays of racist behavior, as a report from Learning for Justice titled "Hate at School" detailed. The report itemizes multiple examples: a middle school student in New York wrote in his textbook that he will lynch the Black husband of a white teacher; a white elementary student in Illinois called all the Black students apes and monkeys; a ten-year-old Muslim girl in Massachusetts got a note saying, "You're a terrorist. I will kill you"; a middle school student in Minnesota told a Latine child that his mother should be in jail with all the illegal immigrants; a fifth grader in Oklahoma drew a swastika and wrote "white power" on his hand.[2]

The New York Times reported in January 2024 that hate crimes in school have continued to increase, doubling between 2018 and 2022.[3] In North Carolina in March 2022, Ashley Palmer, a parent of a Black middle school student, revealed her son Jeremiah had been "sold" by a "slave master" in a mock slave auction held by his classmates.[4] In October of the same year, a video circulated of several players of a high school football team in Northern California reenacting a "slave auction" in the locker room.[5] In February of 2023, several students at Diablo View Middle School in New York passed out cotton balls to classmates to mock Black History Month.[6] That same month, on the other side of the country, a Black sixth grader at Pepper Tree Elementary School in California was subjected to a series of racist drawings from her classmates, including one that said, "To: my favorite monkey," and another directed to "my favorite cotton picker."

Compare those findings to Christopher Rufo's inane assertion that "America remains the most tolerant, welcoming, and diverse society in history."[7] Rufo's pseudo-intellectualism is revealed by the fact that in all of his "research" on race and education, he never mentions any of these quotidian acts of anti-Blackness and racism in schools. And as the "Hate at School" report reveals, most of the incidents of hate reported by educators were not addressed by school leaders: "No one was disciplined in 57 percent of them. Nine times out of 10, administrators failed to denounce the bias or reaffirm school values."

Nevaeh Wharton certainly experienced the lack of accountability for the people who caused her harm. When her mom, Jala Sue, got in touch with the principal of her daughter's school to ask him to take seriously the racist Snapchat slave auction, she was met by what she described as indifference. "When I called there was no alarm at all," Sue told me. "I was just told not to worry about it and 'It's being investigated—not a big deal.'" After feeling blown off by the school administration, Sue said she feared for Wharton's safety and decided to call the police, but that experience, too, was "very disappointing." Without support from the school or the police, it became clear to Sue that those in positions of authority just "wanted this to go away."

Wharton managed to get through that first day after finding out about the auction, and she slept on the problem. The following morning, she woke up with a sense of determination and said to herself, "I'm going to do something about it. I needed to tell people—this has to get out. If I don't speak up, I don't think anyone will." Despite her trepidation, Wharton began speaking out publicly about what had happened. "I was really nervous to speak at first, just because of the town that I live in. And I didn't know if I would receive judgment. The first interview I did they took a picture of me, and I asked that they not show my face for the story. There are some racist people in the area we live in and they're the scary ones to me." But as she began to share her story, she gained more confidence, and she decided to take her case to the school board. Her mom went to the podium and spoke first, while Wharton stood by her and managed to overcome her stage fright to add a few of her own thoughts on the situation. At the next school board meeting Wharton attended, the board was considering a diversity, equity, inclusion, and belonging resolution proposed by the Social Equity Task Force (formed in the wake of the 2020 uprising) as a way of addressing the mock slave auction incident.

When Wharton and her mom got to the meeting, it was packed with those who had heard about the social media slave auction and the resolution on the agenda. People with a wide spectrum of perspectives spoke, not only about the mock slave trade, but about the diversity, equity, inclusion, and belonging proposal, newly polarized by Fox News by linking it to CRT. Nevaeh was overwhelmed, eroding her confidence to speak. Many older white people were there, many of whom Wharton knew weren't even parents in her district. They spoke about why there is too much education about racism occurring in school—even charging that Black people were making up instances of racism "to get attention." "All these history books need to be burned," Nevaeh recalls one educational arsonist saying about any text that included what they believed to contain CRT. "It's the Devil's work."

But many other families of color had come to the meeting to testify to their experience of racism in the schools. Wharton summoned the bravery to speak. Yet as she sat there listening to the experiences of other students—including Native and Asian students—who had also faced racist bullying at school, Nevaeh realized she wasn't alone. "This time I went up to the mic alone without my mom—standing in front of all these people—to testify to the school board. It was so scary. My heart was beating so fast. And what made it even worse was the sound on my mic cut out, which was very embarrassing. But I spoke." I could see a glimmer of pride in her eye as she remembered all she overcame to tell her story that day. It was then that Wharton pulled the truth alarm at the school board meeting. She said, "My name is Nevaeh Wharton. I was one of the people sold in the slave trade. This is unacceptable behavior. The students who did this must have a consequence—they need to learn the truth about Black history and what slavery was." Then she asked the board, "How many more students have to come up here and tell you that we want to learn, that we want to be educated so things like this don't happen again?" And then she told them that she was there not just to support the passing of the diversity, equity, inclusion, and belonging resolution but to strengthen it. And then she turned around and walked away.

As she stepped away from the podium, the majority of the room rose to their feet with applause. But there were noisy uncritical race theorists who persisted in attempting to disable the truth alarm, even in the face of a high school girl's passionate plea to provide antiracist education so that white students wouldn't think it's OK to put their Black peers up for auction. Disturbingly, the spectacle of children of color debating their humanity to crowds of people weighing the issue has become a regular feature of American-style freedom.

Wharton's words helped to get the diversity, equity, inclusion, and belonging resolution passed by the school board. The resolution stated that the Traverse City school district opposed "racism, racial violence, hate speech, bigotry, discrimination and harassment." In addition, it called for diversity training for teachers and school libraries to carry more books by authors of color.[8] Yet Traverse City's uncritical race theorists persisted in trying to curb any effort to heal from the violence of the Snapchat slave trade; they denied the need to learn about structural racism and protested any discussions of race in school.

"I've never seen any sort of discrimination. People in Traverse City are just kind," Lori White, a 41-year-old mother of two, told *The Washington*

Post; astounding words for someone from a town that had just revealed Black students being auctioned on social media. Sally Roeser, a 44-year-old white mother of two, chimed in to explain a major tenant of uncritical race theory: "We were all brought up not to take someone's race into consideration. That's what we're guaranteed in America." Hannah Black, another white parent, told the school board that the equity resolution was "laced with critical race theory."[9] While losing the vote on the DEI and belonging resolution, these voices succeeded in pressuring the school board to dissolve the Social Equity Task Force that would have done ongoing monitoring work to address racism in the schools.

Wharton said she remained unsure about her safety at school after going through this whole process. She reported still hearing students using slurs and telling racist jokes, making it clear that the school board's half measures weren't going to be enough to provide BIPOC students the healing and safety they deserved.

The problem certainly isn't limited to white kids harassing Black peers; racist administrators and educators have also harmed students of color. For example, in 2022 a white teacher in Texas told his class, "Deep down in my heart, I'm ethnocentric, which means I think my race is the superior one";[10] in Utah, a principal forced a student group called "Black and Proud" to be renamed;[11] and in Kankakee, Illinois, a white teacher was caught on video calling one of his Black students a "fucking nigger."[12] A white Cincinnati police officer yelled the same obscenity and racial slur at a Black student at Western Hills University High School in 2022,[13] and police stationed in schools around the country have been some of the most consistent anti-Black role models for youth. According to the Advancement Project, more than 80 percent of students who have been assaulted by school police since 2011 have been Black,[14] and the American Civil Liberties Union (ACLU) reports this anti-Blackness intersects with sexism in a particularly vicious attack on Black girls: "Nationally, Black students are more than twice as likely as their white classmates to be referred to law enforcement. Black students are three times as likely to be arrested as their white classmates, and in some states, Black girls are over eight times as likely to be arrested as white girls."[15]

Leading uncritical race theorists—intellectually dishonest hucksters who make the rounds on the talk show circuit—decry examples of white kids who felt uncomfortable in a class because a teacher had students do a privilege walk, but don't have a mumbling word to say about Black students being put up for auction, threatened with genocide, abused with racial slurs, attacked by police, or any of the other litany of examples of Black students dealing with hate and racial violence.

McCarthyism, Neo-McCarthyism, and Beyond

The Attack on Antiracist Educators

Educators who have taught the truth about racism and oppression have always represented a threat to the uncritical race theorists at the helm of US political and economic power. For that reason, there is a long history of persecution of antiracist educators—especially when they are Black women or women of color. The Reconstruction era was a particularly dangerous time for antiracist educators, as the White League's murder of 17-year-old Black elementary school teacher Julia Hayden on August 22, 1874, in Tennessee grimly demonstrated. In 1956, the legendary teacher and civil rights organizer Septima Clark was fired from her lifelong career as an educator in South Carolina for refusing to quit the NAACP. Mamie Till-Mobley, who had become nationally known after her son Emmett Till was murdered in Mississippi in 1955, began teaching in the Chicago Public Schools in 1960, but she failed the district's oral exam that would have allowed her to become a full-time teacher with benefits because the board of examiners thought she was on an "ego trip."[16] In Vaughn, New Mexico, on February 28, 1997, the chief of police hand-delivered suspension letters to sisters Nadine and Patsy Córdova—two junior and senior high school teachers—who were targeted by uncritical race theorist for teaching about Chicano history and supporting student organizing.[17] In 2015, New Jersey educator Marylin Zuniga was fired for consenting when her students asked if they could write get well letters to the ailing Mumia Abu-Jamal—a journalist and former member of the Black Panther Party who was convicted (in a trial widely disputed for violating his constitutional rights) in 1982 of fatally shooting a Philadelphia police officer; a crime he, and a global movement for his exoneration, has always maintained he is innocent of. These stories of repression are not isolated incidents, but rather represent the ongoing attack faced by educators who dare to teach about racism and oppression.

One of the most intense periods of repression against educators teaching the truth about racism and inequality occurred during the second Red

Scare following World War II. The intensity of anticommunist hysteria directed at teachers during this time is difficult to overstate. Educators were, as Eugenia Kaledin put it, "considered dangerous influences on the general public, [and] were singled out for special scrutiny."[18]

Across the country, thousands of leftist professors and teachers were dismissed from schools under suspicion of being communists—the vast majority of whom had no affiliation with the Communist Party. The entire teaching core of Los Angeles—some thirty thousand educators—were forced to submit to loyalty investigations. In 1950, state legislatures around the country passed more than three hundred laws dealing with subversive practices, including many that directly went after teachers.[19] This included twenty-eight states that mandated loyalty oaths for teachers, thirty-eight states that passed general seditions laws, and thirty-one states that prohibited membership in subversive groups.[20] Alabama passed Legislative Act 888, which required all publishers of "instructional material" to pledge that their materials, and anything cited by them, were not the work of a "known advocate of communism or Marxist socialism." In Sapulpa, Oklahoma, educational arsonists set books aflame, reducing to ashes their supposed subversive portrayal of sex and socialism.[21] A member of the Indiana state textbook commission declared *The Adventures of Robin Hood* should be banned from schools because she believed the story was part of "a communist directive in education" to advocate for "robbing the rich to give to the poor."[22]

Some of the most hostile anticommunist attacks of the era ambushed the educators of New York City and the union that came to represent a majority of them, simply called the Teachers Union. When Wall Street's greed triggered the Great Depression, unlike in any other educator unions in the country, teachers in New York City who were members of the Communist Party (and other class struggle activists) gained influence over the Teachers Union executive board. In his indispensable history of the Teachers Union, *Reds at the Black Board*, honest historian Clarence Taylor points out that while the Communist Party was undoubtedly the strongest organized influence inside the Teachers Union, the union represented all of the teachers. The Teachers Union newspaper published reports from teachers fighting in the International Brigades during the Spanish Civil War, developed antifascist curriculum, fought against IQ testing and tracking, advocated for the hiring of more Black teachers, emphasized "whole child" education, analyzed textbooks for racial bias, and produced Black history supplements.[23]

One of the Teachers Union's most important interventions was its text-book campaign, which exposed the racist depictions of Black people, antise-mitic representations of Jews, xenophobic portrayals of immigrants and colonial subjects, and degrading commentary toward labor. In April 1948, the Teachers Union issued a pamphlet, *The Children's Textbooks*, identifying several books used by the New York City schools that made children "pray to anti-Semitism, Jim Crow and racism." Another pamphlet, in 1950, was titled *Bias and Prejudice in Textbooks in Use in New York City Schools.*[24] In *Bias and Prejudice*, the union revealed a passage in the textbook *Our United States*—a book approved by the New York City Board of Superintendents—that made the following assertion: "It was often a happy life for the slaves. They had no cares except to do their work well." A passage in *United States in the Making* asserted that "slaves of the South were considerately treated. . . . They were in most cases, adequately fed and cared for and they submitted in general to their lot without protest." *Bias and Prejudice* pointed out that in the rare instances when textbooks did acknowledge Black resistance to slavery, it was with ridicule—so that Nat Turner, the enslaved leader of a rebellion in 1831, was described as "illiterate," "ignorant," and "a religious fanatic."[25]

Beginning in 1951, the Teachers Union celebrated Negro history week—established by Carter G. Woodson in 1926—by printing a special Black his-tory supplement in the *New York Teacher News*. This supplement included "excerpts from works by African American poets, novelists, historians, and social scientists . . . [and] other materials for teachers and parents concerning children's books on African Americans were also made available."[26]

In 1949, the New York State Legislature passed the Fineberg law, mak-ing it permissible for school districts to fire educators affiliated with any "subversive organization." Over the course of this attack, more than four hundred teachers in New York City alone were purged from the school sys-tem after being labeled communists.[27] Typically, these teachers were brought before a closed-door hearing convened by the New York City superinten-dent of schools, William Janson. He would ask the question "Are you now, or have you ever been, a member of the Communist Party?" Educators who answered yes were summarily fired. Educators who exercised their Fifth Amendment right not to answer would undergo an onerous investigation that culminated in a trial by the school board.

Laws, policies, and pressure from the corporate media were imple-mented to enlist students as soldiers in the Cold War rather than nurture their spirit of critical thinking and curiosity. In the *American Legion Magazine* of May 1949, for instance, John Dixon wrote:

> Above all else we need a renaissance of patriotism in America's history classrooms, an informed and aggressive patriotism. . . . No teacher should be employed in any American history classroom who does not believe whole-heartedly and without any reservation in American free enterprise, in representative government, and in the preservation of the dignity and independence of the individual citizen.[28]

"Aggressive patriotism." Not inquiry about why so many workers were compelled to go on strike because they were subjected to unlivable wages, or why so many Black people were getting lynched by white supremacists. Not curiosity about the contradiction between the espoused freedoms of America and the show trials of "subversives" who demanded higher wages or a federal antilynching law. Just obedience to American free enterprise.

One of the primary functions of the anticommunist attacks of the postwar era was to arrest any progress toward racial justice in a country that confined Black people to second-class citizenship. The movement to achieve equal pay between white and Black educators emerged during this time in several places, including in Tampa, Florida, where, in 1943, Black teachers successfully sued in federal court to overturn unequal state salary schedules. Similar campaigns by Black teachers were organized from 1944 to 1945 in Charleston, South Carolina; Columbia, South Carolina; Newport News, Virginia; Little Rock, Arkansas; and Birmingham, Alabama. In addition, Black parents organized campaigns to increase funding to schools that served Black children, albeit with less success.

Taken together, the political, labor, and educational activism led by Black people in the postwar years made important gains for African Americans. As Philip S. Foner pointed out, "The median income of nonwhite wage- and salary-earners had risen from 41 percent of the white median in 1939 to 60 percent in 1950."[29]

Despite the vigor of the mid-1940s antiracist organizing, progress toward expanded civil rights was halted by the early 1950s as a result of anticommunist and white supremacist attacks. As historian Manning Marable explained, McCarthyism "retarded the Black movement for a decade or more"[30]—meaning that major racial justice campaigns of the 1940s were cut short and delayed for many years because of the Red Scare.

In so many cases around the country, educators during the Cold War who advanced any discussion of racial justice, solidarity between white and Black people, or antiracist accounts of Black history were quickly labeled as part of a communist conspiracy against America and disciplined or fired. Such was the case in Chicago when Superintendent Herold Hunt was accused of "allowing communist influences in the school" because he offered mild support for a curriculum that supported the teaching of Black history known as the Supplementary Units for the Course of Instruction in Social Studies. This curriculum was championed by Black truth teacher Madeline Morgan (as detailed in the book *A Worthy Piece of Work* by honest historian Michael Hines). Hunt (who had no affiliation with communism) was subsequently removed from his position and replaced by Benjamin C. Wills, an unabashed uncritical race theorist who "defended the prerogatives of white parents unremittingly over Black demands for justice," including to maintain segregation with neighborhood schooling.[31] Although the plan of the cold warriors was to label any antiracist pedagogy as communist and permanently ban it— similar to the strategy of uncritical race theorists today with the term "critical race theory"—the eruption of the Civil Rights Movement finally broke the handcuffs McCarthyism had cinched so tightly on liberation movements and resulted in unprecedented struggles for school desegregation, ethnic studies, and student rights.

In the current era of truthcrime legislation, the attacks on antiracist educators have escalated to levels not seen since the Red Scare. With over 160 educators reporting having been pushed out or fired from their jobs for teaching about racism as of June 2022[32]—a number that was surely much below the actual total at the time—we have entered an era in education with distributing similarities to the hysteria of the Cold War era that targeted educators who taught about racism and inequality.

Besides the firings and punitive policy measures, physical violence against educators has increased dramatically in the last few years. Former president Donald Trump went so far as to literally urge his supporters to fight to the death against CRT, saying at a rally in March 2022, "Getting critical race theory out of our schools is not just a matter of values, it's also a matter of national survival. We have no choice, the fate of any nation ultimately depends upon the willingness of its citizens to lay down—and they must do this—lay down their very lives to defend their country."[33]

Given Trump's call to arms that resulted in death and mayhem during the January 6th attack on the Capitol, we can be certain that his brigade of followers has interpreted his death wish quite literally.

This kind of vitriol against teaching about structural racism has had appalling results. "It is too bad that your mother is an ugly communist whore. If she doesn't quit or resign before the end of the year, we will kill her, but first, we will kill you!" This death threat was made in a letter directed toward one of the adult children of Brenda Sheridan, a school board member in Loudoun County, Virginia. The letter was delivered to her home shortly after Christmas and is emblematic of a disturbing trend of hate speech, neo-McCarthyism, and violent threats targeting educators across the country. Reuters conducted an investigation in 2022, speaking with 33 board members from 15 states and reviewing threatening messages obtained through public records requests. The findings revealed over 220 such messages in various districts, with officials or parents from 15 counties reporting threats deemed serious enough to involve law enforcement.[34]

Threats against educators in response to right-wing opposition to mask mandates and teaching about structural racism reached such a level of crisis that the National School Boards Association wrote an open letter to President Joe Biden asking for federal intervention to stop the threats and physical attacks on educators and school board members:

> America's public schools and its education leaders are under an immediate threat. . . . [M]any public school officials are also facing physical threats because of propaganda purporting the false inclusion of critical race theory within classroom instruction and curricula. . . . We ask that the federal government investigate, intercept, and prevent the current threats and acts of violence against our public school officials through existing statutes, executive authority, interagency and intergovernmental task forces, and other extraordinary measures to ensure the safety of our children and educators.[35]

The revival of McCarthy-era tactics to attack teachers today is striking. Multiple right-wing websites have listed the names of those who signed the Zinn Education Project's "Pledge to Teach the Truth," along with the communities in which they work. As the Zinn Education Project wrote, "Their goals are clear: to incite harassment and spread fear," and they have reported that dozens of educators from across the country have informed them of being attacked, everything from "personal attacks on social media to calls for their investigation and removal at school board meetings, from smears in local media to in-person harassment at back-to-school nights."[36]

Many high-profile examples of this current attack on honest educators have occurred since Trump launched the national attack on CRT, and many others have gone unreported. Uncritical race theorists who have threatened, doxed, fired, or pushed out teachers are working from a McCarthyism playbook designed to intimidate the rest of the educators into avoiding classroom inquiry that explains the history of racism and oppression. The educators who have put their bodies on the line, sacrificed their mental health, and lost their jobs in pursuit of smuggling the truth to kids are critical to understanding the historical era we are in and the education system that shapes the nation.

The Ghost of Robert E. Lee

The onset of the neo-McCarthyist era we are in came into sharp focus when a veteran educator in Florida, Amy Donofrio, faced attacks for advocating for her Black students. "I've taught for thirteen years, pretty much almost entirely at public Title I high schools," Donofrio told me when I spoke to her in August 2021, not long after she had been fired in the wake of the recently ratified bill in Florida banning CRT. She was ostensibly fired for flying a Black Lives Matter flag in her classroom, although the story is so much more twisted and outlandish than that.

"I started off teaching in Ohio for the first three years of my career and then moved to Florida, to Jacksonville, Florida. And I've taught here at Robert E. Lee High School, home of the Generals, for the last nine years." The heightened inflection of Donofrio's voice signaled her anguish at having to work in a school named after the Confederate general; a school that was for whites only until the 1971–1972 school year.[37] Donofrio continued by recounting the violence of organized forgetting that had taken place in her school district long before the attack on CRT began. "We're in a city that is so oppressive. And I know oppression is a major issue in America in general, but Jacksonville is a really special kind of place. Out of the twelve schools named after Confederate leaders in the state of Florida, Jacksonville has six of them. There was a high school down the road from us that was named

Nathan Bedford Forrest High School—literally the founder of the KKK. And that did not change until 2014!"

Donofrio's Robert E. Lee High School also got a name change, but the process was pure pandemonium. At the beginning of the 2020 uprising, Donofrio recounted, "Someone shared a petition to change the name and under that pressure, our school board approved moving forward with a process for considering changing the name." But the process differed from other schools who were forced to remember the racist history invoked by their school's name. "Instead of just voting as a board on whether to change it or not, like pretty much every other school board in the country that had schools named after Confederates, from what I could tell we were the only ones that started hosting community meetings to decide if the name should change," Donofrio remembered. "The meetings were hosted in our auditorium where people could come and speak and give public comment on how they felt about the name change."

That's when the mayhem of organized forgetting was unleashed. The community meetings in the school auditorium to consider a name change "became pep rallies for white supremacy," Donofrio agonized. "People showed up with Confederate-colored pompoms and then when someone would say a racist comment, they all would start shaking their pompoms. Nobody had seen anything like it."

Donofrio attended the first hearing in February to advocate for her Black students. But the vast majority of people who spoke at the meeting were white alumni who favored clinging to the schools' namesake—the commander of the Confederate Army who led his traitorous troops into the bloodiest battles of the Civil War, killing countless Union soldiers in his failed attempt to permanently enslave Black people. Donofrio raised her voice as she recalled that in the meeting, "These people were saying things like, 'In the Bible it says that Jesus was not against slavery. In fact, he said that slaves are to obey their masters.' Such inflammatory and outrageous racism. And they were allowed to say it. It was hate speech." Donofrio started filming the spectacle because "people need to know what's being said here." Her video compilation of those hearings went viral on X (formerly Twitter), receiving some 400,000 views. Eventually the school's name was changed to "Riverside."

The degradation of Black students wasn't limited to voices in the debate over the name of the school. The violence of organized forgetting cut down students' understanding of history inside the schoolhouse as well. Donofrio said, "I looked at our history books really closely this year because I wanted to know what students were learning on these topics. And our US history book, that's the Florida history book, when referencing enslaved people says, 'Some slaves in Florida remained loyal to their owners and stayed behind to help with the home.'"

Donofrio's careful interrogation of the curriculum, and the countless extra hours she put in, earned her the deep respect of her students. Amiyah Jacobs, then a senior at Robert E. Lee High, said, "Since we are a Title I school, not everybody has access to the right resources. So she helps out with kids who need hygiene or food or even help applying to college. She was just very sweet. And she cared for the students. It wasn't always just about 'Do your work.'"[38] Donofrio earned that kind of loving admiration from her Black students by listening to their needs, interrogating her own assumptions, investigating how her own identity as a white woman shows up in the classroom, offering tangible aid, and taking action against anti-Blackness.

Her role in joining with her students to help found a group called EVAC out of a leadership class she was teaching—a class mostly comprised of Black male students—helped her earn this trust. Donofrio gave an assignment called "sharing your story" based on Plato's *Allegory of the Cave* about prisoners who had lived since they were born chained in a cave facing a blank wall. The prisoners see shadows projected on the wall from objects passing in front of a fire behind them and come to believe those images are all there is—until one of the prisoners gets free and unbinds everyone's chains and leads them to light. "I would ask them to think about what they had been through that has shaped who they are—shaped how they saw the world and ask them about what they would need to do to leave the cave," Donofrio told me. "EVAC is 'cave' backward. And so it's the responsibility of everybody who's liberated to return back to the cave to liberate others."

The EVAC program helped lead many students to the light, reframing Black youth as "at hope" instead of "at risk"—and EVAC students joined Donofrio to do a Tedx Talk to explain. One EVAC student won first place in the national "Harvard Kind Schools Challenge" when he turned a bulletin board into a celebration of students who were dealing with different pressures and social issues. "Every month there's a different topic. One month it was having an incarcerated parent. One month was about losing a sibling. Another one was about homelessness. And every month kids throughout the school could apply to share their story. We would interview them, we would take their picture, and then we would type it up. We would post it on the bulletin board, and we had

stickers for other students to use to show support. It was like Facebook." The
EVAC students gained notoriety for their community engagement and were
invited to the White House to meet President Obama. "When we got back, we
were literally hosting the most powerful people in the city, not to guest speak
to the kids, but to learn from them and take notes from them. They even got
their picture on the front page of *The New York Times*," Donofrio recalled.

The program was so successful at supporting Black students that it was
shut down. "The school told me, 'Due to lack of funding we'll have to cut
the EVAC class,' but it was one of my six classes, so it didn't cost the school
anything," Donofrio told me. "That started four years of hell. Four years of
having to fight for a class that had changed so many lives." But it's what happened next to Donofrio that would grab the nation's attention.

In October 2020, a former member of the EVAC movement, Reginald
Boston, was killed by the Jacksonville police. Not long after, Donofrio put up
a flag in her classroom that read "Black Lives Matter." But the flag wasn't only
about police violence. She told me, "I wanted students to be able to walk in
and just be able to take a breath. That's the feeling I just keep coming back to.
At a school that was named Robert E. Lee, at the time, I want them to know
that this classroom was a safe space."

Yet, as Donofrio discovered, working to create a safe space for Black
children comes with consequences. The man who Donofrio had captured
on video claiming that Jesus supported slavery found her Facebook page and
doxed her. "He scrolled down to my November posts, where I had posted,
'The school asked me to take down the Black Lives Matter flag, #no, (it violates zero policy).' And he took a screenshot of that. And he said, 'This is
unacceptable. The flag needs to come down, people should complain.'" The
next day when Donofrio checked her email she found a message from her
principal that said, "You need to remove the flag by the end of the day or it
will be removed for you." Donofrio recounted, "I chose option B. And then
the next day I was given a letter saying I was being put under investigation
and removed from my classroom. They then sent me to what we call 'teacher
jail.'" "Teacher jail" references the practice of removing educators from their
school and requiring them to report to a designated location for the entire
workday. Donofrio explained what it was like to be banished from her school
to serve this sentence for believing that her Black students' lives matter:

I was placed in a dirty warehouse without any windows until the end
of the school year... You have to just go and just sit there while they are

reviewing your case. At any given time, there's maybe fifteen teachers in teacher jail. And it was also striking how it was predominantly Black male teachers there even though less than 5 percent of teachers in Duval County are Black males. The disparity was shocking.

In March 2021, the Duval school district announced Donofrio would be removed from her classroom while they investigated "several allegations."[39] The Southern Poverty Law Center announced in April it was suing Duval County Public Schools on behalf of Donofrio. In May, Donofrio learned about the new Florida bill being proposed that would ban teachers from allowing any discussion of structural racism in a very unique way: she heard Florida Department of Education commissioner Richard Corcoran on the news touting the bill and then bragging that he was firing her. "I'm getting sued right now in Duval County, which is in Jacksonville, because there was an entire classroom memorialized to Black Lives Matter," Corcoran said during a presentation at Hillsdale College. "We made sure she was terminated and now we're being sued by every one of the liberal left groups who say it's a freedom of speech issue."[40] In reality, Donofrio had still retained her position, at that point, but was serving her time in teacher jail. Yet before the summer concluded, the school board granted Corcoran's request, firing Donofrio and resolving her lawsuit out of court. This wasn't the end of her troubles. Shortly after her dismissal, the state initiated another inquiry to determine if Donofrio's teaching license should be completely revoked.

Donofrio was incredulous. "I found out about these bills via a recorded speech from the head of our Florida Department of Education in which he announced that I was terminated," she said. "And then he announced that he was coming up to Jacksonville two weeks later to sign a bill to ban teaching the truth about racism. And he did it." When Donofrio was removed from the classroom, students created a petition calling for her to be reinstated that garnered over seventeen thousand signatures.

"It felt like waking up in a horror movie," Donofrio told NBC News. "Not just for what it means for me—which is obviously terrifying, this is my career, this is my life's work—but horrifying because of the message it sends to teachers throughout the state of Florida."[41]

The uncritical race theorists had triumphed in this battle, and it's worth considering what victories against antiracist teaching look like; they look like removing a sign from a room that affirms the lives of Black students in a school named after a homicidal white supremacist; they look like firing an award-winning teacher who supported her Black students to become nationally recognized for their scholarship and advocacy; and they look like Black students not going to college because they didn't get the support they needed. Despite the firing of Donofrio, they haven't been able to stop her from continuing to support the struggle for antiracist education, and she has spoken out about her case and supported other teachers around the country who have been targeted for teaching truth. At this point, the ghost of Robert E. Lee believed he had finally won the war. However, as you will learn in chapter 4, Donofrio turned out to be a Confederate ghostbuster, and her struggle would end up serving as an inspiration to educators around the country.

"All Kinds of Really Wild, Hateful Stuff"

The Attack on Honest Educators

"Better get out of town before people show up to your class room [sic] to make you leave this town," one man threatened elementary school teacher Kirsten Sierra, who teaches in Richland, Washington. Sierra received physical threats for signing the Zinn Education Project's online "Pledge to Teach the Truth." Sierra told the *Tri City Herald* that she signed the pledge because she supports teaching all parts of history, including events that can make some people uncomfortable. "I have families that are Muslim, families that are Jewish, and a family that is Hindu," Sierra explained. "I want all of our families to feel like they are seen and acknowledged. . . . I want us to teach the truth and acknowledge the past."[42]

But not everyone agrees with those goals. The right-wing Freedom Foundation described the signing of the pledge as a "commitment by K–12 teachers to instruct their students to judge people by how they look, rather than the content of their character." The Freedom Foundation's commitment to using its wealth to promote uncritical race theory and to target antiracist educators is having an undeniable impact. A screenshot was captured of a message sent to Sierra by someone named Ryan Olsen, who warned her of the consequences for publicly declaring she would teach the truth about systemic racism and oppression: "You will not make it here. I would unsign or put away your sheep ways. We will F--K YOU UP."[43]

As the attack on CRT has gained momentum, more and more honest educators have been steamrolled. There are too many of these stories to recount them all, but even examining a few of them here will reveal the kind of McCarthy-era tactics being imposed on education. Markayle Gray, a Black teacher at Charlotte Secondary School in North Carolina, was terminated when he assigned his seventh-grade class *The New York Times* best-selling book *Dear Martin* during Black History Month—a novel that deals with a teenager's emotions after being racially profiled by law enforcement.[44] Kim Morrison, an English teacher at Greenfield High School in Missouri, was fired for teaching the same book. Katie Rinderle, a ten-year veteran educator at Due West Elementary School in Cobb County, Georgia, was fired from her fifth-grade teaching position for reading *My Shadow Is Purple* in class—a book she purchased at her school's Scholastic book fair about being true to yourself and moving beyond the gender binary. Tyler Rathe, an experienced teacher at Jenks Middle School in Tulsa, Oklahoma, was fired for displaying a number of flags representing LGBTQ+ identities.[45] Twenty-two-year veteran educator Elissa Malespina lost her job as a teacher-librarian at Verona High School in New Jersey after a performance review that cited her book displays on race and LGBTQ+ themes.

When reviewing the cases of educators terminated for honest teaching about race, gender, or sexuality, it is striking that most of those targeted are beloved veteran educators, without any prior record of being disciplined, who give inordinate amounts of their time to youth beyond the classroom. It is precisely the educators who are most successful in inspiring youth to see the value of education that are often the most vulnerable to truthcrime laws. As you have already learned, that was certainly the case with Amy Donofrio. But when you put her story next to the many other longtime educators who have dedicated their lives to nurturing youth, a disturbing pattern emerges. These educators were targeted because they were widely celebrated as experts who promoted critical thinking and engaged students in meaningful conversations about what kind of society they want to live in.

Consider the story of sixteen-year veteran teacher and baseball coach Matthew Hawn, who was fired for teaching about white privilege—lessons prompted by the riot at the Capitol on January 6th—at Sullivan Central High School in Sullivan County, Tennessee. "I was given dismissal papers the same day that the state of Tennessee passed their anti-CRT bill," Hawn told the media.[46] Hawn's transgression was allowing students to read an essay by best-selling author Ta-Nehisi Coates and a poem by Kyla Jenée Lacey. "I have students reaching out to me saying, 'Hawn, you're a good teacher,' 'We miss your class,' 'I learned so much,'" Hawn told me when I interviewed him about his ordeal in December of 2022. "And then you have the people you work for saying, no, those students are wrong; this guy should be dismissed from his job and never allowed in another classroom in Sullivan County again." The support from his students and truth teachers around the country certainly buoyed Hawn's spirits, but his teaching career in Sullivan was sunk, nonetheless.

Summer Boismier, an exemplary high school English teacher at Norman High School in Oklahoma with almost a decade of experience, didn't even assign a banned book, but she was nevertheless attacked and fired. "I have been getting messages saying I should be lynched or that I should be sterilized so I can't breed," said Boismier. "All kinds of really wild, hateful stuff." The desire to murder this teacher was provoked by her clever resistance to Oklahoma's HB 1775, which restricts how race and identity can be taught. "Teaching in Oklahoma right now, you are just waiting for the person who is going to turn you in," explained a former Norman Public Schools teacher, who wished to remain anonymous for fear of retaliation in an interview with the *Daily Beast*. "It's very much like *1984*."[47]

When school administrators worried students could access books at school with themes prohibited under the new law, Boismier unfurled red butcher paper to cover up her entire classroom library. But she didn't stop there. Boismier took a black marker and wrote, "Books the state doesn't want you to read" in large letters across the butcher paper covering each of the shelves. Her next stroke of genius was to put up QR codes that provided students a link to apply for a Brooklyn Public Library card—which would grant them access to any online book in their collection in any state—with a note saying, "Definitely don't scan this." There was no law stating you couldn't tell students the truth that the state doesn't want you to read certain books. And there was no law that said you couldn't tell students not to scan a QR code that would allow them to apply for a library card. Nonetheless, administrators put Boismier on administrative leave—and Oklahoma Secretary of Public Education Ryan Walters sent a letter to the state Board of Education demanding Boismier's teaching certification be revoked. Walters took it even farther, claiming that Boismier provided "access to banned and pornographic material to students." All this because educational closeters charged that the QR code she provided could potentially allow students to access books such as *Gender Queer*, a memoir about exploring gender identity and sexuality that won an award from the American Library Association.

After the news of Boismier's defense of free speech in the classroom broke, a teacher at Norman High School reported that Boismier had "been doxed and is worried people may show up to her apartment." Boismier was understandably frightened for her safety and had to find a different place to stay. These outrageous attacks on Boismier ultimately convinced her to resign from her position in late August 2022. Despite being slandered as an indoctrinator, a groomer, and a pedophile, the solidarity Boismier received—along with the strength of her convictions and the fact that teachers are accustomed to chaos and adversity—allowed her to endure the ordeal without losing her humor. "I am a high school teacher and this stuff doesn't scare me," she laughed in her reply to a question from the media. "You're going to have to try harder than that."[48]

In Waukesha, Wisconsin, another colorful story of educational repression was visited on a cherished educator. One day a Heyer Elementary School student informed her mother students were banned from singing the Miley Cyrus and Dolly Parton song "Rainbowland" at the school concert. "Nope, we're not allowed to sing that song anymore," Sarah Schneidler recalled her daughter saying. "In the song, there is a lyric that says, 'different colors, every [kind] coming together,' and in Waukesha, there's been a lot of pressure to get rid of things like that, [such as] talk of diversity and talk of inclusion," Schneidler told CNN.[49] The 2017 duet between Cyrus and Parton says that it would be "nice to live in paradise" to be "free to be exactly who we are," away from judgment and fear. Waukesha School District superintendent Jim Sebert upheld the school administration's banning of the song, declaring that it "could be perceived as controversial."[50]

The song censorship upset Heyer Elementary School first-grade truth teacher Melissa Tempel, a National Board–certified public educator with more than twenty years in the classroom who has written and organized for social justice education most of her adult life. "My students were just devastated. They really liked this song, and we had already begun singing it," Tempel told NPR. "These confusing messages about rainbows are ultimately creating a culture that seems unsafe towards queer people."[51]

Instead of lauding Temple for opposing educational closeting and defending the humanity of her LGBTQ+ students, the Waukesha school district fired her. "I was greeted after spring break by police, the deputy superintendent, my principal, and one of the school board directors and the head of HR, and I was told that I was immediately placed on leave," Temple told me when I interviewed her in September 2023. You read that right: a police officer was waiting for her in the office because she made a public statement supporting kids singing a song about rainbows—an egregious situation that serves as a metaphor for the era we are living in. Thankfully, Temple didn't have to face this intimidation alone and parents rallied to support her. "AEW stands in support of Melissa Tempel, who is an outstanding educator," wrote the Alliance for Education in Waukesha. "This Superintendent and Board began the march toward marginalization last year, and it has only served to stoke fear and sow distrust in the Waukesha Community, which has yielded a pattern of bullying against anyone who calls out the district's bias and harassment."[52] You know the country is careening into the paranoia and repression of the Red Scare and Lavender Scare McCarthy era when children are banned from singing songs about rainbows.

Some people have the mistaken idea these kinds of attacks on educators happen only in states dominated by Republican Party politicians. Those people don't know Crystal Visperas. Visperas is a fifteen-year veteran educator who was teaching eleventh-grade AP language arts and American history at Eastlake High School in Sammamish, Washington—in a school district just twenty miles east of Seattle that she described to me in an interview as "pretty progressive." Visperas, who identifies as a Brown Filipina, told me in a February 2023 interview that the predominantly white high school she taught at had a lot of "families that come from tech fields and have a high socioeconomic status."

"I always wanted to be a teacher and I think it's because of an incident in third grade," Visperas explained to me.

> My third-grade teacher chose each student to represent different countries. I was so excited to participate because many people didn't know I was Filipino, and I was so glad to get to tell people about that. And then she said, "No, you are going to be the Korean girl." My teacher, who was a white woman, was obsessed with Korea for some reason. She dressed me in traditional cultural clothes and forced me to memorize *Silent Night* in Korean and sing it in front of the class. I knew then, even as a little third grader, that we deserved better education.

Visperas grew up in one of the few families of color in a small town out-side of Houston, Texas, and taught for many years in her home state before moving to Washington.

"My students are really wonderful," Visperas told me, recounting how many of them—both white and BIPOC—were excited to have their first-ever teacher of color. But not long after she started teaching at East Lake High School 2019, a student asked her if Colin Kaepernick was protected under the First Amendment when he kneeled during the national anthem. Visperas explained that Kaepernick was protected and also explained that even students in school are protected if, for example, they do not wish to recite the Pledge of Allegiance. "A couple days later, my principal came in and said, 'Hey, there was a complaint about your teaching,'" Visperas recounted. "I was just devastated. I just cried. I said, 'What am I supposed to do? How am I supposed to teach history in this school?' But I decided to just keep moving forward. I decided I would just stick to the given curriculum . . . because I was afraid."

For a time, Visperas tried to protect her job by skirting controversial topics. But then a student told the class that "if a teacher believed in white supremacy, they should totally be able to teach." The student asserted white supremacist students deserved to be able to see themselves in their teachers. Despite this abhorrent view, Visperas reminded herself that this was a child who was still learning and who she had the opportunity to support them to develop better ideas. Visperas was teaching online because of the pandemic and just after the January 6th white supremacist attack on the Capitol—com-plete with people waving Confederate flags—she took the opportunity to help her class better understand the destructive nature of white supremacy. She developed a lesson that she shared with others in her humanities department that highlighted the harm of the Capitol riots on Black and Brown people.

The following October, Visperas learned from her school administra-tors that a student had made a secret recording of that lesson without her consent. That video, along with complaints about her Black Lives Matter flag in the classroom, was sent to a particularly bellicose local right-wing radio host. At this point Visperas went from lamenting the difficulty of teaching the truth about race to her students to fearing for her physical safety, emo-tional well-being, and career. "It hit me then that I'm going to be doxed on social media. . . . What do I need to tell my parents? I was scared for my life." Even though the vast majority of her students loved and supported her,

Visperas decided she had to take a leave of absence and make preparations for when the radio host turned his mob of uncritical race theorists on her.

Over three dozen Eastlake High School educators signed on to a letter that was directed at the Lake Washington School Board and administrators, calling on them to protect the school employees—specifically the immediate physical and emotional safety of Visperas—and to uphold the district's equity policies. "As district officials, you have the power to be the loudest voices in the room when it comes to defending and protecting Crystal and all of us," the letter read. Some five hundred people signed an online petition directed at the Washington State superintendent of public instruction and the governor in support of Visperas.

Despite these important solidarity campaigns, Visperas said she never received support or protection from school officials. Fearful for her safety, Visperas ended up resigning from her job. "The district and school need to stand up for teachers, especially BIPOC teachers, who are asking students and fellow colleagues to fight for justice and human rights and not the easy gaslighting route of kindness, diversity and building bridges," she told the *Washington Education Association* magazine. "Students are brave and bold when you push them to dig into history and facts and ask questions about what they believe in and about the systems around them. Why can't adults do the same?"[53] Kahleb Richwine, one of Visperas's students, described what her teaching had meant to him:

> As a former student of hers, I can verify that Vispy did an incredible job of taking that ardent passion for English and reflecting it onto her students. Be it live enactments from Shakespeare's *Macbeth* or "Vispy's Vocab of the Week," she's been wildly successful in making English as interesting to her students as it has always been for her, and, in turn, exposing why she followed the major she did to become that incredible teacher we all needed.[54]

Visperas had taught her students how to read not only the word but also the world—the true goal of education according to critical pedagogue Paulo Freire.[55] Yet because of relentless attacks from uncritical race theorists, students would no longer benefit from Vispy's Vocab of the Week or her insights about structural racism. It was because she was so effective in empowering her students by giving them the tools of literacy and critical thinking that she was targeted. Visperas, like so many beloved truth teachers around the country, was turned into an example of the kind of repression dedicated truth teachers could expect when their school districts don't defend them.

Antiracist Administrators under Attack

It is not only teachers who have been attacked by uncritical race theorists; principals and superintendents have also been fired or pushed out, with Black administrators enduring the worst abuse. We already know the story of James Whitfield in Texas. But compare his story to what happened to a Black superintendent in a northern blue state. In August 2020, Rydell Harrison became the first Black superintendent of the Easton, Redding, and Region 9 School Districts, which covers two mostly white small towns in southwestern Connecticut. Harrison was hired following the murder of George Floyd and in response to the hundreds of students and recent alumni who wrote to school board members describing racist incidents they'd experienced or witnessed at school. The Easton, Redding, and Region 9 districts had recently established a task force and allocated money to address the racial climate in schools.

However, things changed after those emboldened by the January 6th, 2021, riot at the Capitol began labeling Harrison an "activist" who wanted to indoctrinate students with CRT. Uncritical race theorists began packing school boarding meetings, which would last late into the night, to denounce any education effort to challenge structural racism. A conservative group called "Action for a Better Redding" sent a mailer to community members urging people to complain about Harrison, featuring Harrison's Facebook post condemning the conspiracy theories that led to the Capitol riot. Another group, founded by residents who no longer had kids in the district, sent out mailers suggesting there was no racism in the schools. The relentless attacks took a toll and at the end of June 2021, he announced his resignation. "People have asked me, 'Was it one flyer too many?' And it wasn't just this one thing," Harrison said. "It was the collection of all of these pieces and the emotional and personal toll to be a Black man doing this work and facing very blatant attacks left and right."[56]

Sometimes the attack on administers has been so unscrupulous that you have to laugh to keep from crying. For example, district officials in Byram, Mississippi, launched a war on books—and giggling. Assistant Principal Toby Price of Gary Road Elementary School was fired for reading a second-grade class the best-selling children's book *I Need a New Butt*. On March 1, 2022, Price filled in when the regularly scheduled reader didn't show up for the virtual book event. The kids predictably enjoyed the book, but shortly after the illicit reading, the humorless principal questioned whether Price's book choice was appropriate; it contained cartoon butts and references to flatulence, after all. Two days later, Delesicia Martin, superintendent of the Hinds County School District, made an ass of herself by firing Price. The school board upheld throwing Price out on his rear end, noting the book dealt with, among other things, "bodily functions." If you were thinking, "Yeah, but bodily functions are a wellspring of comedy," you haven't yet reckoned with the descent into ruin that book banners and history deniers are sure will result from this kind of filth. Price was reduced to tears when he realized his time as an educator—seven years in elementary school classrooms and about thirteen years in administration—was over. "I miss Field Day. I miss the Fun Run," Price said. "We had stuff planned for Star Wars Day. This sucks. I have three kids at home and I had 600 at work."[57]

In Eureka, Missouri, Brittany Hogan, the only Black woman in the Rockwood School District's administration, resigned from her position as diversity coordinator in 2021 after threats of violence grew so severe the district hired private security to patrol her house. Aisha Grace, who replaced Hogan, also resigned after only a year on the job. After years of harassment and threats, Terry Harris, a Black man who was leading diversity and inclusion work as the director of student services, left Rockwood after seventeen years to try to heal himself and his family. "I am leaving so that I can feel safe in my body and in my workplace—mentally and emotionally. I am resigning in order to return to feeling valued as one of the region's most innovative, student-centered educators," Harris wrote in an email to colleagues.[58]

An angry mob of uncritical race theorists drove Cecelia Lewis, a Black woman, out of her new job in Cherokee County, Georgia, as the director of DEI—and then continued the harassment into her next job in nearby Cobb County, until she resigned from that position as well. These irate parents believed that Lewis was coming to bring CRT to their schools, which was ironic since at that point she wasn't even familiar with what CRT was. Although Lewis was hesitant to tell her story at first, she finally explained these harrowing events in an interview with ProPublica a year later.[59]

One Cherokee County School Board meeting "nearly ended in an anti-CRT riot," with the crowd that had gathered outside beating against the building's windows screaming "No, no, no!" One man in the crowd screamed, "I'm furious!" and another, "We're going to hunt you down!"[60] That's when kids at the board meeting started to cry and had to be escorted out.[61] Although the kids were certainly frightened, the protesters apparently also terrified Superintendent Brian Hightower even more. He had announced Lewis's hiring in March 2021, and then at this school board meeting, only a few months later, he declared, "While I had initially entertained and publicly spoken to the development of a diversity, equity, and inclusivity, DEI plan, I recognize that our intentions have become widely misunderstood in the community and it created division. To that end, I have concluded that there will be no separate DEI plan."[62]

Lewis made a fresh start in the nearby Cobb County School District, becoming a social studies supervisor. But the angry hive of uncritical race theorists from Cherokee County used a private Facebook page to swarm Lewis, report on her whereabouts, and monitor her employment. A woman fumed, "I am appalled that anyone would advocate for the racist, sexist, and Marxist ideology that is Critical Race Theory." "I did nothing but showed up to work, signed a contract, agreed to do what I was asked to do in the job description," Lewis said. "And yet again, I'm getting attacked."[63]

Unsurprisingly, the racist complaints against Lewis persuaded the pliant district officials to ostracize and demean her from the very beginning of her new job. When Lewis started the job, she was asked to create a slideshow presentation to introduce herself to her colleagues. Then she was instructed to cut the presentation to only one slide. Then she was told she would not be introduced at all and was relegated to the back of the room at the meeting to flip the slides for someone else's presentation.

It didn't get any better from there. She was told her "emails to social studies teachers would need to be vetted before she could hit send (not a single one was approved)." And then she was assigned to work on a "special project," which consisted of the demeaning task of reviewing thousands of educational resources that had already been approved and adopted by the district. "It was pretty much them tucking me away," Lewis said. "Every meeting was canceled. Every professional learning opportunity that I was supposed to lead with my team, I couldn't do. Every department meeting with different schools, I was told I can't go." At the end of August 2021, Lewis submitted her two-week notice to resign her position.[64] This is what institutional racism and sexism look like. Although this may be a particularly iniquitous example, institutions that marginalize and degrade Black women are not only real, but commonplace. Cecelia Lewis's example shows, once again, that the educators with a proven track record of being effective were intentionally targeted by uncritical race theorists.

#LegalizeBlackHistory and Take Queer Studies Out of the Closet

The Florida Department of Education . . . does not approve the inclusion of the Advanced Placement (AP) African American Studies course. . . . As presented, the content of this course is inexplicably contrary to Florida law and significantly lacks educational value.[65]

This decree, issued on January 12, 2023, in a half-page memo by the Florida Department of Education, casts an ominous shadow over the entire discipline of Black studies with its suggestion that a course in the subject with a comprehensive approach "significantly lacks educational value." One uncritical race theorist called the new AP class perverse—and I'm not making this up—because it was created by scholars of African American studies. "It shouldn't be a surprise that an AP curriculum developed with the input of practitioners of African American studies at the university level would contain all the same perversities and warped ideas," Rich Lowry wrote in the *New York Post*.[66] Clearly some believe that white politicians with no experience teaching, and even less engaging with Black history, would be better suited to design the course.

As ludicrous as it is to believe that professors of African American studies shouldn't be included in an African American studies course, unfortunately, it appears that the College Board—the creator of the AP class—agrees. After the Florida Department of Education, led by Commissioner of Education Manny Diaz Jr., and Florida Governor Ron DeSantis criticized the content of the new AP African American studies class, the College Board decided to celebrate Black History Month—officially releasing the curriculum on February 1—by stripping much of the subject matter that the Black history deniers had objected to and purging the works of leading scholars of Black history. Some of the scholars stricken from the AP African American studies curriculum include Kimberlé Crenshaw, Roderick Ferguson, Audre Lorde, Nikki Giovanni, bell hooks, and Keeanga-Yamahtta Taylor.[67]

The Florida education department had specifically stated that it objected to these six themes in the AP African American studies course:

- Black Queer Studies

- Intersectionality

- Movement for Black Lives

- Black Feminist Literary Thought

- The Reparations Movement

- Black Struggle in the 21st Century

Commissioner Diaz clearly rejected those six themes because his department feared what happens when people learn an intersectional approach to Black history that illuminates how overlapping systems of power have oppressed all Black people—including Black women, Black LGBTQ+ people, working-class Black people, and others. In an extravagant celebration of foolishness, Governor DeSantis explained why the AP African American studies class should be banned: "This course on Black history, what are one—what's one of the lessons about? Queer theory. Now, who would say that an important part of Black history is queer theory? That is somebody pushing an agenda on our kids."[68]

The vicious ignorance of DeSantis's statement exposes either his limited historical knowledge of Black history or his cruel distain for it. DeSantis asks us, "Who would say that queer theory is an important part of Black history?" Try one of the many legendary Black LGBTQ+ artists, musicians, authors, organizers, and activists who have transformed US culture and politics—people such as Lorraine Hansberry, James Baldwin, Pauli Murray, Audre Lorde, Ma Rainey, Bessie Smith, Bayard Rustin, Stormé DeLarverie, Marsha P. Johnson, and so many others. The inextricable link between Black history and queer theory is glaringly obvious to those who have studied social movements. The Harlem Renaissance can't be fully appreciated without understanding the flourishing Black queer culture and nightlife that was a defining feature of the era, including the drag ballroom scene. The annual Pride Festivals that occur in scores of cities around the country—generally the largest demonstrations in support of LGBTQ+ people each year—originated from a 1969 rebellion led by Black and Brown queer people, including Marsha P. Johnson, when police raided the Stonewall Inn gay bar in Manhattan's Greenwich Village. As Dominique Hazzard wrote, "Queering Black history means canonizing Marsha P. Johnson as a matriarch of Black America." But she also explains, "Queering Black history goes wider and deeper than the inclusion and re-centering of queer folks. Remember that 'queering' also means reworking. We must rework and complicate the stories we tell about the Black figures we are familiar with."[69] This underscores the inextricable connection of Black studies and queer theory and the need to study both in tandem. Learning a more complex version of the history of Black organizers, as well as learning about broader communities of Black people than only the few African Americans included in most textbooks, is exactly the kind of queering of history that frightens Florida officials.

The attack on Black LGBTQ history follows from DeSantis's so-called "Parental Rights in Education bill"—better known as the "Don't Say Gay" bill—which bans any discussion of LGBTQ+ issues in Florida schools. This educational closeting bill has had predictable results. "The Don't Say Gay bill claims to be for parent rights," one queer Florida public school parent told researchers, "but my rights have been taken away since its passage. My right to send my daughter to school freely, my right to live without fear of who I am, my right to not be discriminated against based on my sexual orientation, and my daughter to not be discriminated against based on her parents' sexual orientation."[70]

This bill and others like it around the country not only enforce educational gag orders to halt important discussions about human sexuality, but they dehumanize the LGBTQ+ teachers, students, and families that make up the school community. "The bill that liberals inaccurately call 'Don't Say Gay' would be more accurately described as an Anti-Grooming Bill," tweeted Governor DeSantis's spokesperson, Christina Pushaw. "If you're against the Anti-Grooming bill, you are probably a groomer or at least you don't denounce the grooming of 4-8-year-old children."[71] This reprehensible rhetoric—labeling queer people as pedophiles—is extremely dangerous. Floridians know damn well what can happen when LGBTQ+ people are seen as less than human; the deadliest homophobic attack in US history occurred at the Pulse nightclub in Orlando, Florida, on June 12, 2016, when a gunman killed forty-nine people and wounded fifty-three more. Moreover, considering that 32 percent of LGBTQ+ students nationally report having seriously considered suicide in the twelve months prior to taking the survey, Florida's homophobia and transphobia masquerading as education can have deadly consequences.[72]

Equating queer teachers to pedophiles has a long and despicable history in the United States and specifically in Florida. During the late 1940s and 1950s, the combination of the Red Scare and the Lavender Scare (that was used to attack LGBTQ+ people) led to the firing of thousands of teachers around the country.

Karen Graves explains in her book *And They Were Wonderful Teachers: Florida's Purge of Gay and Lesbian Teachers* that between 1957 and 1963, Florida officials led a homophobic crusade against queer schoolteachers that resulted in their interrogation and firing and the revocation of their teaching certificates. These educators were forced to appear before boards composed of all men from the office of the superintendent of public instruction, law enforcement, and an investigation committee.

The Johns Committee was established by the Florida legislature in 1956 to scrutinize "organizations, persons, or groups whose activities would constitute a violation of Florida laws, violence, or be inimical to the well being and orderly pursuit of business and personal activities of a majority of citizens."[73] Although the legislation didn't directly state which organizations would be targeted by the committee's anticommunist attack, it was well known that its purpose was to dismantle the Black freedom struggle— including the National Association for the Advancement of Colored People and other civil rights organizations working for desegregation. As Jeff Woods wrote in *Black Struggle, Red Scare*, "Segregation and anti-Communism acted as the mutually reinforcing components of an extreme Southern nationalism."[74]

The Johns Committee was also employed to persecute educators— often single women suspected of being lesbians—whom they pressured to name their sexual partners and asked outrageous questions of, such as "How long have you had homosexual tendencies?," "When was the first time you engaged in homosexual acts?," "How often do you have sex with another woman [or man]?," "What caused you to become a homosexual?," and "What kinds of sex acts do you practice?"[75] By April 1963, the committee had revoked the licenses of seventy-one teachers and had identified another one hundred "suspects." As one woman who lived through these witch hunts recalled in the book *And They Were Wonderful Teachers*: "All the women I know who were teachers had been called into the principal's office and questioned for several hours. Sometimes there were other authority figures there. Sometimes they had been yanked right out of their classes and marched down to the principal's office. They were told that they were 'under suspicion' because of their marital status. Now those women still lived in fear."[76]

Just as the Red Scare and the Lavender Scare were used to purge teachers from the late 1940s through the early 1960s, the attacks on what uncritical race theorists and educational closeters have labeled "critical race theory" and "gender ideology" are being used today to fire educators and exclude discussions about structural racism, sexism, transphobia, and homophobia.

Educational closeting has had deadly consequences, as the story of sixteen-year-old nonbinary, transgender, two-spirit Native American student of the Choctaw Tribe in Oklahoma named Nex Benedict reveals.[77] In 2023, Oklahoma censured the state's only nonbinary representative and signed a bill into law forcing public school students to use the bathroom associated with their gender assigned at birth. Benedict was in the school bathroom on February 7, 2024, when they were beaten to the ground by three girls, suffered head trauma, and blacked out. Benedict's grandmother (and adoptive parent), Sue, took them to the emergency room after the fight, then home again. The next day, Benedict was brought back to the hospital and soon after was pronounced dead. The official cause of death was ruled a suicide, after the toxicology report found a lethal mix of antihistamines and antidepressants in their system. Yet LGBTQ+ advocacy groups have rightfully put Benedict's death in the context of the ongoing bullying, transphobia, and physical abuse. These organizations have shown how attacks on transgender youth, such as by the Libs of TikTok account run by educational closeter and far-right social media influencer Chaya Raichik, contributed to the bullying and beating Benedict endured.

Raichik gained notoriety for posting transphobic videos targeting teachers and librarians. In 2022, Raichik made a video attacking one of Benedict's favorite teachers, who then resigned.[78] The movement for queer studies classes, transgender participation on school athletic teams, gender-neutral bathrooms, and LGBTQ+ affirming policies and programs is a life-and-death struggle that honest educators have to put at the center of their work.

It should be underscored that the attack on queer and trans youth isn't only happening in Florida. Over the past few years, educational closeting bills—especially those targeting trans people—have proliferated in states across the country. Seven states have laws explicitly banning any discussion of LGBTQ+ people or issues throughout all school curricula. Four states restrict how schools can discuss "homosexuality" in specific curricula (e.g., sex education). Six states require advance parental notification of any curricula related to LGBTQ+ people and allow parents to opt their children out.[79] Many of these states also have laws prohibiting gender-affirming medical treatment for transgender minors and restricting transgender athletes from participating in girls' and women's school sports teams.

Seventeen-year-old Ava Kreutziger was in her high school English class at Benjamin Franklin High School in New Orleans when she learned about the enactment of legislation that could negatively affect LGBTQ+ students, such as herself. Overwhelmed with emotion, she excused herself to the bathroom, where she encountered two classmates already in tears. Speaking to the Associated Press about the politicians who have been attacking LGBTQ+ youth, Kreutziger said, "I just hope they can see something in us that's worth saving." Kreutziger and her peers have witnessed firsthand the life and death consequences from the mental health challenges faced by LGBTQ+ students, who were four times more likely to attempt suicide during the pandemic compared with their heterosexual peers.[80]

In previous years, students from Kreutziger's high school in New Orleans organized walkouts to voice their opposition to anti-LGBTQ+ measures. However, in 2024, a group of students decided to take a different approach: they staged a play, drawing from their own experiences, right on the steps of the state Capitol. The students hoped that a theatrical performance would evoke empathy and help those in power see their humanity and the issues they go through as young queer people.

Louisiana state representative Raymond Crews, a Republican who authored a bill seeking to prohibit schools from using a child's preferred pronouns without parental consent, was questioned about the opposition to his law and replied, "We can't ultimately be responsible for people's feelings." If only little Raymond had grown up going to a school that emphasized social and emotional learning and caring about others' feelings—a lot of young people could have been spared from his callous vindictiveness.

More than 80 percent of LGBTQ+ students in the US who attended in-person school at some point in 2020 and 2021 experienced harassment or assault. Fewer than 30 percent of LGBTQ+ students report that their classes include any LGBTQ-related topics, and only 8 percent said their schools had policies supporting transgender and nonbinary students.[81] This neo–Lavender Scare is an unconscionable assault on the well-being of LGBTQ+ youth and educators that will immiserate lives and claim casualties until a mighty solidarity rises up to end educational closeting.

Free Palestine Pedagogy

"Our students demand to learn the truth even if a small group of powerful, mostly wealthy, white adults is threatened by that," insisted Michael Rebne, a teacher at Wyandotte High School in Kansas City. "At this moment we are seeing a rise in both Islamophobia and antisemitism stoked by the same right-wing forces that seek to further marginalize LGBTQIA+ students and the voices of Black, Indigenous, Latinx, Asian and all people of color. We need to set the record straight and see that we are stronger united."[82] Educators in the United States unwilling to turn their lessons into press releases for Israel's far-right prime minister Benjamin Netanyahu have faced harsh censure, especially since Hamas attacked Israel on October 7, 2023, killing around 1,200 people. Since then, Israel has killed tens of thousands of Palestinians, enforced collective starvation, bombed schools and hospitals, and committed a host of other war crimes—atrocities that honest educators believe students have a right to learn about. Radhika Sainath, a senior staff attorney at Palestine Legal, which defends the free speech rights of Palestine advocates, revealed the alarming escalation in these attacks: "We've had an exponential surge in requests for legal help. It has been like nothing we've seen before." In just the month of October 2023, the organization responded to nearly two hundred reports of "suppression of Palestinian rights advocacy"—almost as many incidents as they addressed in all of the previous year.[83]

The repression of education about Palestine has contributed to the proliferation of violence against Palestinian youth. Six-year-old Wadea Al-Fayoume was stabbed by his family's landlord twenty-six times and killed in October 2023. In November 2023, Hisham Awartani, Tahseen Ali, and Kenan Abdulhamid, three Palestinian college students, were walking together in Burlington, Vermont—two of them wearing kaffiyehs—when a hateful assailant shot and wounded all three and left Awartani paralyzed from the waist down.

The crackdown on advocates for Palestinian rights has taken various forms. According to Sainath, individuals have faced consequences ranging from job terminations due to supportive tweets or social media messages about Palestinian human rights to student critics of Israel being doxed and listed on a website called "College Terror List," aiming to render them unemployable. Death threats have even been made to students and teachers.[84] An elementary charter school in Los Angeles fired two teachers for sharing "a lesson on the genocide in Palestine." A school in Illinois banned students from wearing a kaffiyeh scarf—a Palestinian cultural symbol. In Palm Beach County, Florida, a first-grade teacher was investigated by the school district and put on administrative leave for asking the superintendent to "publicly recognize the Palestinian community" while communicating about the violence in the Middle East.[85] Four teachers in Montgomery County, Maryland, were placed on administrative leave for public expressions of support for Palestinians. The Decatur, Georgia, school district suspended their equity coordinator for sharing "Resources for Learning & Actions to Support Gaza."[86] In Fort Lauderdale, Florida, fifteen-year-old Palestinian American Jad Abuhamda was expelled from Pine Crest School because of social media posts—not from him, but from his mother who wrote about the "collective brutality" that Israel was waging against Palestinians.[87] Several universities have suspended campus chapters of Students for Justice in Palestine, including Columbia, Brandeis, George Washington, and Rutgers.[88] Many politicians—both Republicans and Democrats—were more outraged by the students who camped out in tents on college campuses in the spring of 2024 to protest genocide than they were by Israel bombing Palestinian refugees in their tents. Many of these peaceful college student protesters were arrested, suspended, or denied graduation because they spoke out against genocide.

These neo-McCarthyist tactics to prohibit honest education about Palestine aren't new, even if they are intensified. Steven Salaita was fired from the University of Illinois after he publicly criticized Israel's 2014 military assault on Gaza with tweets such as, "Only Israel can murder around 300 children in the span of a few weeks and insist that it is the victim."[89] Bahia Amawai was an educator who worked for a school in a suburban district outside of Austin, Texas, as a speech-language pathologist working with elementary school children with autism, disabilities, and speech impediments. She was fired in 2018 when she refused to sign what amounted to a pro-Israel loyalty oath that demanded she "not boycott Israel during the term of the contract."[90]

And it isn't only red states that have attacked educators critical of Israeli policies or education that seeks to allow students to see the full humanity of Palestinians. Nearly fifty years after the Third World Liberation Front strikes at San Francisco State and University of California, Berkeley, created the first ethnic studies courses, California governor Gavin Newsom signed a bill in September 2016 to create an Ethnic Studies Model Curriculum, which would "provide direction for districts interested in implementing high school ethnic studies courses." In August 2019, the draft curriculum went up for public comment. However, a "well-organized right-wing campaign headed by a pro-Israel lobby committed to preventing any critical discussion of Israel, flooded the CDE [California Department of Education] demands to remove the Arab American curriculum—especially all mention of Palestine—and the anti-colonial, anti-racist framing of the entire curriculum."[91] Then the California Department of Education and Governor Newsom caved. A formidable coalition in support of California's Ethnic Studies Model Curriculum emerged, including the Association for Asian American Studies, the Arab American Studies Association, Black Lives Matter, Jewish Voice for Peace, veterans of the 1968 student strikes for ethnic studies, and many internationally recognized scholars, such as Angela Davis and Robin D. G. Kelley. "Progressive Jewish educators and activists made it clear that the pro-Israel lobby does not speak for them," wrote truth teacher and co-coordinator of the Teach Palestine Project, Jody Sokolower.[92]

During this struggle, a student named Hedaia addressed California's Instructional Quality Commission, the body charged with overseeing the process. "I am a Palestinian Arab student," she said.

> Do you know how it feels to be called a terrorist by your teacher and classmates? It's dehumanizing. As much as I tried to assimilate at my high school, I was always a scary Arab with a hard name to pronounce. This is how I grew up, facing Islamophobic and Arab slurs in and out of school. Explaining myself in classes where Arabs and Muslims are mentioned for one day each year: on Sept. 11. My people are not the stereotypes. We are teachers, students, health care workers, politicians, everything. By removing Arab American studies from the central curriculum, you are removing the existence of people who have contributed to this society and need to be represented in a positive light. Representation matters.[93]

There is no question that antisemitism is also on the rise; but it's important to understand that the uncritical race theorists who have attacked antiracist teaching are the same ones who are primarily responsible for the rise in anti-Jewish sentiment—not Palestinians or hundreds of millions of people around the world who have participated in the movement for a cease-fire in Gaza. Remember that when protestors confronted the neo-Nazis in Charlottesville, North Carolina, who chanted, "Jews will not replace us," then president Donald Trump said there were "fine people on both sides."[94] This contributed to the fact that when Trump attacked CRT in the wake of the 2020 uprising for Black lives, anti-Black education policy also coincided with a rise in antisemitism.

In 2022, the McMinn County School Board in Tennessee voted unanimously to ban the Pulitzer Prize–winning graphic novel *Maus*. In Texas, the Carroll Independent School District held a training for educators, where the executive director of curriculum and instruction explained in an online forum to teachers how to determine which books teachers can keep in classroom libraries. In despicable remarks captured on an audio recording, the director instructed teachers to remember the requirements of the new Texas anti-CRT law, "and make sure that if you have a book on the Holocaust, that you have one that has an opposing, that has other perspectives"—an abhorrent, antisemitic expression of uncritical race theory that asserts there could be a legitimate way to deny the Holocaust happened or show support for the Nazi genocide of more than six million Jewish people.[95] In the context of Governor Ron DeSantis's "Stop WOKE" act, a school in Indian River County, Florida, banned the book *Anne Frank's Diary: The Graphic Adaptation*—a 2019 retelling of the diary Anne Frank wrote while hiding out for two years with her family during the Nazi occupation of the Netherlands.[96] In addition, DeSantis directed his department of education to ban two textbooks about the Holocaust.[97]

At the same time DeSantis's policies have bolstered antisemitism, the governor is one of the most zealous defenders of Israel's genocide of Palestinians. For example, he has called for banning Palestinian refugees from entering the United States and boasted that he sent weapons and ammunition to Israel from the state of Florida to aid the destruction of Gaza.[98] Additionally, despite his outrage over cancel culture, DeSantis issued a ban on Students for Justice in Palestine on Florida's college campuses.[99] This aligns with a larger trend where the right suppresses educational initiatives that aim to honestly confront antisemitism while unequivocally endorsing Israel's attack on Palestinians. This support for Israel isn't rooted in genuine concern for the Jewish community; rather, it serves to bolster the Israeli state as a strategic ally to the United States in the oil-rich Middle East. Christopher Rufo demonstrated this when he offered his colonial strategy for using education to help maintain Israeli and US military power: "Conservatives need to create a strong association between Hamas, BLM [Black Lives Matter], DSA [Democratic Socialists of America], and academic 'decolonization' in the public mind. Connect the dots, then attack, delegitimize, and discredit. Make the center-left disavow them. Make them political untouchables."[100]

The strategy of trying to make anyone who opposes genocide in Gaza a "political untouchable" has largely been advanced by attacking supporters of Palestine as being antisemitic. In doing so, they not only disregard the outpouring of Jewish activists nationwide advocating for a ceasefire but also dangerously intertwine the fate of the Jewish diaspora with the Israeli government's war crimes—thus fueling actual antisemitism.

The largest and most influential human rights organizations in the world—including Amnesty International and Human Rights Watch—have described Israel as an apartheid state.[101] South Africa brought Israel up on charges of genocide at the International Court of Justice, arguing that Israel has been "intentionally directing attacks against the civilian population, civilian objects and buildings dedicated to religion, education, art, science, historic monuments, hospitals, and places where the sick and wounded are collected; torture; the starvation of civilians as a method of warfare; and other war crimes and crimes against humanity." The International Court of Justice then issued a preliminary ruling finding the claim "plausible" and issued an order to Israel requiring them to take all measures within their power to prevent acts of genocide and to allow basic humanitarian services into Gaza. United Nations secretary-general António Guterres described Israel's relentless bombing of Gaza as turning it into a "graveyard for children."[102] Jewish Voice for Peace issued a statement saying, "The Israeli government has declared a genocidal war on the people of Gaza. . . . This war is a continuation of the Nakba, when in 1948, tens of thousands of Palestinians fleeing violence sought refuge in Gaza. It's a continuation of 75 years of Israeli occupation and apartheid."[103]

On November 7, a group of Palestinian children held a press conference outside the al-Shifa Hospital in Gaza City, pleading for the world to intervene to stop Israel's relentless bombing campaign. "Since October 7, we've faced extermination, killing, bombing over our heads—all of this in front of the world," one young spokesperson for the group implored in English. "They lied to the world that they kill the fighters, but they kill the people of Gaza, their dreams and their future. Kids of Gaza run out of their hopes and wants."

The children of Gaza are asking the world to stop lying. Honest educators believe that those who oppose Israeli repression and genocide—a movement made up of hundreds of millions of people all over the world—should not be censored in the classroom and that students have a right to learn about the movement for a free Palestine. "Young people are now watching genocide live streamed on social media as we speak, thousands more children are starved, injured, and murdered with weapons purchased with our United States tax dollars," the children's book author of *Our Skin*, Megan Madison, told me when I asked her about why it was important to resist truthcrime laws. "They don't just want to ban books. They want to hurt trans kids. They want to silence Black progressive leadership, and they are preying on the trauma of Jewish people . . ." As challenging as it can be to teach truth about Palestine in the current period, as *Rethinking Schools* editorialized, "We should understand and take hope in the reason this backlash has grown in intensity: More people than ever are refusing to stay quiet in the face of racism and injustice."[104]

The Attack on Higher Education and Diversity, Equity, and Inclusion

Although uncritical race theorists first pushed truthcrime laws in K–12 education, they are rapidly franchising their attack to colleges and universities. "Younger voters are the issue. It comes from years of radical indoctrination—on campus, in school, with social media, & throughout culture," Wisconsin governor Scott Walker whined on X when the GOP underperformed in the 2022 midterm elections. "We have to counter it or conservatives will never win battleground states again."

With this in mind, nearly half of the truthcrime legislation uncritical race theorists introduced in 2022 regulates colleges and universities.[105] In addition, the American Association of University Professors (AAUP) found that lawmakers introduced more than one hundred "academic gag order" bills since 2021.[106] As of 2023, legislatures had introduced forty bills around the country that restrict colleges from having DEI offices, and at least nine states have enacted truthcrime bills targeting colleges and universities.[107] Some of the bills include harsh punishments for universities caught teaching the truth about racism. The most common penalty is the loss of state funding for truth-crime violations. Other proposed legislation allows individual students to sue public universities for having been exposed to an honest education about racism, as is the case with the so-called "divisive concepts" bill that was signed into law in Tennessee in April 2022.[108] Despite the hysteria that college students are bombarded with woke indoctrination, a 2023 study by the nonprofit Open Syllabus found that references to gender appeared in less than 5 percent of college classes, while race was mentioned in just 0.3 percent. Furthermore, terms such as "critical race theory," "transgender," or "Marxism" were scarcely included, appearing in fewer than 1 in 1,000 class syllabi.[109]

The attack on DEI initiatives at the college level has proven to be uncritical race theorists' next major objective in its war on woke. "With D.E.I., right-wing activists hope to build a broader coalition by tapping into a common-sense perception of its inherent unfairness," wrote Keeanga-Yamahtta Taylor. "Moreover, by casting antisemitism as adjacent to the alleged anti-white racism of D.E.I., this effort has the potential to draw Jews and others concerned about antisemitism into the right's campaign of grievance politics."[110]

This was the strategy that was used to fire Claudine Gay, the first Black president of Harvard University. Gay faced charges she wasn't curbing pro-Palestinian demonstrations on Harvard's campus after Hamas's October 7 attack on Israel. Once the right began this line of attack, they quickly followed with charges that she had engaged in plagiarism, which they used as evidence to charge that Gay had unfairly benefited from DEI programs. Gay resigned in early January 2024, after a disastrous congressional hearing. Christopher Rufo celebrated by writing on X, "SCALPED," invoking the gruesome practice of white colonists who sought to eradicate Native Americans. Hedge-fund billionaire Bill Ackman, one of the uncritical race theorists leading the attack against Gay, wrote that that Gay was made Harvard's president only because of a "a fat finger on the scale." After her resignation he declared, "DEI is racist because reverse racism is racism, even if it is against white people." Billionaire Elon Musk agreed, saying, "DEI is just another word for racism."[111]

The attack on DEI is central to uncritical race theorists' advancement of the master narrative of "reverse racism"—a concept they have propagated to end Affirmative Action programs in higher education. The superstition of reverse racism persists because it is a useful fiction for the richest 1 percent of society, whose power depends on convincing the vast majority of white people that the very real problems they face—such as unlivable wages, inadequate health care, or unaffordable housing—are not due to the hording of wealth by billionaires but are produced by the anti-white beliefs of Black people or immigrants. As Trump told *Time* magazine during his 2024 campaign for president, "I think there is a definite anti-white feeling in this country and that can't be allowed. . . . I don't think it would be a very tough thing to address, frankly. But I think the laws are very unfair right now. And education is being very unfair, and it's being stifled . . ."

This kind of rhetoric from elites is having a clear effect on society. According to a May 2022 University of Maryland Critical Issues Poll, nearly a third of white Americans report they have seen "a lot more" discrimination against white people in the past five years, and despite growing inequity and open displays of white supremacy in the schools and beyond, a majority of white Americans do not believe that there has been a rise in discrimination against Black and Latine Americans.[112] These beliefs are starkly contradicted by every measure of racial disparities. For example, FBI data shows more than 11,634 hate crime incidents in 2022, with Black people making up 52 percent of the victims despite constituting only 14 percent of the population.[113] Additionally, the average white family (at $171,000) has almost ten times the wealth of the average Black family ($17,150).[114] The goal of eliminating DEI programs at the university level is connected to their broader strategy of redefining racism as any effort to combat racism.

The idea that DEI is a threat to white people is belied by its widespread implementation in corporate America, which remains overwhelmingly dominated by wealthy white men (of the 533 executive officers in S&P 100 companies, white men represent 7 in 10).[115] The widespread use of DEI in corporate America is often about mitigating frustrations of employees around racism, rather than dismantling the structures of institutional racism. "Having a workforce that is diverse and representative of your stakeholders is good for business," said billionaire Mark Cuban, in response to Musk's tweet in opposition to DEI.[116]

The dismantling of DEI is about delegitimizing any affirmation of people of color and damming even the most tepid challenges to racism. And if they can eliminate DEI programs, it will give them the strength and confidence they need to go after other, more robust antiracist initiatives. That is why many in the Teach Truth movement defend DEI programs against uncritical race theorist attacks. But it's also why many in the movement argue that DEI programs are not nearly enough to effectively challenge racist institutions and structures—and can even hinder these efforts in some instances. "The language of diversity and inclusion, whether intentional or not, can often serve as a way for institutions to abdicate their responsibility for doing their part in dismantling racism and systems of oppression," Benjamin D. Reese argued. "In a country built on the subjugation of Indigenous and Black people, it is going to take more than respect for all differences to deal with the structures and unconscious biases that continue to marginalize—and kill— black Americans."[117] DEI initiatives, often focused on implicit bias and interpersonal manifestations of racism, can help create more empathy in some situations. And there are no doubt honest educators who work in DEI offices who use their position to try to make institutional change. But the goal of including people of color into a systemically racist and inequitable system is not the same as dismantling that system altogether—and most DEI initiatives are about producing individual changes in perspective, rather than about organizing collective struggle against the systems of oppression.

Uncritical race theorists' vitriol against DEI is dangerous, not so much because it erodes the effectiveness of those programs, but because if discourse about even just celebrating diversity is outlawed, it will be difficult to advance a deeper conversation about ripping up the roots of systemic racism.

On the two-year anniversary of the January 6th, 2021, white supremacist attack on the Capitol, Florida governor Ron DeSantis used the symbolism of the day to underscore his political commitment to opposing antiracist education and issued a statement to announce his appointment of six new members to the state's New College thirteen-member board of trustees. The appointees were all, of course, proponents of truthcrime, including Christopher Rufo, who doesn't even live in Florida.

Student protesters met with the new board members on the Sarasota, Florida–based campus, and one boldly challenged their commitment to uncritical race theory, saying, "You claim to support freedom of thought and education yet you support the governor's decision to suppress entire fields of study that he deems disposable. . . . You and him are targeting fields of study that are critical of capitalism, racism, imperialism, misogyny, etc. How is this freedom of thought? What about our freedom to continue learning these subjects without government suppression?"[118]

The new board forced out Patricia Okker, the first woman president of New College, installing Richard Corcoran, a DeSantis ally, as the interim president.[119] Next, the board abolished the office that organized New College's DEI programs. The reason for the attack on New College comes into focus when you consider its student body and its unique approach to education. LGBTQ+ students make up a large percentage of the student body; the college has replaced letter grades with more holistic narrative evaluations; and the college empowers students to design an individual degree plan, while encouraging intensive independent studies to prepare students for writing a senior thesis. Visiting assistant professors Debarati Biswas and Erik Wallenberg explained the importance of this model, writing, "Students and faculty have built an impressive alternative model of education that should be an inspiration for others, not one that is attacked and disparaged by the governor and the new board of trustees."[120]

Yet the attack intensified in May 2023 when the new uncritical race theorists on New College's board of trustees voted to fire one professor without notice or cause and to deny tenure to five others. "It's a drive-by firing," Jeremy Young, senior manager of free expression and education programs at PEN America, commented on the dismissal of Professor Helene Gold, a librarian at New College.[121] Gold, a twenty-year veteran librarian and an open member of the LGBTQ+ community, explained that those who were targeted by the board "have been women, people of color and members of the LGBTQ+ community. So, they're either incredibly cruel or they're just not thinking about what they're doing, which I have a hard time believing."[122]

New College has a proud history of students who joined the Civil Rights Movement and struggles for racial justice. Wishing to reinvigorate that legacy, Biswasi and Wallenberg wrote, "We are here to defend the freedom of students to learn in their chosen environment, with programs and classes that align with the school in which they enrolled. We are here to defend the freedom of faculty members to teach what we have spent lifetimes studying and were hired to help students understand. And we are here to defend the freedom of staffers to organize in support of the diversity, equity, and inclusion that stand as a central community agreement—one that we desperately need in this state and country."[123]

Although the imposition of truthcrime has been particularly harsh at New College, it has become a trend in Florida's higher education system. The presidents of twenty-eight Florida colleges signed on to a statement in January 2023 announcing that "our institutions will not fund or support any institutional practice, policy, or academic requirement that compels belief in critical race theory or related concepts such as intersectionality, or the idea that systems of oppression should be the primary lens through which teaching and learning are analyzed and/or improved upon."[124]

In Mississippi, despite every Black state representative voting against it, the legislature passed Senate Bill 2113 ("Prohibit Critical Race Theory"). Governor Tate Reeves then signed the truthcrime bill into law, which impacts all public schools, including institutions of higher learning, community colleges, and junior colleges.[125] In response, the University of Mississippi's Associated Student Body declared, "Mississippi Senate Bill 2113 undermines the quality and fundamental purpose of public higher education, which the University of Mississippi has financially invested in to bolster its merit and reputation in the past decades."[126] Truthcrime laws are in northern colleges and universities too. Idaho became the first state to pass a truthcrime law when Governor Brad Little singed HB 377 into law that banned CRT, not only for K–12 schools, but also for public universities.[127]

So much of uncritical race theorists' support of truthcrime laws is predicated on the notion that children shouldn't be exposed to antiracist ideas because it is a form of propaganda being used on those too young to understand they are being manipulated. In fact, it is imposing educational gag orders on teachers and mandating schooling that hides the flaws of our country that is indoctrination. Moreover, they end up telling on themselves when they work to impose truthcrime laws in colleges, revealing that it isn't actually the indoctrination of kids they are worried about, but rather that adult college students will trade in uncritical race theory for ideas that challenge injustice. The Goldwater Institute wrote, "In higher education, colleges are trying to build leftist echo chambers with CRT. . . . But the Goldwater Institute is reining in radical DEI and CRT across the nation." Working to stop adults from taking college classes with antiracist themes reveals that in the clash of ideas among adults, they don't believe their ideas can prevail. Because the logic of uncritical race theory disintegrates under investigation like a castle made of sugar in the rain, their only hope is to try to keep students from taking classes that could lead to a torrent of questions pouring down about oppression in the United States.

The Chilling Effect

"I've had conversations with teachers who said things like, 'I'm getting so much pushback for teaching Alice Walker, I'm going to go back to teaching what I used to teach because I don't want the pushback,'" Black Iowa City middle school teacher Monique Cottman told me when I spoke to her in May 2021. Cottman explained that during the fall of 2020 her school ordered one thousand copies of *Stamped: Racism, Antiracism, and You*. However, after some parents complained, the book became optional, and teachers became fearful it wasn't safe to assign it in the midst of a raging debate about whether or not to hide the history of America's racism from children. Cottman, an organizer with the Black Lives Matter at School movement, stressed that while she would refuse to lie to students about structural racism, she was seeing an increasing number of teachers—frostbitten by the truthcrime law—retreat from implementing curriculum about systemic racism that they had begun in the wake of the 2020 uprising.

Besides immiserating the lives of honest and hardworking educators who have been harassed and fired, truthcrime bills have also been designed to discourage countless educators from teaching BIPOC history or queer history. A 2024 study from the RAND corporation found that two-thirds of teachers in the United States have limited discussions of political and social issues in their classrooms—even when they teach in places without truthcrime laws or policies.[128] This means that twice as many teachers are submitting to truthcrime policies than are legally required to. "Oftentimes, it's a really mobilized, very vocal minority of parents in a community," said Ashley Woo, one of the authors of the report. "Not only can parents come up to you and have a verbal altercation, but there's also this idea that they can threaten your reputation through social media, or that they might be able to go to your leaders and threaten your job. . . . Even the specter of that can create a lot of anxiety for teachers."

Karen Kirt, a veteran social studies teacher in Leland Public Schools—a district in Michigan, which has not passed teacher gag-order legislation—said, "We've had to be more careful about how we talk about race, because so many families were upset. *60 Minutes* did an episode a few years ago about how African Americans are watched more when they go into stores, and in the past, I've played clips of that in my classroom, showing that there's still racism in America. I'm not sure I would do that now."[129]

These are only some of the many examples of self-censorship; be sure, a school that hasn't been reported on near you is freezing out antiracist lessons. Once a few teachers are fired for openly expressing their belief that Black lives matter, for suggesting that white privilege is real, or even just for teaching a book by a Black author, it makes every other educator think twice before engaging in any of those practices.

Teacher educators and researchers in Memphis, Tennessee, conducted a 2021–2022 school year study of both practicing and prospective teachers and engaged them in focus group conversations about the new "Prohibited Concepts in Instruction" law that banned any content that suggests "this state or the United States is fundamentally or irredeemably racist or sexist." The findings in their report, "The Chilling Effects of So-Called Critical Race Theory Bans," reveal the sweeping impact of the truthcrime legislation:

> From these focus group conversations, we learned there were significant effects on classrooms, with teachers feeling the need to restrict the ways their teaching engaged with issues of race, racism, and other forms of oppression. These perceived restrictions, in many cases, extended well beyond the specific topics prohibited in the state legislation. Uncertain how to interpret the law's vague language and fearful of the consequences of being "caught" teaching a prohibited concept, most teachers we spoke with described how the new law led them to be less confident in their ability to teach about race and racism, and so they expected to subsequently engage in this type of teaching less often.[130]

As the report rightly asserts, these truthcrime laws are designed to encourage educators to police themselves and constantly arrest their own lesson plans that would develop students' understanding of how power operates in society or how multiracial solidarity can challenge that power.

Yet what teachers in the "Chilling Effects" report also clarify is that the new truthcrime laws aren't the only obstacles to teaching honestly about race. "Many teachers noted that the standardized curricula they were mandated to follow had already erased many of their opportunities to engage students in critical conversations," the report states. "These mandates were enforced via pacing guides, classroom visits by school- and district-level administrators, and minute-by-minute curriculum content scheduling." Truth teachers have long known that even without overtly banning curriculum or books, social justice education is squeezed out of schools through scripted curriculum and high-stakes standardized tests that are used to enforce what educators are expected to teach.

Still, the truthcrime laws have dramatically decreased the space for teaching about Black history, queer studies, and movements for social justice. "Many teachers have been intimidated into teaching what others feel should be taught and not what needs to be taught. Even those teachers I've had who were not afraid to challenge what is accepted had to do so in secret," said Otitodilichukwu Ikem, a high school student from Coronado High School in El Paso.[131] One social studies educator from Florida explained, in a survey by the Zinn Education Project, both the frigid conditions caused by truthcrime laws and the sentiments of many truth teachers who are nevertheless determined to thaw the winter of censorship and lies: "It is creating a chilling effect on education. We continue to teach the truth, but with much less certainty what the consequences will be for doing so."

#ReadBannedBooks

The freedom to read is very important to me. I want to be able to read whatever I want and to form my own opinions on things, and it's harder to do that when books are banned.
—Nineteen-year-old from Texas[132]

A day before the Keller Independent School District's first day of the 2022–2023 school year, the North Texas district fired off a memo announcing a last-minute decision to remove some forty book titles from the shelves of school libraries and classrooms that had been challenged the previous school year. Among the books were the usual targets of uncritical race theorists: supreme literary achievements like Toni Morrison's *The Bluest Eye* (which tells the story of a Black girl whose dark skin brands her as ugly in a white supremacist world and her desire to have blue eyes, which she equates with whiteness) and books that provide vital insights on the LGBTQ+

experience, such as *Gender Queer: A Memoir* by Maia Kobabe. These books, taken together, critique white cis-heteronormativity, so you can understand why they would be feared by uncritical race theorists and educational close-ters. But the banned book that received the most attention was *Anne Frank's Diary: The Graphic Adaptation,* a 2019 retelling of Anne Frank's story, written while hiding out for two years with her family during the Nazi occupation of the Netherlands. Antisemites and puritanical parents, who found Anne Frank's disarming musings on puberty too salacious for adolescents, led the book banning—and it took a nationwide outcry to finally reshelve her diary.

One language arts teacher from a school district in Texas sent a note to the Zinn Education Project describing the ways that censorship of books and truthcrime laws were rolling through the classroom in 2023: "My dis-trict board members have now banned teachers from buying books for their classrooms and will not let our schools buy books either. They would not let me teach *Just Mercy* by Bryan Stevenson for the past two years. I had to remove my 'protect trans kids' poster from my classroom wall. We are not allowed to say 'social-emotional learning' because it's 'tied to CRT.'"

Book banning reached a frenzied state in the Carroll Independent School District in Southlake, Texas, where uncritical race theorists worked to keep children away from what they considered the dangerous ideas of Johnson Elementary's fourth-grade teacher Rickie Farah. Among Farah's subversive credentials are Teacher of the Year. Farah was caught by a parent doing the unthinkable: she sent students home with a book that had antiracist themes. The mother said the book violated her family's "morals and faith"—a sys-tem of belief, apparently, that is offended by the idea that BIPOC have equal rights. Why, in the mother's estimation, should Farah have known the book would expose children to overtly antiracist ideas? Because the book, authored by Tiffany Jewell, was titled, *This Book Is Anti-Racist: 20 Lessons on How to Wake Up, Take Action, and Do the Work.*

Having been caught red-handed promoting antiracism, the school board voted three to two to issue Farah a letter of reprimand in October 2021. Two of the three trustees who voted for the reprimand, Hannah Smith and Cam Bryan, received campaign donations from the parents who lodged the complaint.[133]

Citing Texas law banning lessons that might make students feel "dis-comfort, guilt, anguish, or any other form of psychological distress" because of their race, the district issued a mandatory rubric to evaluate all books in classroom libraries. The district then required trainings on the book-banning guidelines and instructions for disposing of any subversive texts.

This book purge had the desired effect of intimidating schoolteachers who might look at the many examples of structural racism in our society and be tempted to engage students in a dialogue about injustice. A series of educators spoke to NBC on condition of anonymity, for fear of reprisals, about what these new guidelines would mean for their classes. One elementary school teacher said she would have to remove *Separate Is Never Equal*, from her classroom library—a picture book by Duncan Tonatiuh about a Mexican American family's fight to end segregation in California in the 1940s. Another teacher said she would have to purge Lisa Moore Ramée's *A Good Kind of Trouble* because the girl protagonist joins the Black Lives Matter movement. A high school teacher said that she no longer felt safe with a classroom copy of *The Hate U Give* by Angie Thomas, in part because it depicts racist police shootings, and she also said she would probably have to get rid of all of her books by Nobel Prize–winning author Toni Morrison, which deal with issues of racism and sexism.

These experiences of bibliophobia are not unique to Texas. The American Library Association called the rate at which books are being challenged around the country "unprecedented," and Deborah Caldwell-Stone, the director of the American Library Association's Office of Intellectual Freedom, explained, "In my twenty years with ALA [American Library Association], I can't recall a time when we had multiple challenges coming in on a daily basis."[134] According to the ALA, these were the most banned books of 2022:[135]

1. *Gender Queer* by Maia Kobabe

2. *All Boys Aren't Blue* by George M. Johnson

3. *The Bluest Eye* by Toni Morrison

4. *Flamer* by Mike Curato

5. *Looking for Alaska* by John Green (tie)

6. *The Perks of Being a Wallflower* by Stephen Chbosky (tie)

7. *Lawn Boy* by Jonathan Evison

8. *The Absolutely True Diary of a Part-Time Indian* by Sherman Alexie

9. *Out of Darkness* by Ashley Hope Perez

10. *A Court of Mist and Fury* by Sarah J. Maas (tie)

11. *Crank* by Ellen Hopkins (tie)

12. *Me and Earl and the Dying Girl* by Jesse Andrews (tie)

13. *This Book Is Gay* by Juno Dawson (tie)

The ALA disclosed a startling surge in censorship efforts, with a record 4,240 distinct book titles under attack in 2023. This marks a notable 65 percent escalation from the previous year and an alarming 128 percent surge from 2021.[136]

The rise in book bans is happening in states across the country. A Tennessee school district banned the Pulitzer Prize–winning graphic novel *Maus* about the Holocaust, the right-wing parent group Moms for Liberty (MFL) called for the banning of a book about Martin Luther King Jr., and Tennessee pastor Greg Locke gathered scores of congregants for a public book burning.[137] In a Pennsylvania school district, *Brand New School, Brave New Ruby*, and *The Story of Ruby Bridges* were banned—books about the courageous Black six-year-old who became the first African American child to integrate a white Southern elementary school.[138] Idaho passed a bill allowing prosecution of librarians who checked out any book deemed harmful to a minor. A suburban school district outside of Milwaukee, Wisconsin, banned *Queer: The Ultimate LGBTQ Guide* by Kathy Belge and *This Book Is Gay* by Juno Dawson and emailed student library borrowing records to their parents on a weekly basis.[139] A Wyoming public library board fired its head librarian, Terri Lesley, in July 2023 when she refused to remove books.[140] Some of the states with the most aggressive book bans by 2022 included Texas, with 713 bans; Pennsylvania, with 456 bans; and Florida, with 204 bans.[141]

Book-banning laws have put school librarians in a precarious position, threatening them with penalties and even jail time for providing students with books labeled objectionable.[142] Missouri's book-banning laws prohibiting sexual content are so draconian that among the nearly three hundred books removed from school shelves are titles such as *Maus*, an *X-Men* graphic novel, a copy of *Reader's Digest*, and works about artists Leonardo da Vinci and Michelangelo. School librarians or other educators who violate Missouri's truthcrime law, Senate Bill 775, can face up to a year in jail and $2,000 in fines.[143]

The Wentzville School District (just west of St. Louis, Missouri) alone has banned some 220 books, and during the 2021–2022 school year, police showed up on two different occasions at a high school in the district to question a librarian accused of giving pornography to kids because the book collection included titles like *The Handmaid's Tale* and *Gender Queer: A Memoir*. The librarian declined to be identified because she was "worried about her safety," but did tell reporters that it felt "scary" and "surreal" to have a police officer interrogate her about false accusations of promoting pornography.[144] Tom Bastian, the ACLU's deputy director of communications, explained to the *Columbia Missourian* that "it is unconstitutional for Missouri's lawmakers to threaten teachers and librarians with criminal offenses for observing students' First Amendment rights."[145]

In Florida, *The Nation* reported that "Governor Ron DeSantis's crusade against independent thought is leading to bare bookshelves in classrooms as teachers panic about whether their own classroom libraries violate state law."[146] That's because HB 1467, which became law in July 2022, is designed to panic educators about any book in their collection dealing with themes related to race, gender, or sexuality. Formally, the ban requires that all books in school "be suited to student needs" by prohibiting any book deemed pornographic or age inappropriate. However, in practice, this ban has been applied to important books that support healthy racial, gender, and sexual identity development among youth. The law also stipulates that all books must pass inspection and be approved by a school media specialist who has taken a state retraining class on establishing book collections. Yet the Florida Department of Education didn't make the training available until January 2023, which kept Florida school librarians from being able to order books for over a year.

HB 1467 doesn't only prohibit books from schools, it also enforces draconian punishments for violators. Educators caught with contraband books risk facing a third-degree felony, carrying with it up to five years in prison and a $5,000 fine. So as not to run afoul of the law, officials in the Manatee and Duval Counties of Florida instructed teachers to either remove books from classrooms or cover them up.[147] One teacher reported to the Zinn Education Project, "I'm terrified to say anything about enslavement because it might make students 'uncomfortable.' I also can't recommend ANY books because a parent might not like it and then I could be charged with a felony." Another said, "We have educators unable to fulfill Black history month plans due to the lack of diversity in books and due to new laws and regulations on what they can and cannot read."[148]

The Escambia school district in Florida even issued a ban "pending investigation" of—wait for it—*Merriam-Webster's Elementary Dictionary*.[149] Even the dictionary is now too subversive because it does, after all, contain the words "racism," "sex," and "transgender." The satirical Seattle newspaper *The Needling* ran the headline "Florida Bans 'LGBTQ' from Alphabet"—an absurdity rivaled only by the actual policy of banning the dictionary.

Beyond the books that have been explicitly banned, teachers have also reported the phenomenon of "shadow banning." One teacher in Texas revealed this insidious practice to the Zinn Education Project, writing, "My district set up a due process policy for the public to request books to be removed, but instead of this policy being used, leaders in the district are quietly pulling books from shelves so that there's no record of banning. This shadow banning is removing access to books as we increasingly focus on school culture and policy that polices students, forces assimilation, and dehumanizes our children."

An examination of the books targeted for censorship unveils a stark contrast between which books are targeted for banning and which are not. Uncritical race theorists are not attempting to ban books that make Black children uncomfortable, only those they fear challenge racism. As Robin D. G. Kelley wrote, "For example, there are no calls to ban Thomas Jefferson's *Notes on the State of Virginia*, which asserts frequently that Black people are innately inferior to whites—physically, intellectually, and even in terms of imagination."[150] I would add that there are a number of children's books that romanticize America's founding as a slaveholding society that are not being banned, such as *Master George's People: George Washington, His Slaves, and His Revolutionary Transformation*. Books glorifying the founding fathers' enslavement of African people are safely shelved in school libraries around the country, while books that humanize Black and LGBTQ+ people are the targets of truthcrime laws.

Although the censorship of books in schools has recently exploded, it must be acknowledged that incarcerated people have long been victim to banned books and struggle with some of the most draconian restrictions. In fact, more books are banned in prisons and jails than in schools and libraries combined.[151] "The books that the world calls immoral are the books that show the world its own shame," the legendary gay socialist playwright Oscar Wilde wrote in his celebrated novel *The Picture of Dorian Gray*. What does our nation have to be ashamed of today that is causing the banning of books?

One in eight children go hungry in the United States, with 22 percent of Black and Latine children food insecure in the richest nation in the world. Some forty-four million Americans have combined $1.7 trillion in student debt, with Black college graduates owing on average $52,726 in student debt compared with white college graduates, who owe $28,006.[152] More than 80 percent of LGBTQ+ students who attended in-person school at some point in 2020–2021 experienced harassment or assault. Fewer than 30 percent of LGBTQ+ students report that their classes include any LGBTQ-related topics, and only 8 percent said their schools had policies supporting transgender and nonbinary students.[153] The shame of structural racism, transphobia, and homophobia in a country that professes to be the freest nation on earth is a contradiction so acute that uncritical race theorists and educational closeters continue to throw books onto the bonfire in an effort to hide these realities in the smoke of deception.

Conclusion

Education versus Schooling

During his expert seminar to Congress, James Whitfield articulated a cold reality: "Educators who pour their heart and soul into the growth and development of young people have been placed squarely in the crosshairs of political groups who are determined to destroy public education." This wasn't a detached theorizing; rather, it was an eyewitness account of how the gun scope of truthcrime was locked on to his livelihood when he dared to teach his school community the truth about structural racism.

The toll on educators from the relentless attack by uncritical race theorists is incalculable. However, one way to begin to measure the harm is to analyze one recent survey of educators. A report from the National Education Association found "a staggering 55 percent of educators are thinking about leaving the profession earlier than they had planned," and the poll found that a disproportionate percentage of Black (62 percent) and Latine (59 percent) educators—who are already underrepresented in education—are planning to leave teaching. Obviously, many factors drive educators out of the classroom, including fear for their health during a pandemic, lack of adequate pay, and general disrespect. And just as obviously, the war on truth in education has created casualties in the form of BIPOC and honest white educators leaving the profession. As one teacher explained how truthcrime legislation was likely to cause her an early exit from the profession, "I just can't. I can't do this. I really value being honest with students. I really don't think I can navigate teaching in such a watered-down type of way."[154]

There is no doubt these efforts at organized forgetting in our schools are harming educators and students. Illustrative of the injuries being caused is the 2021 survey finding that 44 percent of high school students reported they persistently felt sad or hopeless during the past year and that among youth with suicidal ideas, more than half are transgender and nonbinary, and nearly half are Black.[155] It is clear that Black, queer, and trans youth are suffering from the trauma inflicted by structural racism and oppression in school and the broader society. This harm is exacerbated when their humanity is questioned by policies such as censoring AP African American studies or "Don't Say Gay" legislation.

There are several trends in the attack on students, educators, antiracist curriculum, and books that are important for understanding the uncritical race theorist' plan for education. First, uncritical race theorists are quite comfortable with the explosion of hate crimes at school and the abuse suffered by Black students and LGBTQ students, while opposing any efforts, whether curricular or institutional, to address and prevent these attacks. Second, uncritical race theorists often specifically target the very best educators— the award-winning teachers, the National Board–certified teachers, the wise veterans, and the ones celebrated by their students—to make an example out of so as to dissuade anyone else from antiracist teaching. Third, they not only ban social justice curriculum but also advocate for book bans to limit students' ability to learn more on their own about the information that was banned from the classroom. Fourth, they have designed their attack on education based off the Cold War playbook that combined the Red Scare with the Lavender Scare.

"Education is different than schooling," Crystal Visperas wanted me to know as my conversation with her came to a close. "Schooling is about uniforms and detention and homework and things like that—robotic things. I see education as an act of service to your community and an act of love. Education is a way for people to free themselves and heal themselves. It is a liberatory, beautiful craft. And it is humbling. I have been humbled so many times." Although uncritical race theorists did push Vispy out of her classroom, they ended up making their job of erasing BIPOC people from education harder because now she works as the manager of recruitment and community partnerships for the Seattle Teacher Residency, which seeks to diversify the profession by encouraging more teachers of color into education.

An educator who joined one of the hundreds of *Teaching for Black Lives* study groups around the country explained both the anxiety and determination of truth teachers in this moment: "Sometimes it feels like it is time to hang it up and do something else. Then you remember if not me then who? We must serve as the light to pass the light to others so that our progress forward is reinforced by other generations of educators."[156]

For the honest education movement to succeed in defeating the truthcrime laws, the Teach Truth movement must study how the war on CRT emerged, who funds it, and what their strategies are. The following chapter analyzes the political economy of truthcrime to support the struggle for honest education.

CHAPTER 3

The Political Economy of Truthcrime

Billionaires, Parent Truthcrime Associations, and the Origins of the Attack on Critical Race Theory

We are right now preparing a strategy of laying siege to the institutions.
—**Christopher Rufo,** Manhattan Institute

Koch-funded entities have manufactured this cycle of outrage, and it is dangerous to ignore the role they are playing and their motivations. . . . They are inciting outrages against racial justice, and then using that outrage as a Trojan horse for entrenching radical free market ideology in every institution possible.
—**Jasmine Banks,** executive director of UnKoch My Campus

"Educators . . . have faced online bullying, calling for their jobs," James Whitfield schooled his congressional students at the hearing. "They have received death threats and hate mail. They have reached points of frustration and exhaustion that I have not seen in my near two decades in this profession."[1] How did the United States reach a point where educators face threats of physical violence for teaching the histories of people of color, Black studies programs are illicit, thousands of books are being banned, and students regularly endure racist, homophobic, and transphobic attacks?

To answer that, you will have to acquaint yourself with Christopher Rufo—a "far-right propagandist" (as described by the Southern Poverty Law Center) who styles himself as a kind of clean-cut alternative to the more rough-and-tumble Proud Boys. It's an old strategy; the White Citizens' Councils, offered a veneer of respectability by replacing the hooded robes with blazers and neckties. He is quite clearly working to make white supremacy respectable again—as evidenced, for example, by his support for *Aporia*, a "sociobiology magazine" that experts have characterized as a forum for neo-eugenics and "scientific" racism because of its advocacy for a relationship between race, intelligence, and criminality.[2]

Rufo is a resident of Washington State, and although many imagine that the attack on CRT must be a product of the South, or of a so-called "red state," he got his political start with a failed bid for a seat on Seattle's city council. Rufo showcased his renowned lack of kindheartedness, his brazen racism, and his propensity to disparage those he views as beneath his station in a documentary short he produced to explain why it's harmful to provide housing to unhoused people. Reading off the teleprompter, studio lights shimmering off his dark brown Ivy League haircut, Rufo stares directly into the camera and sneers,

> Activists say that homelessness is a manifestation of income inequality, that homeless encampments under a luxury condo tower is evidence of capitalism's moral and economic failure. . . It removes any concept of fault or responsibility from the equation. . . . They'll cite high rates of homelessness among African Americans, Native Americans, and LGBTQ . . . and argue that this disproportionality is by definition the result of discrimination.[3]

Rufo goes on to declare that the problem with this left-wing narrative is that it "establishes the premise for a policy of unlimited compassion." Having identified the problem with modern society as a surplus of compassion, Rufo's political project proceeds accordingly as he preoccupies himself with new ways to diminish empathy and solidarity among as many people as he can.

Rufo is content to confine his thinking to the generic rhetoric of the conservative news media, shunning intellectualism in favor of adorning his disdain for the poor and people of color with polished talking points from high-powered right-wing think tanks. Rufo's repackaging of mass-produced racist and homophobic narratives has taken him to stratospheric heights of visibility and influence.

Although Rufo had already been working for the right-wing Heritage Foundation and the Claremont Institute, his blastoff into national notoriety began on September 2, 2020, when he joined the *Tucker Carlson Tonight* show on Fox News. Seated in a Seattle studio wearing his customary uniform of a dark suit and collared shirt, with a stock image of the Space Needle as his background, Rufo began his comments by asserting his scholarly credentials: he had been researching CRT for a whole six months. Rufo was eager to share with Carlson the shocking conclusion of his investigation: "It's absolutely astonishing how critical race theory has pervaded every aspect of the federal government." And with those words, Rufo set off a viral payload of lies and disinformation that spread like the omicron variant through the media.

The fact that CRT hadn't, in fact, been taught to any federal workers and is almost completely absent from any of the branches of government was no deterrent to Rufo, who was determined to create a panic, facts be damned.

Rufo continued with his hyperventilation about the scale of the crisis: "What I have discovered is that critical race theory has become in essence the default ideology of the federal bureaucracy and is now being weaponized against the American people." Next Rufo issued a challenge to President Trump with all the gallantry and intrepid valor of a poker cheat, who, employing a marked deck to be certain of the outcome, pushes all his chips into the middle of the table and lays his hand down:

> Conservatives need to wake up. This is an existential threat to the United States. And the bureaucracy, even under Trump, is being weaponized against core American values. And I'd like to make it explicit: The President and the White House, it's within their authority to immediately issue an executive order to abolish critical race theory training from the federal government. And I call on the President to immediately issue this executive order to stamp out this destructive, divisive, pseudoscientific ideology.[4]

For Rufo's daring gamble to pay off, it would require five pitifully obvious things to match up and give him a winning hand. First, then president Trump had to be watching Fox News; second, Trump had to have no idea what CRT actually was; third, Trump had to see an opportunity to advance white supremacy; fourth, Trump had to have such a fragile ego that being challenged in this way would hurt his feelings enough to cause him to want to prove himself; and fifth, Trump had to see an opportunity for self-aggrandizement.

As incalculable as the odds were, each of those circumstances occurred and Rufo had himself a royal flush of political opportunity to promote himself and his rebranded version of uncritical race theory. The morning after Rufo's appearance on Carlson's troglodyte variety show, Trump's chief of staff Mark Meadows called Rufo to see if some kind of a white brotherhood could be forged that could calm the anxieties of those who worried that the 2020 uprising might continue to grow in size and strength until Black lives mattered to the political institutions of America. Rufo recalled the conversation in an interview for *The New Yorker*: "'Chris, this is Mark Meadows, chief of staff, reaching out on behalf of the President. He saw your segment on 'Tucker' last night, and he's instructed me to take action.'"[5]

Rufo was invited to Washington, DC, and he didn't miss his opportunity to add his flickering light to the other dim blubs that made up the gaudy chandelier of white supremacist advisors the White House had gathered. Together, these uncritical race theory crusaders drafted language that would become Executive Order 13950, declaring an end to any trainings for federal employees that were designed to help them understand the way racism or sexism functions in the workplace. On September 4, 2020, Russell Vought, the director of the Office of Management and Budget, delivered the news for Trump with a memo instructing federal agencies to

> identify all contracts or other agency spending related to any training on "critical race theory," "white privilege," or any other training or propaganda effort that teaches or suggests either (1) that the United States is an inherently racist or evil country or (2) that any race or ethnicity is inherently racist or evil. In addition, all agencies should begin to identify all available avenues within the law to cancel any such contracts and/or to divert Federal dollars away from these un-American propaganda training sessions.... The President has directed me to ensure that Federal agencies cease and desist from using taxpayer dollars to fund these divisive, un-American propaganda training sessions.[6]

And there, in one woefully underdeveloped and unsubstantiated essay that would have fared poorly in any language arts or social studies class in the nation, the Trump administration announced the primary concepts they would package as their new iteration of uncritical race theory to attack children of color. Among the concepts and catch phrases they couldn't grasp intellectually but nonetheless chiseled into blunt instruments to wield against the nation's youth included "critical race theory," "divisive concepts," and teaching that the United States is inherently racist. These would become the watch words of the coming onslaught of white power politics that would engulf school districts around the country—North, South, East, and West.

The 1776 Commission

Following the opening gambit of banning nonexistent CRT trainings for federal employees, the Trump administration turned its sights on K–12 public schools and hosted the White House Conference on American History; and, as wild as it could seem to some, the president whose election prompted the *Oxford English Dictionary* to make its 2016 word of the year "post-truth," turned out not to be an authority on historical accuracy. Though it may come as a surprise to some, the president who once invented a Civil War battle that didn't exist to claim his new golf course was on hallowed ground—even erecting a flagpole and installing a fraudulent plaque that inaccurately claimed "Many great American soldiers both of the North and South, died at this spot"—wasn't a reliable reporter on the past.[7]

The summit assembled many of the most base uncritical race theorists in the country to establish Trump's version of the Ministry of Truth: the "President's Advisory 1776 Commission." Trump described it as a "national commission to promote patriotic education" and counter the 1619 Project's work that demonstrates the ways enslavement was fundamental to the US political and economic structure. The event featured a panel of memory hole historians who attempted to replace past events that inconveniently revealed structural racism with what we could call MAGA (Make America Great Again) schooling. In his opening remarks, Trump fumed that antiracist education was contributing to the 2020 uprising:

> The left-wing rioting and mayhem are the direct result of decades of left-wing indoctrination in our schools. It's gone on far too long. Our

children are instructed from propaganda tracts, like those of Howard Zinn, that try to make students ashamed of their own history.

The left has warped, distorted, and defiled the American story with deceptions, falsehoods, and lies. There is no better example than the *New York Times'* totally discredited 1619 Project. This project rewrites American history to teach our children that we were founded on the principle of oppression, not freedom.

Nothing could be further from the truth. America's founding set in motion the unstoppable chain of events that abolished slavery, secured civil rights, defeated communism and fascism, and built the most fair, equal, and prosperous nation in human history. . . . Our youth will be taught to love America with all of their heart and all of their soul.[8]

Trump made it clear that he not only wanted children's minds, but also wanted to strike a Faustian bargain for their souls to stop any critical analysis of race. Curiously, for all the venom he spat against CRT being taught in schools, he didn't name a single critical race theorist or a CRT book that was being used in school. He did attack one of the most beloved historians in America, Howard Zinn, whose *A People's History of the United States* provides accounts of history about the struggles of oppressed and marginalized groups that are often left out of corporate textbooks.

After Trump launched the event by filling up the room with the smoke of deception, his panel of uncritical race theorists spoke, including the anti-people's historian Allen Guelzo (former staff member at the Heritage Foundation), who put a target on the back of the Zinn Education Project with the pitiful lie that the organization's materials are "snuck under the door of unsuspecting teachers."[9] In fact, rather than try to sneak lessons under teachers' doors, the Zinn Education Project makes free, interactive people's history lessons available for download on their website. But what was truly infuriating to Guelzo, so much so that it led him into telling this lie, was the fact that 170,000 teachers, all across the country, have registered on their own volition to use these antiracist, antisexist, social justice lessons.

In his book *Art of the Deal*, Trump invented the concept of "truthful hyperbole"—also known colloquially as bald-faced lies—which he clearly applied to the 1776 Report that came out of the White House Summit on History.[10] The American Historical Association ridiculed the misleading document, saying it was "[w]ritten hastily in one month after two desultory and tendentious 'hearings,' without any consultation with professional historians of the United States"; it contained "falsehoods, inaccuracies, omissions, and misleading statements"; and it was "an apparent attempt to reject recent efforts to understand the multiple ways the institution of slavery shaped our nation's history."[11] The 1776 Report wasn't only god-awful for what was included in the document, but also for what was left out. The American Historical Association wrote, "In listing threats to the ideals of the nation, the report ignores the Confederate States of America, whose leaders, many clearly guilty of treason, initiated a civil war that claimed more than 700,000 lives—more American lives than all other conflicts in the history of the country combined."[12]

Now, equipped with a pseudohistorical document that uncritical race theorists understood as holy text absolving America of sin, they were ready to spread the good word. Fox News led the crusade, attacking "critical race theory" nearly 1,300 times in a three-and-a-half month period from mid-March through June 2020.[13] With the 1776 Commission playbook in hand and liberals on their heels, the GOP and their right-wing billionaire sponsors went on a blitzkrieg of organized forgetting. "We have successfully frozen their brand—'critical race theory'—into the public conversation and are steadily driving up negative perceptions. We will eventually turn it toxic, as we put all of the various cultural insanities under that brand category," Rufo wrote. "The goal is to have the public read something crazy in the newspaper and immediately think 'critical race theory.' We have decodified the term and will recodify it to annex the entire range of cultural constructions that are unpopular with Americans."[14]

That was the plan. But the plan was complicated by the fact that Trump lost the 2020 election. Had Trump won reelection, the crusade would have continued from by the executive branch, but when Joe Biden was elected president, he quickly annulled the 1776 Commission. At this point, many liberals believed that would be the end of this particular story. Surely now that the post-truth president was gone, some of the more impolite and overt attacks on honest education would subside. Or so they thought.

Passing the Tiki Torch from the White House to the State House

While the idea that the attack on antiracist education would desist with Trump's departure from the White House was dangerously naive, there was an understandable reason why many liberals believed it. One reason liberals imagined the issue would go away was that after the right-wing media launched its attack on CRT in September, it dramatically decreased commenting on the topic in October and November; Fox News went from saying "critical race theory" sixty-nine times in September to using the term only four times in November 2020.[15]

Yet a more fundamental explanation for why liberals didn't take the attack on CRT in education seriously when it was first launched relates to the tradition of bipartisan education policy. For a long time, Democrats and Republicans had forged a consensus around what they called "education reform," with both parties agreeing that the most important goals were to privatize schools, reduce teaching and learning to a score on a standardized test, and use test scores to punish students and teachers with what both parties called "accountability." Remember that President Obama maintained, and even exacerbated, the worst aspects of President George W. Bush's bipartisan No Child Left Behind Act with his Race to the Top program—which intensified the privatization of public schooling and the over reliance on high-stakes standardized test scores. One study found that the overemphasis on standardized testing of the Bush administration mushroomed during Obama's administration, with students taking on average an outlandish 112 high-stakes standardized tests from preschool through twelfth grade.[16]

Many liberals believed that after Trump left office, the country would return to some version of this bipartisan education accord and the coveted state of normalcy would be restored. However, there were three fundamental flaws with this line of reasoning. The first problem was a failure to recognize the radical new political vocabulary Trump had taught the Republican Party, which was given an exclamation point on his way out with the January 6th white supremacist attacks at the Capitol. The second flaw in the liberal calculation was that the "normal" times before President Trump weren't worth returning to. Youth of color didn't want to return to the status quo of underfunded and segregated schools that funneled disproportionate numbers of Black and Brown students into prisons and largely erased the contributions of BIPOC in the curriculum. The third problem with the idea that the all-out attack on honest accounts of history would desist with Trump's eviction from the White House was the lack of recognition of how important racism is to maintaining the American social order—and how frightened the richest 1 percent were by the 2020 uprising for Black lives. Billionaires saw the streets filled with multiracial masses of people in the largest protests in US history, and the terror of a society built on racial and social justice flashed before their eyes. Though many Democratic Party strategists either didn't know it or were being paid not to think too deeply about it, a frightened billionaire is a very dangerous thing indeed, and the richest 1 percent were willing to invest heavily in any campaign designed to reestablish the racial division needed for weakening any challenge to their siphoning of wealth from working people of all races.

Thus, the attack on antiracist education was merely transferred from the Oval Office to state capitol buildings, and state Republican legislators fell over themselves in the scramble be the first to introduce truthcrime laws. So, while Trump and his 1776 Commission had been removed from the executive branch of the government, the tiki torch that Trump lit with his desire to char any thinking that questions racism and oppression stayed lit and continues to burn bright.

Educational Philanthrocapitalism

Then and Now

It must be underscored that as brazen as the attack on education is today, wealthy elites have a long history of using their wealth to construct a school system that limits Black education and disallows antiracist pedagogy. This is an approach to controlling schooling with philanthrocapitalism—a form of philanthropy that is designed to pursue profit and maintain the economic dominance of the richest 1 percent of society.

During the early twentieth century, politicians and northern white philanthropists collaborated to advocate for a model of schooling for Black children that would eliminate holistic approaches to education and implement training to produce a labor force of low-wage workers, serving the interests of industrial titans. E. S. Richardson of Webster Parish, Louisiana, explained that if African Americans could learn that "their only true friends are in the South," then "we need have no fear for white supremacy." A white citizen named Cone from Bulloch, Georgia, said, "Teach him honesty, industry, and obedience to law and order"—expressing for many white elites the belief that Black schooling should be limited to encouraging morality, submission, and work skills that would be profitable to white industry.[17] Rosa Parks's recollection of her experience growing up attending the segregated schools of Pine Level, Alabama, in the 1910s and early 1920s confirms that the goals of these white educational architects were achieved: "The schools in the south were the best training ground for teaching Negro inferiority and white supremacy."[18]

In 1902, white industrialists and philanthropists formed an organization called the General Education Board, in part to coordinate their intervention into shaping—and limiting—the nature of Black education. William H. Baldwin was a northern philanthropist and a member of the General Education Board who spoke for many wealthy white industrialists when he said, "The Potential economic value of the Negro population properly educated is infinite and incalculable. In the Negro is the opportunity of the South. Time has proven that he is best fitted to perform the heavy labor in the Southern States. . . . This will permit the southern white laborer to perform the more expert labor and to leave the fields, the mines, and the simpler trades for the Negro."[19]

For Baldwin and other northern white philanthropists, if Black people were properly trained in industrial trades, and, just as importantly, to accept their second-class citizenship, it could result in heightened revenue by sheltering the southern economy from the kind of profit-reducing union organizing that white workers in the North were engaging in. As honest historian Noliwe Rooks asserts, Baldwin believed that this kind of education was essential for enlisting Black people "to break the rising power of the white labor unions."[20] Walter Hines, another General Education Board member and editor of the *Atlantic Monthly*, also saw dollar signs where he should have seen children, saying Black industrial education is not only "good business especially for the South but good business for the entire country."[21] Rooks points out that from the North to the South, from philanthropists to politicians, "the public funding of Black education was not viewed as a right of citizenship, but rather as a way to include Black people in a changing economic order in service to a changing southern economy in a manner mindful of northern industry."[22]

Carter G. Woodson—dubbed the "Father of Black History"—described how the white power structure maintained control of education to "mis-educate" (as he called it) Black children:

> Negroes have no control over their education and have little voice in their other affairs pertaining thereto. In a few cases Negroes have been chosen as members of public boards of education, and some have been pointed members of private boards, but these Negros are always such a small minority that they do not figure in the final working out of the

educational program. The education of the negroes, then, the most important thing in the uplift of the Negroes, is almost entirely in the hands of those who have enslaved them and now segregate them.[23]

To this day, white billionaires—both liberal and conservative—continue to use their wealth to shape schools into miseducation academes. In 1999, the right-wing Koch network began a concerted effort to whitewash US history when it formed the Bill of Rights Institute. "The Bill of Rights Institute (BRI) is the education arm of the network of front groups the Koch brothers use to promote their far-right ideology," Adam Sanchez explained. "The political goal of BRI materials is to ensure students see racism and slavery as flaws in an otherwise spotless U.S. record, rather than woven into the fabric of our country from its inception."[24] The liberal billionaire Bill Gates has used his unfathomable wealth to push policies such as charter schools, which have contributed to further segregating the schools, and he promoted the dramatic increase in the use of standardized testing, which has played a significant role in crowding out critical thinking and social justice education in favor of teaching to the test.

Follow the Money

The Truthcrime Treasury

In a distortion typical of the mainstream media, Hannah Natanson, Lauren Tierney, and Clara Ence Morse, writing for *The Washington Post*, penned this origin story for the drive for truthcrime laws:

> Anxiety first stirred due to coronavirus pandemic-era school shutdowns as some mothers and fathers—granted an unprecedented glimpse into lessons during the era of school-by-laptop—found they did not like or trust what their children were learning.
>
> Soon, some parents were complaining that lessons were biased toward left-leaning views and too focused on what they saw as irrelevant discussions of race, gender and sexuality—laments taken up by conservative pundits and politicians. National groups like Moms for Liberty formed to call out and combat left-leaning teaching in public schools.[25]

In this prevalent discourse, an organic movement emerged in opposition to the left-wing politicization of education because of parents' newfound ability to observe their children's education remotely. Although the mainstream media often portrays the attack on antiracist teaching as a scrappy, grassroots effort by parents attempting to reclaim their children's education, in reality it is a campaign that was initiated by far-right media, financed by billionaires, coordinated by Republican Party operatives, and made possible by the support of right-wing think tanks. If I had been the editor at *The Washington Post* for Natanson, Tierney, and Morse, I would have edited their description of the eruption of truthcrime laws to read like this: "sequestered in their mansions, private islands, and yachts, white plutocrats issue edicts to politicians and the media conglomerates they own about eliminating curriculum that implicates their rapacious accumulation of power and wealth as problems worthy of study, with no regard for the wishes of the vast majority of the diverse families that make up the public schools."

Let's meet some of the billionaires most invested in passing truthcrime legislation. Julie Fancelli, an heir to the Publix grocery fortune, helped finance the January 6th, 2021, attack on the Capitol and is now funneling tens of thousands of dollars to organizations promoting book bans and attacking antiracist teachers. Former secretary of education Betsy DeVos, whose family amassed a fortune from the Amway corporation, has been a longtime proponent of school privatization and is now spending lavishly to support organizations that defend a parent's "right" to insist that the schools lie to kids about racism. Oil magnate Charles Koch, who has long used his wealth for campaigns to eliminate the minimum wage and paid sick leave for workers, as well as to promote climate change denial and right-wing social studies curriculum for schools, is another one of the primary financiers of organizations that promote truthcrime legislation. Barre Seid, the ultra-secretive right-wing electronics billionaire, gave Leonard Leo more than $1.6 billion in 2020 to influence US politics and policy for years to come. Leo is behind the misnamed Free to Learn organization that was active in the 2021 Virginia gubernatorial election of Republican Glenn Youngkin.[26]

Many of these billionaires have invested in efforts to promulgate uncritical race theory in education for decades but escalated those efforts in the months after the 2020 election when former Trump administration officials formed a MAGA cabal with a primary focus on attacking CRT. With Trump's 1776 Commission disbanded by the Biden administration, supporting the newly formed 1776 Project organization became a priority of this new network. The 1776 Project received an early contribution of nearly $1 million from Restoration, a right-wing PAC backed by billionaire Richard Uihlein of Illinois.[27] *Education Week* reported that "[f]rom April 2021 to September 2022, the PAC raised nearly $3 million in contributions and had spent $2.6 million helping school board candidates win their campaigns."[28] This flooding of elections with cash was used to wash away much of the competition. In 2021, the 1776 Project endorsed fifty-eight conservative candidates in New Jersey, Ohio, Virginia, Minnesota, Kansas, and Colorado, and forty-two of them won.[29] In the 2022 midterm elections, about a third of the candidates endorsed by the 1776 Project won their election.[30] And the 1776 Project was only one of many organizations seeking truthcrime bills and the election of uncritical race theorists.

Consider that the *Daily Beast* identified "eight recently created anti-CRT groups which operate at local levels across the country but bear ties to ideological right-wing aristocrats and political operatives. Their backers include former officials in Donald Trump's administration, an executive at a notorious DC lobbying firm, as well as Koch entities and The Federalist Society."[31] One of those organization is the America First Policy Institute, a think tank staffed by former Trump administration officials, which has worked with legislators in at least two states to craft their truthcrime bills.

In addition, the group UnKoch My Campus examined the publications of twenty-eight right-wing think tanks and conservative political organizations with ties to the billionaire-backed Koch network from June 2020 to June 2021 and found "they had collectively published 79 articles, podcasts, reports or videos about Critical Race Theory."[32]

Some of the other billionaire-funded organizations working to outlaw teaching the truth about structural racism include the Heritage Foundation, the Manhattan Institute for Policy and Research, the Alliance for Free Citizens, American Enterprise Institute, the American Legislative Exchange Council, the Concord Fund, and Citizens for Renewing America.

The Manhattan Institute is one of the most established conservative think tanks—with Christopher Rufo among its coterie of uncritical race theorists—and has played a prominent role in turning billionaire funding into ahistorical videos, talking points, articles, and memos that attempt to explain how advocating for racial inequality is not racist. In June 2021 the institute published "Woke Schooling: A Toolkit for Concerned Parents" and used funding from billionaires to distribute their manifesto for staying asleep about racial, gender, and sexuality. In addition, the institute has produced model truthcrime legislation to assist uncritical race theorists in censoring history around the country.[33]

The Koch-funded American Legislative Exchange Council produces conservative model legislation that it exports to states around the country, and the group held a webinar in the early days of attack on CRT called "Against Critical Theory's Onslaught." This forum helped to coordinate uncritical race theorists from around the country, including state legislators, private foundation representatives, corporate lobbyists, and right-wing policy organization staffers.

Citizens for Renewing America has used its list of divisive concepts to draft model legislation that would ban the 1619 Project and any of the concepts therein. In addition, it has produced a tool kit that advises on "how to stop Critical Race Theory and reclaim your local school board."[34]

Far-right conspiracy theorist and Trump insider Charlie Kirk founded Turning Point USA, which hosts the School Board Watchlist, a website that posts the names, photographs, and descriptions of school board members and educators around the country that they are targeting for removal. The group especially objects to any school district that believes in "cultural literacy and sensitivity"—apparently preferring cultural illiteracy and insensitivity.[35]

Since the first days of the GOP's pivot to a focus on truthcrime legislation, the Heritage Foundation has consistently published political perspective briefs to orient uncritical race theorists to the latest talking points that advocate for teachers to lie to kids about history. This kind of advocacy, such as promoting book and curriculum bans to obscure the struggles and contributions of Black people, is familiar work for the Heritage Foundation. The organization got its political start supporting the war against multicultural textbooks in Kanawha County, West Virginia, in 1974, which erupted into violence when educational arsonists targeted schools and the board of education with incendiaries. The Heritage Foundation hired a lawyer at this time named James McKenna to help create the censorship demands of the parents in Kanawha County and provide legal aid to their attack. McKenna elucidated the Heritage Foundation's rationale for engaging in a war on multicultural books: "Picking your fight is important. If you pick the right fight at the right time, it can be profitable . . ."[36]

Following this same playbook today, the Heritage Foundation is attacking antiracist education because it believes it can again be profitable. In

April 2023, the Heritage Foundation released Project 2025—also known
as the Presidential Transition Project—a 920-page blueprint authored by
numerous conservatives, including former Trump administration officials.
Many of the collaborating organizations have received dark money contributions from fundraising groups associated with Leonard Leo. Project 2025
outlines policy proposals to extensively overhaul the federal government's
executive branch in the event of a Republican win in the 2024 US presidential election, and it offers a dystopian vision for a future, where the most draconian truthcrime laws—for example the "Don't Say Gay" laws and bans
on antiracist teaching—are enforced on the entire country. In a Newspeak
dictionary definition of doublethink, the Heritage Foundation defines civil
rights as the attack on people's civil right to learn about the history of the
struggle for equal rights in this passage of Project 2025: "Enforcement of
civil rights should be based on a proper understanding of those laws, rejecting gender ideology and critical race theory." Project 2025 then proposes
federal legislation "that prevents [CRT] from spreading discrimination."[37]

It's important to recognize that the assault on antiracist education and
LGBTQ+ students by right-wing organizations is just one component of a
broader agenda aimed at consolidating power and wealth in the hands of a
very few people. This agenda encompasses attacks on various fronts, including
on voting rights, reproductive rights, immigrant rights, union rights, housing
rights, and more. This is a class of people who seek to profit off of gentrifying
neighborhoods while simultaneously working to gentrify our history so people don't have the lessons that could aid them in building the kind of social
movements it would take to win housing justice. The basic strategy of monied
uncritical race theorists is to take actions that subvert democracy and then
hide their actions by banning people from learning about them.

Take the Concord Fund, for example. Operating as a dark money group
under the alias of the Judicial Crisis Network, the Concord Fund not only
has allocated substantial resources to voter suppression campaigns but also
has allocated over $1 million to eradicate racial justice education in K–12
schools.[38] These efforts are integral to the group's strategy of division and
conquest, which seeks to undermine social cohesion and maintain their
grip on power.

It's imperative to contextualize these attacks within the broader framework of wealth concentration. Currently, the wealthiest 1 percent control
nearly half of the world's wealth, while the poorest half possess a mere

0.75 percent.[39] To maintain this extreme wealth disparity, the elite employ diversionary tactics, such as demonizing drag queen story hours, or comprehensive sex education, or privilege walks as purported threats to societal stability. By stoking outrage over these perceived issues, they deflect attention from their own culpability in siphoning resources from public schools, health care, and other essential services. In reality, the true threat lies in their relentless pursuit of profit at the expense of marginalized communities and the public welfare. Truthcrime legislation, then, serves as a means to perpetuate this agenda by preventing young people from learning the historical lessons of social movements that have challenged inequality and injustice.

Parent Truthcrime Associations

With billionaires and their wealthy think tanks offering a currency printing press to anyone who advocates for outlawing teaching the truth about structural racism, a plethora of uncritical race theorist parent groups were formed, and existing groups received an infusion of cash that made them much more visible. I call these groups "Parent Truthcrime Associations" (PTCAs), and they function similarly to the White Citizens' Councils and the parent groups that built campaigns of "massive resistance" against desegregating the schools after the 1954 *Brown v. Board of Education* Supreme Court decision.

Some of the most prominent PTCAs are MFL, Parents Defending Education (PDE), and No Left Turn in Education (NLTE). These PTCAs share several characteristics. First, PTCAs are overwhelming made up of white parents. Second, they are dedicated to advocating for laws that prohibit teaching the truth that structural racism is foundational to the United States or that ban teaching about gender or sexuality. Third, they employ sophisticated public relations strategies to masquerade as plucky bands of parents self-organizing to defend their kids from being shamed in school by antiracist teachers—rather than admitting they are being funded by wealthy elites as part of the get-out-the-vote strategy for GOP candidates. PTCAs often exploit campaign finance deregulation, stemming from the 2010 US Supreme Court decision in *Citizens United v. Federal Election Commission*, which allows them to hide from the public who is donating to their organization—a practice that produces what has come to be known as "dark money." As Alyssa Bowen and colleagues wrote for *Truthout*, "The funding sources

of many dark money 'parent' groups that cropped up along with the manufactured outrage against 'critical race theory' in 2020 and 2021 are largely
unknown due to weak public disclosure regulations."[40] Still, investigative
journalists have discovered significant connections between PTCAs and
billionaires, as detailed below.

As *Truthout* put it, "'Parents Defending Education' is overwhelmingly
funded by big donors' dark money rather than by 'concerned parents.' . . .
PDE's 2021 990 nonprofit IRS form shows that the group raised more than
$3.1 million in its first year," and pointed out that PDE raised only $77,272 of
that from membership dues.[41] According to the Center for Media Democracy,
nine different right-wing foundations have poured money into PDE, including
Edelman Family Foundation ($200,000), Searle Freedom Trust ($250,000),
Bader Family Foundation ($130,000), and DonorsTrust ($20,250).[42]

PDE has received generous donations from the billionaires Betsy DeVos
and Charles Koch and gained noteriety for its misnamed "IndoctriNation"
map that encourages uncritical race theorists to "submit an incident report"
on their website to intimidate teachers who dare to teach about systemic racism and oppression.[43] Much like what the group Campus Reform does at the
college level, PDE's hope is that by outing individual K–12 schools and educators for antiracist education in a searchable database, they can intimidate
teachers around the country to fear reprisals for teaching about topics such
as slavery, segregation, or mass incarceration. PDE made national headlines
when it sued the Biden administration because it didn't include enough
uncritical race theorists on its National Parents and Families Engagement
Council. The lawsuit led to education secretary Miguel Cardona to disband
the group rather than engaging in a struggle to explain why racial justice
deserves to be a focus of the group.

The PTCA NLTE was founded in the wake of the murder of George
Floyd, by a mom who was horrified that her child could be exposed to
lessons that explained the structural causes of his murder. NLTE founder
Elana Yaron Fishbein is known for her reprehensible uncritical race theory, as when she dismissed anti-Black police violence, racist attacks at
school, and the rise in anti-Black hate crimes, arguing that "black bigotry towards whites" is a "very real problem." NLTE also prides itself on
transphobic trolling, as when the organization told LBGTQ+ people to go
"back to Trans-sylvania." NLTE emerged from the fringes of the internet
and gained a sizeable following of extremists when Fishbein was a guest

on Fox News's *Tucker Carlson Tonight* and *The Ingraham Angle*. Progress Michigan reports that NLTE has been backed by Tucker Carlson and a Koch organization.[44]

Of all the PTCAs, MFL is perhaps the most ironically named, bigoted, politically connected, and well funded. MFL was cofounded by Tina Descovich, Tiffany Justice, and a school board member from Sarasota, Florida, Bridget Ziegler—the wife of Florida Republican Party chairman Christian Ziegler. Bridget Ziegler has led vicious attacks on the LGBTQ+ community, including championing Governor DeSantis's "Don't Say Gay" law that limits the curriculum to cis-heterosexual representation, yet admitted in December 2023 to having engaged in a same-sex relationship when a woman accused her husband of raping her and revealed that Bridget had participated in a threesome with them.[45] Former Sarasota student Zander Moricz put these events into perspective when he stepped to the podium at the December 12, 2023, school board meeting and, addressing her directly, stated,

> Bridget, our first ever interaction was when you retweeted a hate article about me from *The Nationalist* while I was a Sarasota County school student. You are a reminder that some people view politics as a service to others, while some view it as an opportunity for themselves. . . . Bridget Ziegler, you do not deserve to be on the Sarasota County School Board. But you do not deserve to be removed from it for having a threesome. That defeats the lesson we've been trying to teach you, which is that a politician's job is to serve their community not to police personal lives. So to be extra clear, Bridget, you deserve to be fired from your job because you are terrible at your job, not because you had sex with a woman.[46]

MFL was founded in January 2021 and incorporated as a 501(c)(4) organization—a designation it uses to try to hide its donors—and by the end of the year had "grown to 135 chapters in 35 states, with 56,000 members and supporters, according to the organization's founders."[47] MFL's cofounder Tina Descovich claimed the growth of the organization and the large sums of money raised were the result of their spirited stick-to-itiveness. "If someone wants to give us a million dollars, we would take it." Descovich said. "But it's just not happening." Descovich, with the characteristic propensity of uncritical race theorists to avoid the truth, credited the groups fundraising success to individual $50 memberships dues and proceeds from the sale of T-shirts.

In fact, MFL is closely connected with powerful Republican Party operatives and has received funding from several conservative organizations. *Politico* reported that billionaire Julie Fancelli donated $50,000 to MFL in June 2022, marking the first contribution to the group's political action committee.[48] Maurice T. Cunningham, author of the book *Dark Money and the Politics of School Privatization*, shined the light of truth on MFL's hidden contributions, writing, "Since its inception Moms for Liberty has managed a fund raiser with former Fox News celebrity Megyn Kelly (top ticket $20,000), co-hosted The American Dream Conference featuring a keynote from former Trump Cabinet secretary Ben Carson."[49] He also points out that they sold out of presenting sponsorships for $50,000 dollars at their national summit, which featured DeSantis, Carson, Senator Rick Scott, and billionaire Betsy DeVos.

These political operatives are all in on MFL's vision of remaking education and politics in the United States. To understand why, it's imperative to examine what they mean by "liberty," a term they quite apparently use as a synonym for censorship, anti-intellectualism, lying, and harassment. You won't catch these moms demanding pay raises for the majority female workforce of educators, decrying the disgracefully high maternal mortality rate for Black women, or organizing campaigns to lower class sizes. Instead, these mothers delight in banning books about Black people or queer people and harassing educators. Exposing the entire truthcrime legislation movement for what it is, the Tennessee chapter of MFL challenged the book *Martin Luther King Jr. and the March to Washington* because of "photographs of political violence" and the book *Ruby Bridges Goes to School* because of "racist remarks."[50] As unpleasant as the truth can be, Martin Luther King Jr. and the Civil Rights Movement did face political violence, and Ruby Bridges, the six-year-old girl who was among the first Black students to integrate a school in New Orleans, faced hysterical mobs of white parents, including those who made death threats against her. But MFL doesn't just want to ban books that teach about racial justice, they also want to replace them with openly racist ones. On its national website, MFL recommends the textbook *The Making of America* by W. Cleon Skousen, where he argues that slavery in the United States was not racist. As he put it, "Slavery is not a racial problem. It is a human problem." As Media Matters explained, "Skousen's book is also sympathetic to slave owners, calling them 'the worst victims' and writing that 'in some ways, the economic system of slavery chained the slave owners almost as much as the slaves.'"[51]

Although book banning and advocating for racist textbooks certainly excites these mostly white mothers, nothing thrills them quite as much as issuing threats and harassing students and educators. The New Hampshire chapter of MFL went so far as to put out what they referred to as a "bounty" of $500 for whoever was first to use the state's new snitch hotline that encouraged parents and students to turn in teachers that they believe have violated the truthcrime law. MFL tweeted, "We've got $500 for the person that first successfully catches a public school teacher breaking this law. Students, parents, teachers, school staff... We want to know! We will pledge anonymity if you want."[52]

MFL's despicable campaigns of harassment continued after Jennifer Jenkins unseated Tina Descovich for a Brevard County, Florida, school board seat. In a piece for *The Washington Post*, Jenkins described just what these educational closeters' definition of liberty was:

> Young children, accompanied by their parents, shouted into megaphones, "Don't touch me, pedophiles!" LGBTQ students tried to speak while adults chanted "Shame!" ... A group of about 15 shouted "Pedophiles!". ... "Be careful, your mommy hurts little kids!" one shouted at my daughter. "You're going to jail!" they chanted.... One coughed in my face while another shouted, "Give her covid!" A third swung a "Don't Tread on Me" flag near my face. My neighbors told me they had seen protesters brandishing weapons in the church parking lot behind my house. The next day, a large "FU" was burned into my lawn with weed killer. The bushes in front of my house were hacked down.[53]

The Proud Boys, designated by Southern Poverty Law Center as an extremist hate group, have aided PTCAs by using physical confrontations and threats of violence in their effort to end antiracist teaching. From Washington State, to California, to Kansas, to Florida, and beyond, the Proud Boys have invaded school board meetings, where they have "shouted racist and homophobic slurs at students." An Orange County, California, radio station quoted school board chairwoman Hillary MacKenzie describing a meeting of the board: "There were two men in Proud Boys shirts and hats ... one wore a stocking over his face ... the other one told our board during public comment that someone should tie rocks around our necks, and we should throw ourselves in a river."[54]

PTCAs are intervening in elections across the country, at every level, on behalf of billionaires. The GOP fell short of its prediction that its attack on CRT during the 2022 midterm elections would produce a "red wave" that they would ride to its goal of achieving a substantial majority in both chambers of the US Congress. Still, Republicans won enough seats to secure a majority in the House of Representatives and reelect incumbent governors in Texas and Georgia. Although they made limited gains at the national level, their focus on school board races helped them elect truthcrime candidates at the local level across the country. As former Trump advisor Steve Bannon said in May of 2021, "The path to save the nation is very simple—it's going to go through the school boards." And by saving the nation, he quite clearly means saving it for white supremacy by suppressing honest education.

To get a sense of how uncritical race theorists are implementing Bannon's strategy, take a look at the school board recall efforts. Between 2006 and 2020, Ballotpedia identified recall efforts around the country against an average of 52 school board members each year; that number shot up to 237 board members in 2021 as the PTCAs led a coordinated campaign against anyone who defended honest history.[55]

Alarmingly, MFL estimated that half of the more than 200 candidates they endorsed in the 2022 midterm elections were elected, including about 61 percent of the group's 67 endorsed candidates in Florida. "It was clear that culture war conservatives scored some victories," *The Washington Post* reported about 2022 school board elections around the country. Many extremely well-funded North Texas anti-CRT school board candidates won their positions in several Dallas-area races, and antitruth Texas Republicans won several seats on the State Board of Education to strengthen their majority.

Yet as communities began organizing to defend education from MFL and other PTCAs, the organizations' fortunes began to change. In the election cycle of November 2023, despite being bankrolled by the richest 1 percent, most of their bids for school board and other elected positions failed, with MFL estimating only 43 percent of their candidates won. Although their extremist agenda is clearly not currently supported by the majority of people, it should be noted that, as of this writing, there are 365 people who have been endorsed by MFL who hold office, and there can be no doubt that PTCAs are becoming an important auxiliary to the Republican Party and central to their electoral strategy.[56]

"Defund the Schools"

Uncritical Race Theory's Privatizing Agenda

Although convincing white parents that their children spend all day at school learning to hate their family is certainly a GOP get-out-the-vote strategy, the motives behind the attack on antiracist teaching go much deeper. As educator and high school social worker Nora De La Cour wrote for *Jacobin* magazine, "By pitting parents against schools, libertarian billionaires and Republican strategists intend to motivate voters in the short term and fully privatize K–12 education in the long term."[57]

The right-wing think tanks and foundations previously detailed in this chapter have long pursued an agenda of school privatization—which includes attacking the teachers' unions that are in the way of the decimation of public education—and are simply rebranding their campaign with anti-CRT rhetoric. Although most uncritical race theorists leading this campaign are titillated by telling lies, Christopher Bedford, a senior editor at *The Federalist*, honestly revealed the real aims of right-wing attacks on antiracist education:

> Our schools—from preschool all the way to graduate programs—have gone seriously astray in a way that no single law can ever hope to fix. Masks, "critical race theory," or whatever you want to call it, are basically just visible sores on our schools. They're painful symptoms of a much deeper sickness. . . . Every year this country spends $640 billion on public K–12 education, and a huge share of that money is going to people with evil ideas who want to poison your children to think the same way. . . . So what's the solution? The answer is to think bigger. . . . Here's what we should do: Defund the schools for real.[58]

Bedford must have been attempting to create a clever spinoff of "defund the police" with his call to "defend the schools"—so he was surely disappointed when legions of parents didn't take to the streets to demand that the funding be slashed to their kids' school. Nevertheless, sycophants like Bedford will continue to lure support from the wealthy because they understand the potential profits that could be made from privatizing education and the importance of training the public not to expect any services for the common good. "When it comes to K through 12 education," said the billionaire media magnate Rupert Murdoch, "we see a $500 billion sector in the U.S. alone that is waiting desperately to be transformed by big breakthroughs that extend the reach of great teaching."[59] Murdoch, of course, wasn't interested in education because he wanted to empower young people, but rather because there were billions of dollars that could siphoned out of public accounts through school privatization.

Christopher Rufo, in a speech titled "Laying Siege to the Institutions," described the strategy of using CRT to scare white families into supporting school privatization, saying, "To create universal school choice, you really need to operate from a premise of universal school distrust." It's important to understand that the term "school choice" came out of the resistance from white parents to desegregating schools after the *Brown* Supreme Court decision and is today used by those who want to replace public schools with charter schools—privately run schools that get public funds—and voucher programs that give money to individual families to send their kids to private schools.

Honest historian Nancy MacLean's book *Democracy in Chains: The Deep History of the Radical Right's Stealth Plan for America* is useful for understanding where the kinds of ideas that Rufo espouses were developed.[60] MacLean credits the fanatical right-wing economist James McGill Buchanan and his partnership with billionaire Charles Koch for helping to develop a "property supremacist" philosophy at the core of the drive to privatize education. Buchanan, a product of the Chicago school of economics that molded many minds into zealous defenders of free-market fundamentalism, became the chair of the University of Virginia's economics department at the very time Virginia state legislators launched "massive resistance" against desegregating public education.

Buchanan and his colleague Warren G. Nutter "offered a plan they believed could salvage what remained of massive resistance while surviving court review. How? Privatize education, but do so on the basis of strictly economic arguments." MacLean wrote, "Their goal was to create pathways for white families to remove their children from classrooms facing integration. School choice had its roots in a crucial detail of the *Brown* decision: the ruling only applied to public schools. White southerners viewed this as a loophole for evading desegregated schools."[61] Raymond Pierce explained how school choice was used to maintain segregation:

> From 1958 to 1980, private school enrollment in the South increased by more than half-a-million students. Hundreds of private segregated schools were opened, and private school enrollments by wealthy, white Southerners increased at a steady pace. What also increased were efforts to fund private schools at the expense of public schools, using vouchers

or tax credits to cover significant percentages of student tuition and operations costs.[62]

One Virginia county went so far as to completely close the public schools altogether from 1959 to 1964—rather than desegregate them—and opened up new private schools for the white children, "while leaving some eighteen hundred Black children with no formal education whatsoever." Although Buchanan and Nutter's plan ultimately failed, MacLean explains, "In these final hours of the massive resistance era, then, can be found the seed of the ideas guiding today's attack on the public sector and robust democracy alike."[63]

It's no coincidence that the plan to privatize public education originated from a racist campaign to maintain Jim Crow schooling, or that many of today's school privatizers are leading a campaign against antiracist education. With billionaires driving education policy, Democrats and Republicans have long collaborated to privatize schools. It's important to note that distinctions exist between the Democrat and Republican plan for how to privatize education; Republicans often tend to prefer the voucher system, where families get money from the government to pay for (a portion of) private school tuition, whereas Democrats often tend to prefer charter schools. When Florida governor Ron DeSantis signed HB 1 in March 2023, he created one of the largest voucher privatization programs in the country. Evoking the language of the school segregationists of the 1950s, DeSantis declared, "This expands school choice to every single student in the state of Florida." By using the CRT scare to frighten people away from the public schools and into accepting the pillaging of public coffers to dole out money to private entities, DeSantis revealed the deeper objective of truthcrime laws.

Teacher Union Busting

Within public employee unions, the 1.7-million-member American Federation of Teachers and the 3.2-million-member National Education Association represent the single biggest sector of unionized workers in the United States today.[64] Uncritical race theorists strongly oppose unions representing educators because these unions serve as crucial barriers to the privatization of education.

As well, unions advocate for higher pay, and increased school funding and, at their best, champion antiracist and social justice causes. "Unions,

collective bargaining, and teacher job protections play a vital role in protecting teachers' ability to teach the truth to students," honest educator and
author Kevin Kumashiro explained. "Unions historically have been on the
front lines of pushing for shared governance, including local control of curriculum, as well as to advance broader human and civil rights, particularly
for marginalized communities. . . . Teacher strikes—within unions and without—in recent years have undoubtedly amplified their voices."[65]

The Chicago Teachers Union, through militant struggles, strikes, and
sophisticated organizing, has won increased pay for its members, fought and
saved schools from closing, and supported the struggle for a mandatory curriculum in Chicago to support students learning about the history of police
misconduct and torture in the city. The United Teachers Los Angeles union
has also led with a social justice union approach, not only striking in 2019 for
better pay, but also to support immigrant students, lower class size, ensure a
nurse in every school, and end random searches of students by police.

The collective power of educators struck fear in the hearts of Republicans during the 2018–2019 "red state revolt" that began in West Virginia
with state leadership of the West Virginia branches of the American Federation of Teachers and the National Education Association holding a strike
vote. The strike launched the "Red for Ed" movement that inspired similar
statewide strikes in Oklahoma and Arizona, as well as widespread actions
by educators in Kentucky, North Carolina, and Colorado and a school bus
driver strike in Georgia. Tens of thousands of educators around the country
engaged in these (often illegal) strikes. Many of these educators, residing
in states with anti-union laws, lacked collective bargaining rights and yet
organized at the rank-and-file level to push their unions and associations
into action. In state after state, these mass strikes forced Republican Party–
dominated legislatures to increase spending on education. In Oklahoma, for
example, the strike lasted from April 2 to April 12 and won a $6,000 increase
in teacher salaries, with support staff salaries increasing by $1,250.[66]

Organized educators who force governments to reinvest in public education and defend educators who teach the truth about racism are a threat to
uncritical race theorists. The question of whether teachers' unions will organize the scale of struggle necessary to defend teachers who honestly educate
about racism and oppression is one that will come to define both the quality
of public education and the very nature of employment in the United States.

The Liberal Fear of Critical Race Theory

"Avoid Teaching Concepts Like 'White Privilege'"

When the attack on antiracist teaching was launched during the 2021–2022 school year, Democratic Party politicians and liberal pundits attempted to stay above the fray and not engage with delusional right-wingers ranting about CRT in school—either because they misestimated the lengths the GOP would go to attack antiracist teaching or because they shared a fear of CRT and hoped it wouldn't become an issue their constituents would ask them to take a public position on.

The Democratic Party's refusal to lead a campaign to defend antiracist teaching stems from its obsequiousness to the same billionaire class that funds the Republican Party. In addition, because the Democrats' reelection strategy is often obsessed with peeling off right-wing voters—instead of rallying their base or motivating the vast numbers of people who don't vote by inspiring them with a vision of economic, racial, and social justice—too many Democratic Party politicians try to avoid the issue of CRT altogether.

When debating conservatives, liberals often assert that CRT isn't being taught in schools. Although it's true that the majority of educators were unfamiliar with CRT until Republicans began vehemently opposing it, the right wing, aided by media platforms, largely succeeded in labeling any form of antiracist teaching as CRT. Consequently, when liberals dismissed the idea of CRT being taught in schools, it came across as disingenuous to many. The liberal strategy of proclaiming, over and over, that CRT is not taught in schools—without engaging in the debate about whether antiracist teaching was appropriate for school—left them vulnerable to attacks by conservatives that they were hiding something. And they were hiding something. Liberals were attempting to obscure the fact that they were scared that taking a bold position in defense of antiracist teaching, ethnic studies, Black studies, or CRT could cost them votes. Because many liberals, like conservatives, were also unfamiliar and afraid of CRT, many of them decided to dodge the larger question of whether CRT *should* be taught.

This liberal confusion and timidity around how to discuss CRT was on display in the 2021 governor's race in Virginia between Democratic candidate Terry McAuliffe and Republican Glenn Youngkin, underscoring much of what is problematic about the liberal response to attacks on CRT. Youngkin gave a full-throated denunciation of CRT as "toxic" and "poisonous left-wing doctrine" that is "flagrant racism, plain and simple."[67] McAuliffe's response was to say, "I don't think parents should be telling schools what they should teach."[68] Although parents who want to criminalize teaching the truth about race, gender, and sexuality must certainly be challenged, that's not what McAuliffe said. In his attempt to sidestep the central issues in the debate— such as whether children should get to learn about struggles against systemic racism—Youngkin came off as instructing parents to stay out of the conversation about what their children are taught. Telling parents that they shouldn't care what their kids are learning was a boneheaded move, and that comment likely played a role in McAuliffe losing the election; a poll conducted by CreativeDirect found 54 percent of all voters said that McAuliffe's statement was a big factor in their decision of who to vote for.[69]

But the problem goes far beyond a gaffe at a campaign stop. McAuliffe may genuinely oppose the GOP's proposed restrictions on teaching about racism in schools, but he doesn't support the important insights of CRT that would help students understand why the governor's race was between two multimillionaire white men.

Because many liberal politicians don't actually support CRT, they are placed in a difficult spot during elections when the Republicans attack it. They know that Republican attacks on CRT play a role in energizing their base, so they must oppose the attack. But they are squeamish when it comes to a rigorous investigation of the way structural racism operates, lest it help propel social movements that could go beyond just challenging the GOP and move toward a broader critique of inequities in America—rooted in white supremacy and racial capitalism—that could upset their own corporate sponsors. So instead of defending CRT, or even just defending antiracist education more broadly without naming CRT, liberal politicians often just monotonously repeat that CRT is not being taught in school.

As the GOP attack on truth in education escalated in the run-up to the 2022 midterm elections, the failure of the liberal strategy to combat the lies became increasingly clear. Even though passing antihistory, anti-CRT laws was quickly becoming the primary reelection strategy for the Republican Party, the Democrats were paralyzed in their ability to defend antiracist teaching because the party as a whole has never been oriented toward uprooting systemic racism; how was it now going to pivot toward defending students' right to learn about it? The Democratic Party is associated with more supportive views of BIPOC and certainly has many antiracist constituents, and it even put forward the first Black president. Yet the Democratic Party, in conjunction with the Republican Party, has long played a key role in maintaining systemic racism.

From its origins as the party of slavery and Jim Crow segregation, to the internment of over 125,000 Japanese Americans during World War II, to exacerbating mass incarceration, to enforcing mass deportations, the Democratic Party has played a central role in maintaining systemic racism. Movements for social justice today must grapple with the fact that President Bill Clinton's support of a crime bill that imposed harsh mandatory sentences was a major catalyst for the explosion of the prison population—a bill that was drafted and championed by then senator Joe Biden. President Obama dramatically increased deportations of immigrants and President Biden followed by imposed harsh border militarization policies.[70] Given this extensive record, it's understandable why Democratic Party politicians have failed to mobilize against laws prohibiting the teaching of truth about structural racism—a true account of this history would implicate their own party.

The Democratic Party's failure to forthrightly confront truthcrime laws has left America's Black youth and youth of color vulnerable to far-right billionaires and their astroturf parent organizations—groups attempting to dominate schoolhouses and turn school board meetings into arenas reminiscent of the White Citizens' Councils who opposed the Civil Rights Movement.

The refusal of the Democrats to defend honest education about race has been so flagrant that it has angered or demoralized wide swaths of its base. The evidence of this is abundant. An op-ed published by a liberal columnist in *The Washington Post* argued, "When Republicans turned an obscure academic topic known as critical race theory into a national boogeyman supposedly poisoning the minds of our youth, Democrats were caught flat-footed. They weren't sure how to react: Debate what it actually means? Explain that it isn't something that gets taught to kids? In the face of relentless conservative demagoguery, they were flummoxed. . . . And Democrats still seem uncertain how to respond."[71] "I get frustrated with the Democrats' lack of movement, to be quite transparent," Revida Rahman—a Brentwood, Tennessee, mother of two and cofounder of the racial equity group One WillCo—told *The Washington Post*. "I think the other side has an engine that is always moving. They have a playbook. They're playing chess and we're playing Go Fish or something."[72] Professors Daniel Kreiss, Alice Marwick, and Francesca Bolla Tripodi argued in an article for *Scientific American*,

> Rather than dismissing manufactured concerns over CRT as fake, Democrats should embrace the robust teaching of America's racial history in our public schools and make an affirmative case for why it matters for American values of fairness, equality and justice. Democrats should then focus on articulating how attacks on CRT are meant to divide people of all races who otherwise share interests. Rather than dismissing these attacks as isolated incidents, Democrats should mount their own sustained and coherent campaign to argue affirmatively for diversity, equity and inclusion programs and for complementary efforts such as the 1619 Project.[73]

This frustration with the Democrats was echoed by *New York Times* columnist Jamelle Bouie, who explained,

> Democrats have notably not delivered on many of their promises. . . . These are not just attacks on individual teachers and schools; they don't stigmatize just vulnerable children and their communities; they are the foundation for an assault on the very idea of public education, part of the long war against public goods and collective responsibility fought by conservatives on behalf of hierarchy and capital. These are not distractions to ignore; they are battles to be won. The culture war is here, whether Democrats like it or not. The only alternative to fighting it is losing it.[74]

William Frey, of the liberal Brookings Institution, suggested that Democrats should stop sitting on the sidelines of the attack on antiracist education and explain to parents "why understanding the history of race in the U.S. is important for their children to learn."[75] Diane Ravitch, one of the most widely read education historians and a critic of school privatization, wrote an important critique of the failure of liberal billionaires and establishment Democratic Party politicians to defend honest teaching about racism:

> The most puzzling aspect of this coordinated effort to suppress the teaching of accurate history is the silence of people who should have spoken up to defend the schools and their teachers. The most prominent no-show on the ramparts is Secretary of Education Miguel Cardona. Last June, he testified before a Congressional committee and was asked about critical race theory. He responded that his department would leave curriculum decisions to states and local districts. . . . Other

prominent absentees from the CRT-censorship-book banning controversy were the billionaires who usually are verbose about what schools and teachers should be doing.

Where was Bill Gates? Although rightwing wing-nuts attacked Bill Gates for spreading CRT, Gates said nothing to defend schools and teachers against the attacks on them. He is not known for shyness. He uses his platform to declare his views on every manner of subject. Why the silence about teaching the nation's history with adherence to the truth? Why no support for courageous teachers who stand up for honesty in the curriculum?[76]

When you consider how vocal Bill Gates has been about education—relentlessly defending his destructive spending of untold millions to privatize education and inundate the schools with high-stakes standardized tests—it is quite telling that he hasn't bothered to defend educators who are being fired for wanting to teach accurate accounts of Black history. Gates once argued, "Education may be the hardest civil rights fight of all."[77] Quite apparently, he's given up even a rhetorical commitment to the fight.

The truthcrime bills proliferating throughout the country are so brazen and openly racist that the required response by anyone interested in truth and justice is very clear: assert freedom of speech, defend academic freedom, and demand that students have the right to learn about Black history and histories of people of color. Education and civil rights organizations understood the moral imperative and threat to democracy that uncritical race theorists represented and began organizing to defend truthful education right away. Yet the Democratic Party has not supported the national mobilizations of educators against the truthcrime bills and has often tried to avoid talking about the issue altogether.

How is it that in the face of one of the largest coordinated assaults on public education and BIPOC students, the Democratic Party could refuse to respond to the Republicans with a coordinated defense of an honest education and forthrightly oppose racism? The answer resides in the fact that an honest account of systemic racism is also threatening to the billionaires who fund the Democratic Party—leading them to remain conspicuously timid in defending educators and students who have been targeted by the GOP.

The failure of the majority of Democratic politicians to mount a sustained defense of antiracist teaching has predictably created room for some Democrats to openly align with the GOP. In March 2024, Democratic US congressperson Wiley Nickel of North Carolina joined eight other Democrats in voting to federally ban any teaching that suggests the United States is "fundamentally racist" in schools that serve the children of those in the military. Nickel defended his vote, saying, "I fully agree that our students deserve an educational environment free from such division."[78]

J. Dionne Jr. defended abandoning the defense of antiracist education, writing, "One thing Democrats should not do: tear themselves apart with arguments over critical race theory itself."[79] Some liberal pundits and politicians have outright rejected honest educators who, at great risk to their careers and sometimes even their personal safety, defend teaching the truth about structural racism. "[I]f Democrats want to win elections—and allow kids to get a meaningful education—they should stop dismissing parents' complaints about 'critical race theory' as nonsensical fabrications. . . . [I]t would make sense to avoid teaching concepts like 'white privilege,'" wrote liberal uncritical race theorist and senior columnist for *Forbes* Natalie Wexler.[80] The message is clear: the discomfort that white parents have with their kids learning about race is more important than supporting youth of color or teaching the truth about structural racism.

In following the Democrats' lead, much of the liberal media has failed to mount a robust defense of antiracist education. While Fox News provided Christopher Rufo a platform to amplify his attacks on CRT, the mainstream corporate media has significantly elevated that platform and brought his message to a broader audience. By granting Rufo an inordinate amount of time and attention, these media outlets have legitimized his unfounded conspiracy theories on race. At the same time, the mainstream media refuses to regularly cover the thousands of scholars, educators, parents, and students who are building the Teach Truth movement; they will, however, provide a platform for far-right extremist groups disguised as grassroots "parent rights organizations" without delving into their billionaire funding.

During his appearance on the *Cuomo Prime Time* show on November 17, 2021, self-proclaimed "old school liberal" Bill Maher joined the GOP's campaign against antiracist education. In a display of what passes for political insight in today's moribund political TV culture, Maher expressed discomfort with antiracist education, suggesting it has gone "too far." He applauded modern schooling for supposedly teaching more about Black history than the film *Gone with the Wind*, which glorifies slavery. However, he cautioned against acknowledging racism as fundamental to the nation, stating, "That's different than teaching that racism is the essence of America. That's what people get upset about." He also argued against antiracist education for "children, who are probably not old enough, or sophisticated enough, to understand this very complicated issue, with a very complicated history."[81] Maher's stance blatantly disregards the reality of Black students who are navigating segregated schools, disproportionate discipline, police abuse, and other aspects of systemic racism on a regular basis. Ready or not, Black and Brown youth are engaging with racism continually—the question is, will they be able to discuss their experiences in class and access the historical context? If *Are You Smarter Than a Fifth Grader* ever features a racial justice edition, perhaps Maher should decline an invitation to participate.

Given the desperate and unhinged attempts by the far right to drag the country back into the McCarthy era and deny the most obvious manifestations of racism, Democrats could have built on 2020 protests for racial justice and launched a campaign against the attacks on antiracist teaching that could have increased both their congressional majority and their moral standing.

Democratic Party pollster Celinda Lake, however, attempted to justify the party's alternative strategy of attempting to sidestep debate on CRT, saying, "I don't minimize the amount that the Republicans are doing to try to energize their base with this issue. But this is not a threat to us. The economy is the much bigger threat than critical race theory."[82] What Lake teaches us here is that not only is the Democratic Party establishment, in fact, minimizing the potential of the Republicans to use the attack on CRT to gain power, but they also view the attack on CRT only as an issue that could impact the election and not so much as one of the most egregious attacks on democracy and youth of color that it is.

If the Democrats refuse to engage in the debate about CRT and antiracist education for fear they will lose the "moderate" voter, the majority of people who believe that more Black history should be taught in school—as polls have demonstrated—are likely to be uninspired and fail to turn out for elections. Consider, for example, that more than 80 percent of registered voters expressed to the Black Education Research Center the importance of teaching public school students about the history of racism and slavery in the United States, as well as its ongoing effects on students and communities.[83] The Democratic Party establishment's hesitancy to vigorously fight against truthcrime laws isn't because they haven't looked at the polls and are unaware that defeating these bills would help them increase their vote total.

Their lack of gusto for racial, economic, and social justice stems instead from the fact that, as with the GOP, they are predominantly funded by white billionaires who see no advantage to teaching students about systemic racism or capitalist exploitation. So while the vast majority of liberals rightly favor striking down laws that prohibit teaching about systemic racism, the powerbrokers in the Democratic Party are not beholden to their base as much as they are to their megadonors.

Conclusion

Billionaires versus Truth Teachers

"To be crystal clear, this is about disrupting and destroying public schools.... We must simply call this what it is ... a ploy to divert public school dollars to subsidize private education in the name of 'choice,'" Whitfield instructed the congressional hearing. "This can't be the way forward. We simply cannot afford to lose true public education."[84]

It is truly astonishing to consider how much money billionaires have spent to advance school privatization, hate groups, campaigns of harassment, and PTCAs. Imagine the visual beauty and musical compositions that could have been created if that money had been invested in art and band classes for millions of kids. Imagine the healing for millions of students and their families that would have been possible if that money was invested in wraparound services of health care, mental health care, dental care, tutoring, job programs, and more. Yet instead, the funding went to supporting mobs harassing school board members, online trolling campaigns of educators, and a slew of legislation designed to dehumanize transgender children and ban honest accounts of history. These are the fiscal priorities of a society that is not well.

Billionaires have two major strategies for reproducing a society, generation after generation, that allows for an unfathomably wealthy few to profit off of the labor of everyone else. The first strategy is repression. When rapacious investment bankers triggered the Great Recession with subprime mortgages and credit default swaps, the Occupy Wall Street movement swept the country and organizers built encampments in public spaces to demand a redistribution of wealth from the richest 1 percent to the other 99 percent. And then, on one weekend, a nationally coordinated effort by mayors saw police attack the Occupy encampments and brutalize those who dared suggest such blasphemies in America as sharing or economic democracy.

During the 2020 uprising, police relentlessly attacked protesters with flash grenades, tear gas, billy clubs, and even live ammunition. When students occupied their own college campus around the country in protest of the genocide in Gaza, police were sent in to break up the encampments.

This kind of state violence has been a permanent feature of how elites use police to contain any challenge to their wealth and power. Although they won't hesitate to use vicious force if necessary, they would prefer if people policed themselves by learning in school to accept the current inequalities. Maintaining an economic system such as ours, where eighty-one billionaires have more wealth than the bottom half of all people on Earth, doesn't just happen by accident.[85] It takes careful investments in institutions that shape ideas, and those investments see the biggest returns in the mass media and the system of schooling. Noam Chomsky has described the political economy of the media and how elites shape popular narratives about society in classics such as *Manufacturing Consent*. Critical pedagogues have described how schooling is used to reproduce hegemony, such as Ira Shor in *Empowering Education* or Michael Apple in books such as *Official Knowledge* and *Ideology and Curriculum.*

One of the central contradictions of schooling in our society is that it is purported to be the great equalizer and the bedrock of success, and yet in practice, education has long been designed to teach children to accept the society as it is—with all of its violence, racism, and inequality. This contradiction is becoming increasingly clear and is leading to the growth of the Teach Truth movement, detailed in the following section of the book.

Part II

Remembering

CHAPTER 4

"We Will Teach This Truth!"

The Teach Truth Movement

*As an educator of ethnic studies, it is so essential that I teach my
students the true history of Black, Brown, and Indigenous people in the United States and around the world. I will not stand
down as legislators try to hide the truth from our students.*
—**Stephanie Melendez,** high school social studies
teacher, West Palm Beach, Florida

*You don't get to tell us what to read. You don't get to tell us
what to teach. You don't get to tell us what to learn.*
—**Kimberlé Crenshaw**

"I've also witnessed large groups of students gain a voice and stand in the
face of this hatred," James Whitfield shared with his congressional classroom as his lesson continued. "I'm so proud of our young people. They give
me great hope!"[1] These inspiring and creative young people Whitfield taught
Congress about are taking action all over the country to defend their right
to learn honest history.

Meet Decatur High School senior Ana Villavasso. She is a painter. She
had never thought of herself as an artist before, but when the pandemic hit,
she was looking for something new to help get her through the isolation of

161

having to shelter in place at home. During this time, she worked consistently to develop her skills, and soon she could faithfully replicate images of people in well-developed portraits.

When in-person classes resumed at her school in Decatur, Georgia, she brought her new talents into the school building. "I think one of the things I was most proud of this year is that I created a mural in my school," Villavasso told me in a July 2022 interview. "Maybe ten feet wide, eight feet tall. I did it all by myself and it's basically five characters painted in different colors of the rainbow, they're just illustrating camaraderie. . . . You don't know what race they are, you don't know who they are, you just know that they're having fun." Villavasso, a young Black woman, explained to me that by painting the people in the mural with bright colors that are not actual skin tones, she was inviting people to both recognize the diversity of people who have different skin colors and project a hope for a day when everyone could see the beauty in each other beyond our current racial constructions. Since creating that mural, Villavasso has gone on to paint many canvases to express herself, often with themes about the struggle for racial justice. "What really brings me joy is being able to express myself and also being able to help others at the same time."

But that hasn't always been possible at school for Villavasso. Over the years she has dealt with many instances of racism at school, but there was one particular incident in sixth grade that first caused her to realize she was being treated differently because she was Black. She was assigned a group project, and as the deadline drew near, her friend hadn't finished her part. Villavasso decided to borrow her friend's iPad while they were at school to help get the project finished and texted her friend to tell her she would bring the iPad back soon. When Villavasso went back to the classroom where the project had been assigned, the teacher began yelling at her in front of the class, "You're stealing, you're stealing"—without even asking Villavasso about the situation. This is the kind of experience that was at the forefront of her mind when the state began passing truthcrime legislation in the schools.

Georgia's truthcrime legislation, HB 1084 and Senate Bills 375 and 377—known to some as the "divisive concepts" bills and to others as the "classroom censorship" bills—were designed to take away "the ability to talk about people who weren't straight, white, Christian men," as Villavasso put it to me. The passage of these bills in the spring of 2022 dramatically altered education because, as Villavasso explained, "You couldn't call the United States systemically racist. You couldn't talk about race. You couldn't talk about critical race theory. But a lot of people think the laws were only critical race theory. It's not only critical race theory. They banned anything that would cause a constructive discussion or an argument within the classroom." Elucidating what was wrong with banning so-called divisive concepts from the classroom, Villavasso told me, "In tenth grade, I was a part of this organization called Students Organized for Anti-Racism. . . . One of the pillars of our organization was to experience discomfort in our conversations. I don't think you're able to learn without ever experiencing any sort of discomfort."

In addition, there were bills banning transgender youth from participating in school sports according to their gender identity. Villavasso opposed all of these bills. "There were a whole bunch of bills, like a stack of them, that nobody was talking about until we organized at Decatur, and then the Georgia youth justice coalition all banded together. We said, 'Is anybody listening right now?'"

In February 2022, Villavasso was in her advisory class. "It was Black History Month, so we were having a whole bunch of presentations about Black history and my advisement teacher mentioned that there were a bunch of bills going around that were trying to limit the conversations that we were having. And she looked at me and she looked at the girl next to me [Vinessa Taylor], who was Black Student Union president. And then she said, 'They need to hear student voices.'" From that very moment, Villavasso committed herself to the struggle for antiracist education. "We're going to do something about this," she replied to her teacher. "In that class period, with four or five other people, we went to the back of the classroom, and we got to work. We created a Google Doc, a comprehensive list of all the things we needed to do. The next week was our February break, so we had to work over a break. People were out of town, but everyone was getting the work done." They decided they would organize a protest in the few weeks they had before the truth-crime bills were set to be voted on.

Villavasso described to me the whirlwind of organizing efforts to plan what they decided would be a school walkout called "Hands Off Georgia," which included creating a website with information on the proposed truth-crime legislation, making a flyer with a QR code that took people to the website, making announcements in teachers' classes, coordinating the event with Georgia Youth Justice Coalition, inviting other schools to participate, and getting media attention. Villavasso told me,

> Vinessa [Taylor] was responsible for contacting other schools. So she went to basically every school that she could find in the Metro Atlanta area and looked up their clubs—looked up the black student union, looked up any ethnically affiliated club that they had, got their email for the faculty sponsor, or the president, or just some name, and contacted them with, "Hey, we need as much students as possible out on this protest." I was responsible for contacting all the adults. There's this one organization in Decatur called the Beacon Hill Black Alliance, and they do a whole bunch of antiracist work around creating safe spaces for Black people in general. I contacted their leader. She helped me with the logistics: microphones, a podium, bullhorns. I had to drive at like 10:00 p.m. to meet in a parking lot with her to get the bullhorn the day before. She also helped me get set up with so many press media outlets. . . . And the Georgia Youth Justice Coalition guided us on how to talk to the press.

The day before the protest, not only was Villavasso securing all the equipment that was needed, but she was also making the final brushstrokes to finish her mural project. As taxing as all of this work was, Villavasso was exhilarated from the feeling that comes from making your voice heard when powerful people want to silence you.

And yet, she was also very anxious. "Our protest took place on February 25th, 2022. I woke up that morning and I told my parents, 'I'm not going to school today. I have this protest.' My parents said, 'Oh, we'll be there.' But besides my parents, I really had no clue who was going to show up. I told my group, 'We did the most we could.'" Villavasso arrived at the state capitol early in the morning to set up for the rally, but as she worked, she began to fear that the outreach efforts had not been strong enough to get a good turnout. But it wasn't too long before a new fear gripped her. "As I'm setting up, all of a sudden I see a whole swarm of people heading down to the Capitol, and I was scared because I realized that now I would have to speak in front of all these people." Over three hundred students from six different schools approached the capitol with chants such as, "Education is a right, this is why we have to fight!" Several young people took to the podium to let the uncritical race theorists in the capitol building know that they had no right to censor truthful accounts of history.

"I came because I am going to school—college—to become an educator, and I want to be able to teach kids proper history," said Decatur
High School senior Kenya Freeman. Yana Batra, of the Georgia Youth
Justice Coalition, spoke to the need to both organize and vote. When Villavasso took the podium, she leaned into the microphone and emphati-
cally declared, "Let those representatives know that their place is not in a
classroom, especially if they're not educators. We need American history.
It's the history of people of color—not only Black history but all people
of color."[2]

Reflecting on that day in her interview with me, Villavasso was beam-
ing: "That was the happiest moment of my life to see the fruit of our labor
paid off. Not only because people are showing out for a cause that genuinely
matters to them, but also just knowing my work actually came true. I'm just
so glad that people found their voice." The confidence that Villavasso gained
in the struggle to ensure that BIPOC history was taught truthfully in the
classroom was a victory in and of itself.

Although the Georgia legislature did pass the "classroom censorship"
bills to outlaw teaching the truth about racism and banned transgender
youth from playing for school teams consistent with their gender identities,
they simultaneously taught students about the depths of structural racism
and transphobia better than they could have learned in any classroom—and
also produced deeply committed young activists. As Villavasso recounted
her experience of the walkout that day, I couldn't help but think of a young
Barbara Johns, who led a walkout of her high school in Virginia in 1951, and
whose case was ultimately one of the legal challenges brought before the
Supreme Court in the *Brown v. Board* decision.

Ana Villavasso's story of students and educators supporting each other
in the struggle for an honest education is one that has been repeated in
schools and communities around the country.

And sometimes their struggles have won.

In August 2020, Pennsylvania's Central York School Board succumbed
to the twisted logic of uncritical race theory and banned a list of more than
three hundred antiracist books, films, websites, and other resources. But
at the September 20 school board meeting, honest educators and students
organized a rally to oppose the censorship. Before the meeting began, seventeen-year-old Central York High School senior Edha Gupta addressed
the gathered protesters and declared, "This ban is a dagger in my heart. I no

longer recognize the Central anymore, the inclusive loving diverse Central that has been a part of my life since preschool."[3]

During the school board meeting, many public speakers continued the call to overturn the bans. "We need an antiracist curriculum because no child should have to be teased because they have a different religion or their skin color is different," one speaker said.

This size and force of this mobilization couldn't be denied and, by a unanimous vote, the board voted to reverse its earlier truthcrime policy. "It took five high schoolers organizing a peaceful walk-in protest . . . to help make sure that our district heard that they, and many others, did not feel represented. They are heroes and should be celebrated as bastions of American freedom and democracy. I want to be clear: These kids did this," said Ben Hodge, a Central York High School theater teacher and cofacilitator for the student Panther Anti-Racist Union.[4]

Confirming Hodge's words, Gupta wrote that night on Instagram, "WE REVERSED THIS BAN. WE DID. THAT!" Gupta went on to say, "Our voices are powerful enough to demand immediate action, and that is EXACTLY what took place tonight."[5] In that moment, the dagger of truth-crime was removed from Gupta's heart, and the process of healing began.

As uncritical race theorists become more extreme in their attacks on truth, a growing Teach Truth movement is coalescing to not only fend off truthcrime legislation but also expand Black studies, ethnic studies, and other antiracist pedagogies. The curricular resistance to the antitruth bills has been varied, creative, overt, covert, and widespread—even if it has received little coverage in the mainstream media. The resistance to truth-crime has included public pledges to refuse to lie to kids about structural racism, marches, rallies, historical walking tours, flash mobs, tablings, petition signing, banned book clubs, op-eds, a "freedom readers" bus tour, and countless acts of "fugitive pedagogy" involving many thousands of teachers who have ignored truthcrime laws and taught their students the truth about racism and oppression.

Although the attack on antiracist teaching has been demoralizing and despicable, the resistance from educators, students, and parents around the country has been beautiful, emotionally moving, and healing. This organized rebellion has set off a truth alarm that is causing people to take action from the streets to the schoolhouse, from the classroom to the courtroom.

Truth Teaching as Resistance

One of the things quite often missing from both conservative and liberal media coverage of what they call "the CRT debate" is a detailed description of what antiracist pedagogy actually looks like. Because the media rarely takes you inside an antiracist classroom, uncritical race theorists have had free reign to mischaracterize the work of truth teachers. The quiet, unknown, fugitive pedagogy of teachers around the country who are honestly educating is a powerful part of the Teach Truth movement.

To appreciate the joy and healing that antiracist lessons produce, I invite you to look beyond the headlines about CRT and evaluate the actual practice of antiracist truth teachers. Consider the following account of how Jordan Jones, a middle school social studies teacher in Pittsburgh, Pennsylvania, taught a lesson written by truth teacher Bill Bigelow called "Reconstructing the South." As the lesson states,

> What kind of country is this going to be? This was the urgent question posed in the period immediately following the U.S. Civil War. When students learn about Reconstruction, if they learn about this period at all, too often they learn how the presidents and Congress battled over the answer to this question. Textbooks and curricula emphasize what was done to or for newly freed people, but usually not how they acted to define their own freedom.[6]

After providing this context to his students, Jones engaged his class in the lesson's simulation activity where the students debate the authentic political questions that faced the country from the era right after the Civil War and evaluate what strategies for creating racial justice would be most effective. The questions students grapple with include:

- Now that the war is ended, who should own and control these plantations?

- Would you be willing to promise the Northern politicians that, in exchange for acknowledging your right to the land, you would continue to grow cotton?

- What do you propose should happen to these Confederate leaders?

- Who should be allowed to vote in the new South? Everyone? Only

168 Teach Truth

168 Teach Truth

formerly enslaved people? Only those who were loyal to the United States during the war?

- How will the Black freedpeople be protected from the revenge of the defeated soldiers and from the plantation owners?

- What conditions should be put on the Southern states before they are allowed to return to the Union?[7]

Jones described his students' experience with this lesson on Reconstruction, writing,

> Students worked together in small groups and independently to answer each of the six questions within the activity. Students were engaged and collaborating effectively. However, the real magic took place when we had a whole class discussion/debate about the best solutions.
>
> There were clearly two ways of thinking for the students involved. On one side were students who were thinking pragmatically and trying to be realistic about what they thought they could have actually accomplished at this point in history. On the other side were students focused on doing what they believed was morally right and what solutions would best ensure the continued liberation of recently freedmen and women.
>
> The back and forth was powerful, and students were highly engaged in the process of not just thinking about history but participating in history.
>
> Finally, at the end of the day was a comparison between the solutions that won the argument and what decisions were actually made in history. The shock and disappointment were palpable.[8]

These students learned about the immense advancements toward building a multiracial democracy that existed during Reconstruction and also discovered how structural racism was reimposed—despite the end of slavery—on society through a vigorous counterrevolution against the expansion of Black rights. For all the hysterics by uncritical race theorists, looking at the actual antiracist lessons being taught reveals highly engaged students grappling with historical lessons relevant to their lives. This lesson exemplified Audre Lorde's insight that "[l]earning does not happen in some detached way of dealing with a text alone, but from becoming so involved in the process that you can see how it might illuminate your life. And then how you can share that illumination."[9]

Jones's method reveals so much about the practice of truth teaching, because while he presented students with the accurate debates of the era, and while he centered the arguments that the Black freedom struggle was grappling with at the time, he didn't tell students what to think. They were encouraged to draw their own conclusions, and, in fact, students disagreed about what action should have been taken at the end of the lesson. Juxtapose this exhilarating engagement of students to American Birthright's uncritical race theory standard number 45 on Reconstruction, which directs students to:

Explain as many as possible of the policies and consequences of Reconstruction. (H, C)

a. Presidential and Congressional Reconstruction

b. The impeachment of President Johnson

c. The 13th, 14th, and 15th Amendments

d. Attempted creation of a free-labor economy in the South

e. Opposition of Southern whites to Reconstruction

f. Accomplishments and failures of Radical Reconstruction (Thaddeus Stevens, Charles Sumner)

g. The presidential election of 1876, and the end of Reconstruction

h. The rise of Jim Crow laws

i. The Supreme Court case, *Plessy v. Ferguson* (1896)[10]

Incredibly, these standards don't suggest students learn anything about the rise of the KKK and the massive terror campaign they and other white supremacist organizations led that killed thousands of Black people during Reconstruction. But it isn't even the neglecting of this history that makes American Birthright so dangerous—the sheer tedium of the directions, which call for the recitation of one fact after another, ensures that students subjected to this curriculum will quickly be lulled to sleep and will be drooling on the desk like a scene out of *Ferris Bueller's Day Off*.

Jones's use of Bigelow's lesson shows why uncritical race theorists find antiracist teaching threatening: it demonstrates that historical events were not predetermined, that people's analysis of problems and how they act on that analysis matters. This is a "people's history" lesson that is instructive to students for helping them navigate today's struggles for justice. This lesson tells students that what they think and what they do are important and that they are not captives of fate or history but can be active participants in shaping the world.

Were students in Jones's class talking about the difficult subject of white supremacy? Of course they were. Reconstruction was the era when the Democratic Party supported the founding of the KKK and other white supremacist organizations to crush movements for racial justice. It was a time when society debated the fate of former white slave owners. Did engaging in these debates about how to achieve racial justice after the war shame the white kids in the class? Of course not—however, the lesson did shame white supremacy. Shaming white supremacy actually affirms the lives of white students and shows them how they can be part of collective struggles for racial justice. Inviting white students to discuss with their peers of color how to achieve racial justice lets them understand that they can have an important role to play in that conversation.

One of my favorite lessons to teach—and one of the most popular in my classes—is called "Teaching SNCC: The Organization at the Heart of the Civil Rights Revolution," and was written by Adam Sanchez. SNCC was one of the most important organizations in propelling the Civil Rights Movement forward to bring down Jim Crow segregation and finally win the right to vote for Black people. Students who learn history out of textbooks often come to believe the Civil Rights Movement was a primarily a few charismatic leaders, rather than appreciating that it was masses of young people that strategized and achieved the major victories for racial justice.

This lesson invites students to imagine themselves as members of SNCC and students engage in debates on the important questions the organization delt with in their fight against Jim Crow. Some of the authentic dilemmas faced by SNCC that students discuss in this simulated Civil Rights Movement–era meeting include "Should SNCC prioritize voter registration or direct action?" and "Should SNCC welcome a thousand mostly white volunteers to Mississippi?" After the students confront some of the main issues SNCC grappled with, they compare the positions they arrived at with those of the actual organization. I've found that once the students end their meeting, they are excited to find out what the SNCC youth actually decided. This brings the history alive in ways that lecturing can never achieve. Gulfport, Mississippi, high school history teacher Cristina Tosto described the power of this lesson:

> We did the Teaching SNCC lesson, where students have a SNCC meeting to discuss plans and make decisions based on real historical events. I wish people could see how the kids were really strategizing and getting into their roles as SNCC members.
>
> It was so encouraging to me as a teacher to see my students understand the grassroots organizing of the Civil Rights Movement. However, it was even more rewarding to watch them engage with the material in a social, emotional, and critical way. They are not only learning history, they are learning skills that can be applied to real-life scenarios.[11]

Isn't it obvious why uncritical race theorists would want to ban this lesson? Students learning that it was young people like them who dragged this nation, kicking and screaming, away from an apartheid system and toward the goal of democracy threatens to suggest that they also possess the agency to challenge inequitable power relations today. When educators and students engage with historical truths such as those in this lesson, they begin to heal from the violence of organized forgetting.

Though all too rare, in some instances educators actually do use CRT to help them provide truthful accounts of US history. High school history and social studies teacher Jania Hoover, who teaches at a predominantly white school in Texas, explained in an article for YES! Magazine that she uses CRT to help her students analyze the New Deal policies of the 1930s. While teaching about how the New Deal helped lift many people out of poverty, she also allows students to analyze how the programs included racist lending practices that helped create segregated communities. "I showed them maps that detailed areas where the FHA guaranteed loans in the city where we live," Hoover explained. "I then showed them current maps showing housing patterns based on race and income levels." Looking at the ways the institutions, policies, and systems maintain structural racism, even when they don't directly mention race, is a hallmark of CRT. Hoover's lesson aided students in understanding their society better, but it didn't shame white kids: "Both Black and White students were blown away at the very real implications of that information. The White students didn't feel guilty, and the Black students didn't feel helpless.... Everyone felt powerful, because they knew information that helped them understand patterns they see on a daily basis."[12]

The Pledge

Besides the countless unheralded educators who are quietly refusing to lie to students about structural racism in their everyday curriculum, many thousands of teachers are also publicly defying truthcrime laws. One powerful example of this defiance is the over eight thousand educators around the country who have signed the Zinn Education Project's online "Pledge to Teach the Truth." The Zinn Education Project launched the online pledge in March 2021 when Republicans began introducing truthcrime legislation in state legislatures. The pledge begins with a quote from Martin Luther King Jr.: "One has not only a legal but a moral responsibility to obey just laws. Conversely, one has a moral responsibility to disobey unjust laws." The pledge goes on to state, in part,

> From police violence, to the prison system, to the wealth gap, to maternal mortality rates, to housing, to education and beyond, the major institutions and systems of our country are deeply infected with anti-Blackness and its intersection with other forms of oppression. To not acknowledge this and help students understand the roots of U.S. racism is to deceive them—not educate them. This history helps students understand the roots of inequality today and gives them the tools to shape a just future. It is not just a history of oppression, but also a history of how people have organized and created coalitions across race, class, and gender. . . .
>
> We the undersigned educators will not be bullied. We will continue our commitment to develop critical thinking that supports students to better understand problems in our society, and to develop collective solutions to those problems. We are for truth-telling and uplifting the power of organizing and solidarity that move us toward a more just society.[13]

Within the first few weeks of posting the pledge, thousands of educators from every state in the nation had signed, demonstrating the mass opposition to truthcrime legislation and the great potential to build a movement for honest education about racism.

Erin Chisholm, a high school history teacher in Glendale, Arizona, was one of the teachers who signed the pledge and included this note: "The truth is worth more than the $5,000 fine the state of Arizona wants to slap on me if I allow my students to become critical thinkers." Elementary teacher Trechiondria Lathan, from Iowa City, Iowa, made this promise: "I will not simply comply with racist laws, or be disrespected, dismissed, and trauma-tized by administrators and political leaders who proudly inflict harm on BIPOC students, families, and educators across the nation. In the words of Angela Davis, 'I am no longer accepting the things I cannot change. I am changing the things I cannot accept.'"[14]

These defiant teachers who have publicly refused to submit to truth-crime legislation have no doubt inspired countless others who have not signed their name out of understandable fear of reprisals, but nonetheless are committed to teaching the truth about racism and refused to remove valuable antiracist books and teaching activities from their curriculum.

It must be underscored that signing the pledge has come with conse-quences for some teachers. *The Daily Wire,* a right-wing publication, quickly began attacking educators who signed the pledge, publishing their names state by state, which facilitated trolls who engaged in campaigns of "harass-ment, intimidation, and physical threats."[15] Jennifer Lee, a high school teacher in Killeen, Texas, was one of the educators who worked to support teachers in her state who endured threats from *The Daily Wire's* piece. Lee spoke with educators facing reprisals for their honest educating about race and encour-aged them to contact the Texas State Teachers Association, her teacher orga-nization and the state affiliate of the National Education Association. "One Texas teacher got a letter from her superintendent saying that they did not appreciate her signing the Teach Truth pledge, and so we talked through the process to join TSTA [Texas State Teachers Association]," Lee said.[16] The Texas State Teachers Association and the National Education Association have pledged to defend educators who are reprimanded for teaching the truth about race. The degree to which the unions follow through on that commit-ment will play a significant role in how willing teachers are to teach honestly about US history.

The Education Spring

Teach Truth and Freedom to Learn Movements

In late May 2022, Republican lawmakers in Ohio introduced HB 322, legis-lation designed to require educators to lie to students about racism. The bill stated, "No teacher or school administrator . . . shall approve for use, make use of, or carry out standards, curricula, lesson plans, textbooks [or] instructional materials" that suggest "slavery and racism are anything other than deviations from, betrayals of, or failures to live up to the authentic founding principles of the United States, which include liberty and equality."[17]

This proposed truthcrime bill deeply disturbed Ohio's educators. Should this bill pass, would educators be required to skip over the constitution's Three-fifths compromise that gifted slave states increased representation in Congress, or the clause that required the reenslavement of Black people who had fled to freedom? Would educators have to whiteout the sentence in the Declaration of Independence that calls Native Americans "merciless Indian Savages" and hide the fact that this racist belief facilitated the colonization and genocide of Indigenous people?

It frightened many educators that they would ever have to ask questions such as these, including middle school technology teacher Heather Smith in Youngstown, Ohio. Yet her fear turned into determination when she learned from the Zinn Education Project about a planned June 12 National Day of Action to stop bills like HB 322. She began searching for where the local Teach Truth rally would be held, but when she couldn't find one, she thought, "Well, why don't I just try to do it myself?"[18] Smith then connected with Penny Wells, the director of the Mahoning Valley Sojourn to the Past, which takes high school students on immersion trips to southern Civil Rights Movement landmarks. Together, Smith and Wells organized a gathering for the day of action at a local swimming pool that had been segregated in the 1940s, and they taught a lesson to those assembled about the history of segregated pools. In addition, an Ohio State Board of Education member joined the rally in defiance of the state legislature and read the board's official resolution against racism and hate.

This kind of grassroots effort of educators learning to be organizers in defense of an honest education occurred all around the country on that day. But getting to this National Day of Action was not automatic, and the movement did take some time to emerge. As the attack on honest education escalated in the months after Trump lost his reelection bid in 2020—and billionaire-funded parent truthcrime associations and right-wing think tanks dramatically accelerated the war on antiracist teaching—inaction from mainstream liberal organizations in the country was profound. As discussed in chapter 3, establishment leaders in the Democratic Party calculated that organizing to defend honest education about race in opposition to the Republicans' strategy of naming everything they despised (things such as socialism, antiracism, struggles for equity) "critical race theory" was a distraction from more important issues. With liberal organizations taking many of its cues from the Democrats, months went by without much coordinated opposition to the attack on truth teaching.

There were, of course, exceptions. For example, the African American Policy Forum, led by Kimberlé Crenshaw, quickly launched "Truth Be Told," a vital campaign of popular education to explain CRT (as opposed to how the GOP was defining it) and to organize people against truthcrime legislation. This leadership helped coalesce other organizations into a national effort to defend honest education about race. In the waning months of 2020 through to the spring of 2021, organizers at the Zinn Education Project also jumped into the void created by many large liberal organizations that were uncomfortable getting involved in the struggle for antiracist education. Joining forces with the Black Lives Matter at School organization, the two groups declared Saturday, June 12, 2021, the first national Teach Truth Day of Action.

Word of the Teach Truth action spread quickly through the vast network of educators around the country who participate in the BLM at School movement, as well as those registered at the Zinn Education Project website. The June 12 national Teach Truth day of action drew hundreds of educators and their supporters, who gathered at historic locations in more than twenty cities to publicly pledge to teach the truth about racism and oppression and highlight the history in their communities that would be prohibited in the classroom under new truthcrime laws. In Waterloo, Iowa, marchers visited several locations that highlighted the impact of segregation and employment discrimination against Black Iowans in the 1950s and 1960s, and Anne Johnson declared at one of the stops, "Willie Mae Wright came to Waterloo in the 1950s. She recalls an employment agency rejected her application because 'they didn't take colored people.'"[19] In San Bruno, California, educators gathered at Tanforan Racetrack, where eight thousand Japanese Americans were incarcerated before they transferred to a long-term lockdown facility during World War II.

In Philadelphia, BLM at School steering committee member and national Teach Truth event organizer Tamara Anderson addressed the crowd, saying, "I love James Baldwin, but I sure would love the day I could stop quoting him and it sounds like 2021." Another speaker at the rally, a twelve-year-old Black student named Jordan Henry, fired up the crowd when he declared, "Up until this point in my education, most of my teachers have taught me how to count, rather than teaching me what counts." When high school teacher Kristin Luebbert was passed the microphone, she explained the history of the land they were standing on: "We are at the site of the house of our first President, the very site where a talented Black seamstress named Ona Judge—one of many people enslaved by the Washingtons—declared her freedom and fled north.... Ona refused to be treated like a candlestick or an heirloom vase. As a human being, she had a right to her freedom—and she took it! She lived as a free person for the rest of her life. We will teach this truth!"[20]

On the same day in Memphis, Tennessee, educators conducted a walking tour to highlight the history of white supremacy that was being whitewashed with the then recently enacted antitruth education bill. Honest educators gathered at the site where Nathan Bedford Forrest, a Confederate general and the first "grand wizard" of the KKK, ran a market to sell enslaved people from 1854 to 1860. The march organizers highlighted that their school, Memphis Grizzlies Prep, was located on the downtown lot once operated by Forrest as a slave market. Alex Iberg, a teacher at the school, asked, "Are we even allowed to talk with our students about our own school? How do we tell the truth and not break the law?"[21]

After giving this history lesson about the ground they were standing on, protesters marched to the marker for the 1866 Memphis Massacre at Army Park and the National Museum of Civil Rights. This allowed truth teachers an opportunity to educate the demonstrators about their city's three-day massacre during the early stages of Reconstruction, when mobs of police and white residents rampaged through Black neighborhoods. They began by targeting Black Civil War veterans, but soon attacked any African American they could find, killing forty-six, injuring 285, and raping five Black women.[22] In addition, educational arsonists burned down twelve Black schools. Students (of all races) who go to school on a slave auction site, and who live in a city whose character was shaped by a horrific race massacre, may feel discomfort when they learn these facts—but they deserve to learn the truth. And all students can draw inspiration from the social movements that led to the abolition of these sites of human trafficking.

Following the success of the first National Day of Action in June 2021, the same sponsoring organizations teamed up with the African American Policy Forum to organize a subsequent national weekend of action as school was starting in many places around the country from August 27 to 29, 2021. Educators, students, parents, and their allies organized events in some 115 cities that weekend. Since these actions, the second weekend in June has become an annual Teach Truth national day of action, and several other national and regional mobilizations have been organized to defend the right to teach accurate accounts of history. In addition, the African American Policy Forum has launched, in collaboration with many other organizations, the Freedom to Learn campaign, including the Books Unbanned Tour and an annual May 3rd Day of Action.

In Minneapolis, in October 2022, passengers boarded three tour buses filled with illicit cargo with the intent to distribute. Aboard were members of the African American Policy Forum, the Transformative Justice Coalition, and Black Voters Matter, who all partnered to launch the "From Freedom Riders to Freedom Readers: The Books Unbanned Tour." These organizations loaded up the buses with some six thousand banned books—including *All Boys Aren't Blue*; *The Bluest Eye*; *Their Eyes Were Watching God*—and began a journey to the South, with many stops along the way, to distribute their contraband materials and register people to vote. Kimberlé Crenshaw helped launched the tour with a speech that connected the freedom reader tour to the 1961 Freedom Riders campaign, organized by the Congress of Racial Equality and the SNCC:

> We know that the same people who want to change the rules when we start winning elections, want to change the rules when we start going out to protest and millions of people join us. The same people who were upset when we took to the streets in all 50 states after the murder of George Floyd are the same people who have decided that they want to take the language of structural racism, of racial injustice, of social justice, out of our mouths, out of our studies, out of our books. We have decided that—just like the freedom riders who said, "you don't get to tell us where to sit, you don't get to tell us where to eat, you don't get to tell us what to drink"—we decided you don't get to tell us what to read. You don't get to tell us what to teach. You don't get to tell us what to learn.[23]

Every stop the buses made had a specific intention—beginning with leaving from the city that launched the 2020 uprising after the police killed George Floyd and the first stop in Kenosha, Wisconsin, where Jacob Blake was shot in the back seven times by police in front of his kids. The bus continued on to some fourteen states and twenty-six cities, including Chicago, Detroit, Toledo (Ohio), Cleveland, Pittsburgh, Baltimore, Washington, DC, Richmond (Virginia), and Raleigh (North Carolina) and ended in Jacksonville, Florida. Recall that the Duval County Public Schools serve Jacksonville, the district the with most banned books in the country. Recall that this was the district that fired Amy Donofrio for her Black Lives Matter flag and ended her highly successful EVAC leadership class. Recall that Duval is where veteran teacher Chris Guerrieri reported that a district administrator told a media specialist to also teach the "positive sides" of slavery.[24]

The annual Freedom to Learn National Day of Action on May 3 has also proven to be an important focal point of the struggle against truthcrime. On May 3, 2023, protestors marched to the College Board's office in Washington, DC, to teach them a lesson about the collective power of the Black freedom struggle—the very kind of lesson they had recently taken out of their AP African American studies course. Recall that the college board deleted from the course all references to structural racism and expunged readings from many of the leading Black studies scholars. Standing in front of the office, Reverend Frederick Douglass Haynes III said,

> We are daring to declare, in front of the College Board we will not have education undermined, we will not have the truth replaced by a lie. We are here because if the truth sets you free, then lies lock you up. And we are too woke to be locked up by a lie taking over our education system across this nation. And so we gather here at the College Board, number one, because we know a liberated people is an educated people. . . . Martin King quoted James Baldwin and wonders if he had integrated our people into a burning house. Critical race theory helps us to put the fire out while discerning who the arsonist is.[25]

Haynes's powerful words suggest that sometimes the worst educational arsonists are not those creeping around the schoolhouse at night with kerosene and a match, but those sitting in boardrooms enacting policies behind closed doors. This was clearly understood by the thirty LGBTQ+ organizations, including many of those with a focus on organizing Black people, who built a campaign calling for College Board president David Coleman to resign.[26] In an open letter, these organizations denounced the "relentless attacks that have led to book banning, curriculum censorship, politically motivated purges of educators, and an exodus of skilled teachers."[27] In addition, the African American Policy Forum, African American Studies Faculty in Higher Ed, and the Freedom to Learn collective launched an open letter to the College Board, stating, "The College Board, a billion-dollar American nonprofit that serves a gatekeeping role in higher education, remained silent when this conservative backlash collided with their stated objectives in launching the course."[28]

In this era, when so many institutions, school districts, and states are championing truthcrime laws, reading programs and study groups featuring banned books have become an important form of resistance. For example, GLSEN—a national organization working to support LGBTQ+ students—started a program called the Rainbow Library. This initiative sends free LGBTQ+-affirming text sets to schools around the country that make a request. "We know that brave actions—by educators, leaders, and community members—show LGBTQ+ youth that they are safe, they belong, and they matter," said Michael Rady, senior education programs manager at GLSEN when I asked him about ways his organization was supporting the national Teach Truth day of action. "In many places, it takes immense courage for an educator to participate in our program. These past few months I have been working with educators whose Rainbow Library books have been seized by administrators."[29]

The Banned Books Book Club offers tool kits for teachers, students, authors, and librarians for resisting book bans, provides lists of important antiracist and antitransphobic books, and has a guide for how to start a banned book club. The Zinn Education Project has created hundreds of study groups for educators around the country on the book *Teaching for Black Lives* (which I coedited with Dyan Watson and Wayne Au)—including in many states that have truthcrime laws. During the 2023–2024 school year, over one hundred *Teaching for Black Lives* study groups were organized in thirty US states and two Canadian provinces. "Building community and networking is an important way to build stamina to face the challenges of teaching in this state's socio political context," Lorena German, a study group participant from Florida explained. "We will continue to teach truth, with inclusivity in mind, from a place of love. Teachers need to know they're not alone."[30] Another participant explained, "Living in Minneapolis especially in 2020 it felt like there was such a powerful surge of hope and change for Black lives and then it fizzled out. I'm still trying to educate myself and others to do better. It's important to me because I want my students of color and my Black students to feel seen and validated in schools."[31]

As these national campaigns develop for honest education, the role of educator unions will be crucial in determining if they cohere into a mass social movement strong enough to take on the billionaire class behind truth-crime legislation. The National Education Association and the American Federation of Teachers have both joined organizing meetings and invested resources in supporting national campaigns to teach truth. The unions have become important allies, and this support has been significant to the growth of the Teach Truth movement. The unions' legal teams have supported law-suits against truthcrime laws, and their organizing departments have con-tributed to the Teach Truth days of action. Still, much more could be done to invigorate an all-out national effort to repeal truthcrime laws and initiate campaigns for Black studies, ethnic studies, gender studies, and queer stud-ies. Additionally, educators around the country who have been targeted by truthcrime laws and fired for their honest teaching about the United States have reported to me that they wish their local union would have offered more support and built a more robust campaign to defend the right to teach the truth. Educator unions must do more to prioritize defending their members from truthcrime legislation. The degree to which rank-and-file educators in the Teach Truth movement organize to invigorate their unions—at the local and national levels—will play a significant role in determining the degree to which the unions expand their campaigns to defend honest education about race, class, gender, and sexuality.

Which Parents Have Rights?

"Parents' rights" has become a rallying cry for the GOP. In 2021, Republican attorney general Todd Rokita of Indiana introduced a Parents Bill of Rights, asserting that educational policy and curriculum should accurately reflect the values of Indiana families. During the same year, the Florida legislature passed an educational closeting bill they titled "Parental Rights in Educa-tion," which they claimed protected the "fundamental rights" of parents by outlawing educators' ability to teach about LGBTQ+ issues. A number of states have begun allowing parents to pursue legal action against school dis-tricts that teach banned concepts.[32]

Yet when uncritical race theorists claim to champion "parents' rights," what they really mean is they support billionaire-funded organizations, primarily driven by conservative white parents, to censor Black history and LGBTQ+ history from school curricula. The most obvious contradiction of the uncritical race theorists' parents' rights campaign is that it quite clearly is not designed for families of color—or even white families that want their children to learn about stories of resistance to enslavement and segregation. LGBTQ+ parents and caregivers, or parents and caregivers of LGBTQ+ children, are also excluded from their narrow definition of parents. In fact, any parent who believes that students are capable of engaging in discussions about aspects of US history that don't leave the country smelling like roses is banished from an uncritical race theory understanding of who qualifies as a parent worthy of rights.

There are, however, actual grassroots parent organizations working to end racist and transphobic censorship in education. These national parent organizations, such as Defense of Democracy, STOP Moms for "Liberty," and Red Wine and Blue (RWB), don't receive funding from billionaires. RWB has emerged as a leading national network of multiracial suburban women. It was founded in 2019 by Katie Paris in Ohio and has rapidly grown to become one of the largest progressive grassroots groups. With a membership now approaching half a million, RWB emphasizes the importance of fighting disinformation, opposing book bans, and winning local school board campaigns. One of its most popular organizing efforts has been creating study groups around banned books.

Formed soon after truthcrime bills began proliferating, HEAL (Honest Education Action & Leadership) Together is a national initiative of the Race Forward organization working to build a movement of parents, students, educators, and community members for honest education in school districts across the United States. HEAL Together supports grassroots community partners across nineteen states and dozens of school districts, with tools such as a handbook of equity-based policies that have been implemented in school districts around the country and grassroots organizing trainings to help communities resist truthcrime laws.

There have also been important local and regional parent organizing efforts to defend kids from the violence of organized forgetting. For instance, the Missouri Equity Education Partnership (MEEP) has done impressive work to mobilize parents and communities in defense of inclusive education.

Heather Fleming, a Black woman whose children attend school in the Francis Howell School District, formed MEEP in 2021 with the aim of organizing chapters in the state's 554 school districts to battle those advocating for truthcrime policies. MEEP's work took on a special significance in response to the Francis Howell School District's decision to cancel Black history and literature classes in December 2023, allegedly because they contained elements of CRT. The move by the district's all-white school board sparked outrage and protests within the community, prompting MEEP's grassroots efforts to counter the narrative perpetuated by well-funded astroturf organizations. As Fleming emphasized, "They're telling our students to just 'shut up and dribble.' They're telling our kids, 'You'll never be human enough for us to treat you like equals.'"

In Florida, Jules Scholles founded Support Our Schools to counter MFL. Aiming to bolster her numbers, Scholles worked to form coalitions with existing groups such as the NAACP. Scholles has seen the attack on the school by MFL and other PTCAs: "They're ruining our schools, and they're not stopping. You've got no masks, you've got no vaccines, you've got no CRT, you're about to get no teaching anything that makes white children feel bad, why are you still so effing angry? Like why are you still coming to these meetings so juiced up and angry?"

Understanding the historical context behind the call for "parental rights," particularly in its current push to ban antiracist curriculum, is crucial for comprehending its contemporary significance. This rallying cry gained prominence following the Supreme Court's landmark *Brown v. Board of Education* ruling in 1954, which declared racial segregation of children in public schools unconstitutional. "This same frenzy occurred after desegregation when educators tried to add Black achievements to school texts," said Leslie Fenwick, dean emerita of the Howard University School of Education and dean in residence at the American Association of Colleges for Teacher Education. "White parents burned books, physically threatened white teachers who tried to teach the more inclusive curriculum, and pressured school boards not to adopt books and curriculum that featured anything Black, by asserting that doing such was a divisive and communist trick."[33]

In contrast to this kind of paranoia and racism, BIPOC parents and caregivers have long led efforts to assert the collective rights of families of color to have their children learn honest accounts of US history that include all the people that live here. For obvious reasons, uncritical race theorists have never embraced efforts from these parents.

Institutional Resistance to Truthcrime

Although much of the resistance to truthcrime policies and legislation has been the result of educators, students, and parents leading grassroots efforts, there have been a few important examples of entire institutions joining the struggle to teach truth.

In October 2022, in response to the Placentia-Yorba Linda Unified school district's banning CRT, Cal State Fullerton announced it would no longer place student teachers in the system's K–12 classrooms. This was a dramatic announcement given Cal State Fullerton is one of the biggest providers of teachers to the district's public schools. Leaders in the university's College of Education explained that principles of DEI and social justice and tenets of CRT are foundational to their program, and they wouldn't be able to properly educate their teacher candidates in a district that disallowed important instruction about structural racism. This action by the College of Education shows the potential power that teacher education programs could have around the country if they were to decide that teaching the truth about racism was nonnegotiable.

The Brooklyn Public Library provided another example. Linda Johnson, president and CEO of the library, refused to just watch in horror as the book bans proliferated around the country and decided to take action. Johnson and her colleagues began by reaching out to libraries in Texas to see how they could support anticensorship efforts, but they feared such actions would cause them to lose accreditation or funding. "We decided, well, we'll do this ourselves," Johnson said. The result was "Books UnBanned," an initiative launched by the Brooklyn Public Library in April 2022 that allows anyone aged thirteen to twenty-one in the United States to access banned books by requesting a free digital library card. The library offers 350,000 ebooks and 200,000 audiobooks with no wait-list for cardholders. A year after launching the program Johnson said the library had issued library cards to people in every state. "We've issued about 7,000 cards and we've circulated almost 90,000 books," she said.[34]

Although there are more examples like these, the fact that there aren't too many more examples of entire institutions—such as school districts or corporations—who have forthrightly organized to oppose truthcrime laws gives lie to uncritical race theorists' claims that America's institutions have been captured by critical race theorists.

Rays of Truth in the Sunshine State

Some of the most concerted efforts to stop truthcrime legislation have taken place in Florida, where Governor Ron DeSantis made the attack on honest education the centerpiece of his failed bid for the presidency. "We're going to keep on teaching it," 82-year-old Marvin Dunn, a professor emeritus at Florida International University, told *The Washington Post*. "This is the antidote to the DeSantis-izing of history."[35] Dunn was born in the central Florida city of DeLand in an orange grove barn and grew up under the harsh Jim Crow laws of the state; he recalls being prohibited from going to the white beaches and only being able to access the beaches designated for "colored" people.

Dunn has made it clear that he is done with DeSantis's racism and isn't afraid to defy truthcrime laws. Although Florida's laws may inhibit many students from having honest conversations about Black history and white supremacy, Dunn has organized statewide "Teach the Truth" tours to take high school students to historically significant places to the Black freedom struggle. He conducted his first tour in January 2023 and took more than two dozen Miami high school students and their family members to a museum that marks where Black truth teachers and civil rights activists Harry T. Moore and Harriette V. S. Moore were killed when an educational arsonist planted a bomb under their house on Christmas Day 1951. "These are things that nobody knew, it's like it was swept under the rug," said Shanika Marshall, one of the parents who took her son on the tour. "I feel very strongly that this history needs to be told. There's no shame, it just is what it is, but it needs to be put at the forefront so we can all try to get past it."[36]

More than two hundred people joined Dunn on January 8 for a walking tour of the site of the Rosewood massacre, which occurred one hundred years before on that same month. The Rosewood massacre began on New Year's Day in 1923 when a white woman in the town falsely accused a Black man of beating her. A white posse soon formed and began a lynching and burning campaign that destroyed the rural Black community. Amid the carnage, educational arsonists burned down a Black school. Lizzie Jenkins, the niece of a

Rosewood school teacher, recalled long ago, "It has been a struggle telling this story over the years because a lot of people don't want to hear about this kind of history. But Mama told me to keep it alive, so I keep telling it."[37] Despite corporate textbook erasure of this brutal chapter in history, Jenkins's mama's directive to keep the story alive is being fulfilled by educators like Dunn.

But it hasn't been easy, and sometimes truth teaching even means risking your life. During one of Dunn's previous tours to teach the history of Rosewood, a neighboring property owner drove by and yelled racial slurs at the group. The man drove away, and then came back, speeding down the dirt road and nearly hitting Dunn's adult son. According to a police report, 61-year-old David Emanuel began yelling that he had to deal with "busloads of these Black bastards" whenever they came to Rosewood.[38]

Seventeen-year-old Mikese Lovett, a junior at Miami Edison Senior High School, accompanied his mother, Chauntel Walters, on the January 8 tour of Rosewood. Lovett told the *Post* his history class only spent about a week on Reconstruction and the Jim Crow era, with only a brief mention of Rosewood—and he wasn't taught about any of the many other incidents of racial violence in Florida. "We don't go into depth," he said. "They just scratch the surface." Walters graduated from a Florida high school in 2010 and said she had never heard of Rosewood or any of the other episodes of racial violence or Black resistance Dunn showed them. "They have to be able to teach this to kids in school," Walters said. "We need to know our history, all of it." In his book *A History of Florida: Through Black Eyes*, Dunn wrote, "Almost all of Florida's painful racial past has been whitewashed, marginalized or buried intentionally. But I was born here. I know Florida's flowers and her warts."[39] And despite the truthcrime laws, many young Floridians now also know the healing power of remembering the past.

Dunn isn't alone in his quest to legalize Black history in Florida. On April 3, 2003, high school English teacher Adam Tritt was up at dawn in Melbourne, Florida. After working the full school day, Tritt drove to support an event to distribute banned books to youth and their parents. Tritt, his wife, and a dozen other volunteers gave out some nine hundred contraband books that evening. "The town where I teach has 150,000 people and not a single bookstore," Tritt told the Zinn Education Project. "There is no decent public transportation for people to get to a library. Banning books from schools denies young people access to them."[40] To address the problem, Tritt established "Foundation 451," a reference to the dystopian story about educational arsonists, *Fahrenheit 451*. Foundation 451 helped to organize many similar book events throughout the preceding year and has encouraged educators and parents in states with book bans to organize against censorship, speak out at school board meetings, and meet with principals to persuade them to join the struggle. "We need a flood of parents writing emails to the principals and school boards," he said.[41]

Hundreds of students across Florida walked out class on February 23, 2023, heeding the call from the Dream Defenders in opposition to the state's truthcrime legislation and DeSantis's plan to outlaw all DEI initiatives at Florida colleges and universities. Scores of students from University of South Florida, University of Florida, Florida State University, and other higher education institutions rallied around the state. Students spoke out against the ban on AP African American studies, the "Don't Say Gay" bill, and DeSantis's demand that public universities hand over health data of trans students seeking gender-affirming care. Speaking for many that day, Tiya Hareland told ABC News, "As a trans person its very scary to live in the state of Florida right now. . . . It feels like they are trying to get rid of us."[42]

While most protesters were college students, some high school students also joined in on the statewide walkout. On February 15, Eric Franzblau was in his aerospace class at Plantation High School when the principal, Parinaz Bristol, walked in. Franzblau took the opportunity to inquire if he could ask her a question. She consented, and Franzblau told her about the upcoming day of action against educational censorship that was being organized and asked if he could participate in the walkout. "She was like, 'You can't do that, it's too political, we can't sanction that for our campus,'" Franzblau recalled. Franzblau decided to seek advice from friends about what to do, and a classmate in his statistics class told him, "Yeah, dude, we should totally have this protest, do a walkout. People need to know at this school that we're not going to be silent." "I was incredibly nervous," Franzblau told the *South Florida Sun Sentinel*, explaining that he didn't want to get in trouble, but he believed strongly in his right to speak out on these issues.[43]

Despite having his request denied by the principal, Franzblau refused to relinquish his right to express his beliefs about education and continued organizing. He created group chats, posted on social media, and designed a poster that read "Join the walkout this Thursday, Feb. 23 to protest Ron DeSantis during your eighth period and tell a friend!!" along with peace signs and a Black solidarity fist overlaid on an image of DeSantis's face.

Then, two days before the walkout, a school security officer pulled Franzblau out of class and escorted him to the principal's office where an administrator instructed him that he was forbidden from distributing materials promoting the protest. Then they took it further. The uncritical race theorists in charge decided that rather than inquire what was motivating Franzblau to be so invested in his education that he was willing to spend his free time organizing to defend his right to learn, they instead threatened him with suspension. Bristol also sent out an email and a robocall to parents that stated,

> We have been made aware that a student-coordinated walkout might [take] place at our school tomorrow, Thursday, February 23rd, regarding recent state education decisions. . . . I want to emphasize that this potential walkout is not a school-sponsored activity. While we support student activism, we must maintain safe and secure learning environments for all students and staff. We encourage students to remain in class. Any student leaving campus without authorization or violating school rules will face appropriate disciplinary consequences.[44]

In the face of threats and intimidation Franzblau didn't blink and instead called their bluff. A day after being threatened with suspension (one day before the walkout), a school security officer again pulled Franzblau out of class and marched him to the principal's office. Franzblau assumed that Bristol was now going to suspend him. Instead, however, the principal offered him a deal: he could either hold the walkout in the first or last fifteen minutes of the school's eighth period. Franzblau texted his friends to ask what he should do, and they counseled him to accept the offer. Reluctantly, Franzblau chose to hold the walkout during the first fifteen minutes of eighth period. "Initially I took the fifteen-minute guideline as a loss," Franzblau said. "A fifteen-minute protest, what really is that?" But as he thought about it, he realized it was a victory, if a small one. "Because I was so adamant, that's how I got the fifteen minutes," he said. "They had to cave in."

When the eighth-period bell rang, and Franzblau headed out to the track. His heart sank when he only saw one other person out on the field with him. But then a rush of some 150 students came streaming out of the building. They chanted, "Hey ho, hey ho, Ronny D has got to go," "We say gay," and "We say trans." In addition, on the other side of the fence organizers from the Dream Defenders showed up to support, including CJ Staples, who tossed his megaphone over the fence. Franzblau used it to give a speech and then passed it to his friend from statistics class, who also spoke out.

Franzblau's story illustrates the difficulty in making change and the many tactics uncritical race theorists will use to curb free speech. Although it may have been a small step, the passion and persistence of these students allowed them to get off the uncritical race theory plantation, if only for a short time, and inspired students around the country to advocate for their right to learn, despite threats and intimidation.

"Your Actions Are Unconstitutional"

The Legal Effort to Defend Truth Teaching

Regan Killacky is a public school teacher in Edmond, a city on the northern edge of the Oklahoma City metropolitan area. After being directed to avoid conversations on race and gender in his classroom due to Oklahoma's passing of truthcrime bill HB 1775—or as opponents have called it, the "antiracism teaching ban"—Killacky became one of the plaintiffs in a lawsuit against the state, filed by the ACLU, the Lawyers' Committee for Civil Rights Under Law, and others civil rights groups. The October 2021 filing made it the first federal lawsuit to challenge a truthcrime law. The antiracism teaching ban in Oklahoma has resulted in officials instructing teachers to refrain from using terms such as "diversity" and "white privilege" in their classrooms, and in the removal of such classics as *To Kill a Mockingbird* and *Raisin in the Sun*, among others. "H.B. 1775 limits my ability to teach an inclusive and complete history within the walls of my classroom, ultimately restricting the exact type of learning environment all young people deserve—one free from censorship or discrimination," said Killacky.[45] When this case finally comes to trial, educators in the state where the 1921 Tulsa Massacre occurred will discover if it will become legal to teach truthfully about white supremacist violence and the structural racism that caused the state to refuse to compensate the Black families who lost their loved ones and livelihoods in the massacre.

This legal battle in Oklahoma highlights the fact that the fight against truthcrime is happening not only in classrooms but also in courtrooms. The

ACLU, the NAACP Legal Defense Fund, the Southern Poverty Law Center, the Lawyers' Committee for Civil Rights Under Law, as well as the legal teams of the National Education Association and the American Federation of Teachers, are some of the leading litigators working to overturn book bans and educational gag orders around the country.

Legal action proved pivotal in Mississippi when, in January 2022, Ridgeland mayor Gene McGee withheld $110,000 from the public library with an educational closeting ultimatum for librarians: remove LGBTQ+ literature from your shelves or lose funding. The ACLU of Mississippi threatened legal action, and their staff attorney McKenna Raney-Gray wrote in a letter to McGee, "You have no authority to undertake such measures, and your actions are unconstitutional."[46] Following the letter, the Ridgeland Public Library funding was reinstated.

Under Virginia Code 18.2-384—a law that had been dormant for decades before being dusted off in 2022—any individual can file a petition to the state claiming that any book is obscene. On May 18, 2022, the Virginia Beach Circuit Court issued orders finding "probable cause to believe" *Gender Queer* and the fantasy novel *A Court of Mist and Fury*, by Sarah J. Maas, were "obscene for unrestricted viewing by minors" and initiated proceedings to block the sale and distribution of the two books.[47] By June of that year, several independent bookstores joined the ACLU in filing a joint motion demanding the state court dismiss the obscenity proceedings against the two works. "The First Amendment is clear—disliking the contents of a book doesn't mean the government can ban it," the ACLU argued.[48] On August 30, the court dismissed the attempted ban.

After Governor DeSantis signed the "Stop WOKE" act into law in April 2022, two immediate legal challenges emerged. One lawsuit, filed by the Foundation for Individual Rights and Expression (a college free-speech group) on behalf of a University of South Florida professor, student, and student group, argued that the truthcrime bill violated the First Amendment. They contended that the legislation aimed to restrict discussions on vital historical subjects, citing an instance where an educator was pressured not to teach about segregation in baseball and Jackie Robinson's role in breaking Major League Baseball's color barrier.[49]

Then in November 2022, US district judge Mark E. Walker ordered a temporary injunction against portions of the truthcrime bill known as the "Stop WOKE" act (now called the "Individual Freedom Act"). Judge Walker began his court order with the first sentence of George Orwell's dystopian novel *1984.* "'It was a bright cold day in April, and the clocks were striking thirteen,' and the powers in charge of Florida's public university system have declared the State has unfettered authority to muzzle its professors in the name of 'freedom,'" the judge wrote. "This is positively dystopian."[50]

"This is a huge victory for everyone who values academic freedom and recognizes the value of inclusive education," said ACLU senior staff attorney Emerson Sykes. "The First Amendment broadly protects our right to share information and ideas, and this includes educators' and students' right to learn, discuss, and debate systemic racism and sexism."[51] However, although colleges and universities were temporarily spared from some of the worst aspects of truthcrime law, DeSantis found other ways—such as firing the president of the New College and replacing her with the former GOP House speaker and education commissioner Richard Corcoran—and the law remains in place for K–12 education.

In March 2024, a high school teacher and two students from Little Rock Central High School filed a federal lawsuit against Arkansas's ban on CRT and what the state calls "indoctrination"—also known as Black history—in public schools. Specifically, they demanded the state overturn its decision to withhold credit for the AP African American studies course. This challenge carries a significant symbolism, at least for those still allowed to learn that Central High School was the site where nine Black students bravely integrated the previously all-white school amidst death threats, harassment, and intense opposition. "Indeed, defendants' brazen attack on full classroom participation for all students in 2024 is reminiscent of the state's brazen attack on full classroom participation for all students in 1957," the lawsuit said.

At present, lawsuits challenging truthcrime bills have been initiated by a range of stakeholders, including educators, students, parents, teachers' unions, and civil rights organizations across at least seven states, including Arizona, Arkansas, Florida, Missouri, Oklahoma, New Hampshire, and Tennessee. "The main constitutional arguments against education gag laws about race are based in the First and Fourteenth Amendments to the United States Constitution," Harry Chiu, a joint legal fellow at the Southern Poverty Law Center and Southern Education Foundation, told me. "The Fourteenth Amendment includes a due process clause, which is basically a fairness guarantee for people who face punishment under the law. It requires that laws that punish conduct be clear enough so that people understand what they can and cannot do. Education gag orders across different states often have the same unclear language. For example, like most other states with gag orders, Georgia's HB 1084 bans teachers from 'advocacy' of the idea that the United States is 'fundamentally racist'—without defining either term." In addition, states that prohibit teaching that causes "discomfort" are equally vague in their failure to define the term and also violate the Fourteenth Amendment.

Chiu also explained to me that the First Amendment protects students' right to receive information in school without unconstitutional state censorship. "While the state can regulate curriculums, it cannot do so for purely partisan reasons without actual educational benefit," he said. For example, it would be illegal to ban all lesson plans written about one political party or the other. Truthcrime legislation violates the First Amendment by mandating a political perspective in classroom discussions of race and racism. This is because, for example, when truthcrime laws are enacted, they allow educators to teach that racist law enforcement policies are anomalies or the product of a few bad apples, but not that they reflect broader systemic discrimination against Black people. "Students need to learn about different views on this important issue in order to understand the society they live in," said Chiu.

As lower courts rule on the bans of antiracist teaching around the country, those in the Teach Truth movement have their eye on a potential US Supreme Court decision that would determine if the national clock rings thirteen and truthcrime becomes official policy of the nation. "It's very difficult to know where the current Supreme Court will go," Chiu said. "We all know that the conservative justices have a six–three majority, so that might lean toward upholding these gag orders, which are exclusively Republican in origin. However, the fact that these laws are written so vaguely may lead them to stopping states from enforcing them against teachers under the Fourteenth Amendment. The First Amendment argument on behalf of students is more difficult," he told me. "Conservative judges frequently prioritize traditional areas of state authority, and states have a lot of legal latitude in determining the form and content of public education."

As history has demonstrated in many past Supreme Court decisions, the rulings they issue are not only the result of the legal arguments made by attorneys. The size of the social movements surrounding any given court case can be decisive when justices weigh the impact of their ruling on their own historical legacy and the consequences their ruling might have for generating more social unrest.

Conclusion

"Teachers Not Only Will Fight . . . We'll Win"

"Every student, regardless of faith, race, socioeconomic status, sexual orientation or any other factor," Whitfield continued in his lesson to Congress, "deserves to be seen, heard, valued, celebrated, engaged, inspired, empowered, and loved each day." As malicious as the attack by uncritical race theorists and educational closeters has been, the Teach Truth movement has achieved important victories toward this vision of a beloved classroom community.

In Illinois, the movement tallied a win when they got the legislature to pass the Teaching Equitable Asian American Community History Act in 2021, to require all K–12 social studies classes to include Asian American and Pacific Islander history and challenge stereotypes about Asian identity. Nevada passed a law in 2021 that directs history, science, arts, and humanities classes to include the contributions of people of color and people with disabilities. After many years of struggle in Seattle, Black families, youth organizers, and Black Lives Matter at School activists achieved a great victory in 2021 when the Seattle Public Schools launched its first Black studies course as part of its new Black Education Program. Seattle Public Schools wrote, "The Black Education Program is also partnering with our Native Education and Ethnic Studies programs in developing educator resources to support our 'Decolonizing Social Studies' and implement our decolonizing approach across all subjects, beginning with middle school."[52] The struggle to expand and maintain these programs is ongoing, but the creation of them shows the power of collective struggle. *Truthout* summarized some of the other wins for the movement, writing,

> In March 2021, California legislators passed a bill to make Black studies a high school graduation requirement for every student beginning in 2030. Other states—among them Arizona, Colorado, Connecticut, Illinois, Indiana, Maine, Nevada, New Jersey, New Mexico, New York, Oregon, Rhode Island and Vermont—have followed suit and have drafted standards of their own to authorize or mandate instruction that goes beyond Eurocentric knowledge. Most took effect in the 2022–23 academic year.... Meanwhile, cities like New York have launched pilot programs that zero-in on LGBTQIA+, Black, and Asian American and Pacific Islander history.[53]

One of the most inspiring wins for the Teach Truth movement happened in Florida in June 2024. As detailed in chapter 3, Governor DeSantis intended to use Amy Donofrio as an example to show, as he put it, that Florida is "where woke goes to die" by targeting her for the Black Lives Matter flag in her classroom.[54] While the state attempted to revoke her teaching license, grassroots organizing and Donofrio's fighting spirit successfully helped convince a judge to allow her to continue teaching in Florida.

Donofrio hopes her experience inspires other teachers. "Affirming Black students should never put a teacher's license at risk," she said. "In Florida, 64 percent of public school students are of color and I hope this can show that teachers not only will fight for our right to uphold our professional responsibility to them—but that we'll win."[55]

This chapter began with an inspiring, yet unsuccessful, bid to stop classroom censorship legislation in Georgia. It's important to note, however, that this struggle did lay the groundwork for subsequent victories against truthcrime legislation in Georgia. Alex Ames is one of the founding members of the Georgia Youth Justice Coalition, and she described these victories, speaking at the May 2023 "Our Freedom to Learn" forum sponsored by HEAL Together. She said,

> It has been an incredible three years at GYJC [Georgia Youth Justice Coalition] since we first started building young people's power towards education justice, and towards multiracial democracy. Just this spring, we defeated the largest voucher [bill] in Georgia's history. We stopped, "don't say gay" legislation, for the second time in two years—they keep coming back. We halted policies criminalizing librarians or banning gender affirming medical care. And we won 25 million for public school counselors that our students need. And last year we halted every book ban in the state.... I also should mention we just won the largest public school budget in the entire history of the state of Georgia.[56]

Although the Teach Truth movement might not have the deep, bespoke suit pockets of truthcrime financiers or the authority of US institutions, a formidable coalition of educators, students, parents, caregivers, and community organizers have the power of solidarity and the truth on their side. It is certainly true that the Teach Truth movement has lost some important struggles and is unevenly organized around the country—owing in large part to the fact that the bulk of establishment Democratic Party politicians and their orthodox adherents have either tried to avoid the issue of antiracist education or have worked to actively undermine it. However, millions around the country are gaining a world-class education today about the intellectual violence inflicted by uncritical race theory. And some of these people have begun to engage in the kind of struggles that are a prerequisite to achieving social justice. As connections in the Teach Truth movement networks grow, and as the movement scores more victories, the potential to build a truly massive rebellion against all manifestations of systemic racism increases. Recall that the happiest day of Ana Villavasso's life was the day she helped so many others find their voice against truthcrime legislation in Georgia, and know that countless others who experience the joy of solidarity will be attracted to joining the struggle to defend honest education.

Look out. The movements that finally burst through McCarthyism produced one of the largest eras of social protest in US history, including the Civil Rights Movement, Black Power uprisings, anti–Vietnam War agitation, women's liberation organizing, struggles for LGBTQ+ liberation, anticolonial insurrections, disability justice activism, ethnic studies insurgencies, labor unrest, and student revolts.

As I write, our society is in a liminal space between uncritical race theory and the forming of a great resistance against the very concept of truthcrime. When the next round of uprisings breaks through today's neo-McCarthyist, anti-CRT, neoliberal policies, we will see what kind of upheaval it produces. I don't know what that rebellion will look like exactly, but I do know that persecution begets defiance, and oppression inevitably courts resistance.

Be assured, truth teachers won't just be watching, or even just teaching about this rebellion—they will be in the streets with their students forming a sea of humanity that will shipwreck all the fear, lies, punishment, and demagoguery of uncritical race theorists. This burgeoning of collective empowerment will be rooted in an understanding of the past that leads to the creation of an alternate future too grand for billionaire truthcrime law advocates to even imagine. This practice of imagining and acting to create a better world will be deeply healing for all who participate.

CHAPTER 5

The Radical Healing
of Organized Remembering

If you stick a knife in my back nine inches and pull it out six inches, there's no progress. If you pull it all the way out that's not progress. Progress is healing the wound that the blow made. And they haven't even pulled the knife out much less heal the wound. They won't even admit the knife is there.

—**Malcolm X**

"I beg of you to take these threats seriously and do all you can to support us," Whitfield pleaded to his congressional pupils during his expert lesson at the hearing. The threats he endured for speaking out against systemic racism, and the threats in general to honest education, were the dagger of racism Malcolm X described in the above quote. The urgency in Whitfield's voice revealed the wound was still fresh, the stiletto had yet to be removed, and it was imperative for politicians to admit that it was, indeed, there.

Malcolm's enduring image of a blade sunk deep in the back of Black America was in response to a reporter's question as to whether racial progress was being made, and it explains more than just the violence perpetrated on Black people; it also describes the deceit that accompanies the violence and even begins to suggest a process for healing.

The idea that uncritical race theorists can stab Black people in the back at the same time they claim that not only did they not cause injury but there isn't even a knife accurately describes truthcrime laws and the attack on anti-racist teaching. If our education system is ever going to be an intellectually and emotionally nurturing environment for all students, our society will have to acknowledge that there is a knife, that the knife needs to be fully removed, and that an intentional process of healing will have to be implemented. "If we don't know our history, how can we come up with our own point of view? How can we grow?" asked Re'Kal Hooker, a seventeen-year-old student from the Living School in New Orleans, who opposes truthcrime legislation. "We are still discriminated against and I feel like young kids will think it's just something that happens, like it's natural, or something they can't get away from."[1]

I propose we care for those harmed by the violence of organized forgetting with what I will call the "radical healing of organized remembering" (RHOR). The radical healing of organized remembering identifies collective efforts in education—but also in social movements—to uncover purposely concealed historical lessons that are vital for recovering from historical trauma and building healthy struggles for justice. Trauma is not only inflicted by physical acts of violence but also by the erasure and distortion of historical truths. When BIPOC youth are denied lessons about their culture and history it negatively impacts their self-esteem, their understanding of their own agency in the world, and their ability to envision how to help create a more just society. The RHOR emphasizes the importance of reviving knowledge that has been incapacitated by epistemicidal attacks through facilitating collaborative efforts between schools, social movements, and communities to learn historical truths that have been obscured or denied.

There are many things that can traumatize people, but one of them certainly is the denial that the trauma was caused in the first place and the obscuring of the systems that have perpetuated the harm. Deep healing begins from learning suppressed truths, acknowledging the systemic forces that have perpetuated harm, and actively working to dismantle them. Through interactive lessons, storytelling, artistic expression, and community engagement, the RHOR aims to restore agency to those who have been disempowered and support them in defining their own identity and contributing to the struggle for a more equitable society.

The concept of radical healing was developed by honest educator, author, and organizer Shawn Ginwright. "Radical healing refers to a process that builds the capacity of people to act upon their environment in ways that contribute to well-being for the common good," Ginwright teaches. Ginwright's framework of radical healing has been an important tool for helping to support BIPOC youth in schools around the country. He explains that a "healing-centered" approach to education is needed to support young people. As he writes, "Healing in this context also means that young people develop an analysis of these practices and policies that facilitated the trauma in the first place. Without an analysis of these issues, young people often internalize, and blame themselves for lack of confidence. Critical reflection provides a lens by which to filter, examine, and consider analytical and spiritual responses to trauma."[2]

The observation that young people need to develop an analysis of the structures that cause them harm to heal from trauma is vital. When a physical wound is healing—say from a knife in the back—a disruptive process occurs in the body when white blood cells (which fight off infection by clearing bacteria and preparing the wound area for tissue growth) cause inflammation before the tissue can regenerate. Similarly, healing from historical trauma through "organized remembering" is disruptive to bodies of knowledge that have excluded people of color, and that disruptive process is a prerequisite to cultural healing. As Resmaa Menakem explains in his book *My Grandmother's Hands*: "Genuine healing is a temporarily disruptive process. This is true not only for individual bodies, but for the collective Black body—and the collective American body—as well. Just as the human body creates inflammation to heal, wise social activism creates the social and cultural disruptions needed to help a culture heal and grow up."[3]

However, there are many kinds of social bacteria that attempt to impede this healing process. Judith Herman, a leading psychiatrist and researcher of trauma, made this penetrating insight about the harm caused by banishing historical memory in the opening paragraphs of her vital book *Trauma and Recovery: The Aftermath of Violence—from Domestic Abuse to Political Terror*:

> The ordinary response to atrocities is to banish them from consciousness. Certain violations of the social compact are too terrible to utter aloud: this is the meaning of the world *unspeakable.*
>
> Atrocities, however, refuse to be buried. Equally as powerful as the desire to deny atrocities is the conviction that denial does not work. Folk wisdom is filled with ghosts who refuse to rest in their graves until their stories are told. Murder will out. Remembering and telling the truth about terrible events are prerequisites both for the restoration of the social order and for the healing of individual victims.[4]

When I read these words, they leapt off the page and entered my spirit. I am someone who carries significant trauma in my body. Herman's analysis of the connection between the trauma I hold and the political decisions that shape the social order I live in is quite precious to me. I have coped with posttraumatic stress disorder from having survived, along with my family, the devastating 2010 earthquake in Haiti that killed hundreds of thousands of people—and also from witnessing the United States and the United Nations dramatically increase the death toll by prioritizing guarding private property rather than distributing lifesaving water and food in the immediate aftermath when so many trapped in the rubble just needed a drink of water to stay alive. I spent several days after the earthquake assisting an emergency medical technician in providing first aid to badly injured Haitians and experienced children dying as I attempted to help save their lives. I witnessed hundreds of bodies being scooped up by bulldozers and thrown into the backs of trucks. Even writing this recollection increases my heart rate.

In addition, I carry "historical trauma"—a term coined by Dr. Maria Yellow Horse Brave Heart in the 1980s to explain the impact of colonization, forced relocation, assimilation, and genocide of Native Americans. Writer Jasmin Joseph explains that the interrelated concept of intergenerational trauma "was first identified in the 1960s among the children of Holocaust survivors and has since been applied to Indigenous groups of the Americas and Australia, as well as victims of genocide or ethnic cleansing, such as Armenians in Turkey."[5]

On my father's side I carry the historical trauma from my African ancestors who endured the *Maafa*—a Swahili word meaning "Great Disaster," referring to the genocide of the transatlantic slave trade that resulted in Europeans killing millions of Africans. On my mother's side I carry the trauma of *Medz Yeghern*—an Armenian phrase meaning the "Great Catastrophe," referring to the Armenian genocide that took the lives of my great-grandfather Ardash Hagopian's family and over one million other Armenians. Although most Americans are aware that the system of slavery occurred—in however distorted a way—even a basic awareness of the Armenian genocide has been denied students ever since the Turkish government sought to annihilate Armenians, beginning with the arrest of 250 Armenian intellectuals on April 24, 1915. The Armenian genocide was a twentieth century test case that helped convince the Nazis that they could get away with the Holocaust; as Adolf Hitler put it, "Who, after all, speaks today of the annihilation of the Armenians?"[6]

Because Turkey has been an important ally to the United States in the oil-rich region of the Middle East, the United States actively participated in the cover-up of the genocide and refused to acknowledge that it occurred for over one hundred years. It wasn't until 2021, for crying out loud, that the United States finally accepted the reality of the Armenian genocide that much of the world, save Turkey and Israel, had recognized long ago. This kind of suppression of the truth was described masterfully by Herman when she explains the analogous drive of a domestic abuser and the violent acts of governments to seclude their deeds away from any public reckoning:

> In order to escape accountability for his crimes, the perpetrator does everything in his power to promote forgetting. Secrecy and silence are the perpetrator's first line of defense. If secrecy fails, the perpetrator attacks the credibility of his victim. If he cannot silence her absolutely, he tries to make sure that no one listens. . . . After every atrocity one can expect to hear the same predictable apologies: it never happened; the victim lies; the victim exaggerates; the victim brought it upon herself; and in any case it is time to forget the past and move on. The more powerful the perpetrator, the greater is his prerogative to name and define reality, and the more completely his arguments prevail.[7]

I grew up in close proximity to perpetrators of the violence of organized forgetting. I was acutely aware that on my dad's side, the horrors of slavery my ancestors were subjected to were often taboo to discuss in school, and on my mom's side, my family had endured a genocide that almost no one I knew had ever heard of and was denied by the US government. This was disorienting and created internalized shame as I grew up. Because of both my traumatic experiences in Haiti and my identity and heritage, I have had to be very intentional—with the help of brilliant therapists—about working through stress, anxiety, fear, and hypervigilance that is caused by various forms of trauma; and I have also learned from social movements that the cataclysmic political decisions of elites who control governments—which they have worked diligently to deny—are at the root of this trauma.

When the US government finally acknowledged the Armenian genocide, members of Armenian communities around the country reached out to me to join celebrations of Armenian resistance and culture, and I came to know the radical healing of organized remembering. It was truly a medicinal experience to join a forum to mark the 106th anniversary of the Great

Catastrophe, which was convened to build community, celebrate Armenian art and culture, and recognize Armenian elders whose lifetime of work had finally achieved the recognition of the genocide by the US government. In that moment, blinking through tears, I experienced the truth of Herman's point that remembering the terrible events of history can be so vital both for the healing of individual victims and for the renewal of society. This observation is of great importance to the discussion of today's history deniers who wish to banish the terrible realties of structural racism from consciousness.

I have also known the power of collective healing from intergenerational trauma on the other side of my family, as I shared in the preface to this book. In my quest to learn about my Black ancestors, I discovered that they had more to pass on to me than only the trauma of being violently stolen from Africa and trafficked to America—they also bequeathed their vitality, jubilation, creativity, and resilience.

This resilience has been cultivated, in part by guarding and passing on the value of *Sankofa*, the word the Akan People of the Ghanian region of Africa use that literally means "go back and fetch it." Sankofa is also an Andikra symbol represented by a bird with its head turned backward while its feet face forward and carrying a precious egg in its mouth, symbolizing the need to look back and learn from history to move successfully into the future. Truth teachers Joyce King and Ellen Swartz explain that all students need access to "heritage knowledge"—a group's cultural memory—and it is especially vital for Black students' healing process to learn about African history and culture. "This system has been quite effective at inducting children into societies where inequalities and dominance are taught as inevitable, conformity and obedience are rewarded, cultural heritage is eased or distorted, and profit is favored over ethnic standards," write King and Swartz.[8]

Despite this long history of denying Black history, African Americans and other subjugated populations have transmitted their stories of resistance to oppression throughout the generations. But the persistent withholding of this history from schoolchildren has produced centuries of social and racial illiteracy.

We would do well to consider the legendary novelist and truth teacher Toni Morrison's idea of "disremembering" from her book *Beloved*—a story about the enduring trauma of slavery that itself is being disremembered in school districts around the country that have banned it. As scholar and truth teacher Eddie S. Glaude Jr. writes of *Beloved* in his book *Democracy in Black*,

"Disremembering enables the characters in the novel to ward off, tempo-rarily, the pain of past events. Disremembering blots out horrible loss, but it also distorts who the characters take themselves to be. Something is lost."[9]

Although confronting a painful truth can be overwhelming for an iso-lated individual—and disremembering it can be an important coping mech-anism—remembering a trauma can be therapeutic when faced collectively. For example, if Black students are isolated in predominantly white class-rooms and taught Black history as only the history of enslavement—and not about the resistance to enslavement or the African societies the predated colonization—that remembering can actually be traumatizing rather than healing. Confronting trauma without a caring community, whether that trauma is an individual experience or historical trauma, can be retrauma-tizing. This underscores the necessity of building a beloved classroom com-munity to help students heal from trauma. In my classroom, we start each day with the West African Andikra phrase *Boa me na me mmoa wo*—"help me and let me help you"—embodying the concept of interdependence. Edu-cators such as Curtis Acosta, in the Mexican American Studies Program in Tucson, Arizona—before it was attacked and shut down by the state—used the Mayan phrase *In Lak'ech* ("You are my other me") to greet students and build cooperation.

In *Collective Trauma, Collective Healing*, psychologist Jack Saul asserts, "One integral step to recovery is public acknowledgment, and therefore val-idation of, the communal story experienced by the survivors. Affirmation of a broad range of experiences is the most helpful healing."[10] Just as individ-uals can heal from trauma through the acknowledgment of the harm, class-rooms of children can heal from the violence of organized forgetting when their histories and communal stories are validated. "The core experiences of psychological trauma are disempowerment and disconnections from oth-ers," writes Herman. "Recovery, therefore, is based upon the empowerment of the survivor and the creation of new connections. Recovery can take place only within the context of relationships; it cannot occur in isolation."[11] Con-sequently, building strong relationships and beloved communities is at the heart of the radical healing of organized remembering.

This observation by Herman resonates deeply with my personal jour-ney of trying to heal from my traumatic experiences in Haiti and with my experience with students in the classroom. Both therapy and participation in social justice movements have been instrumental on my road to recovery. The collective remembering I have engaged in about Haitian and African American history has been healing for me as an individual in a similar way that the history has been healing for the Black freedom struggle when it has remembered and applied these lessons it has learned from the past. As Cynthia Dillard, truth teacher and author of *The Spirit of Our Work: Black Women Teachers (Re)member*, puts it, "Our healing begins in gathering together to (re)member. (Re)membering is a catalyst for healing and creation. . . . [D]iasporic Black folks draw our strength from memory and acts of (re)membering to construct what it means to stand anew, whether through forced movements like the transatlantic trade in humans or in migrations of other kinds."[12]

Fugitive Pedagogy and Organized Remembering

Black people have long created communities of resistance that have helped to cultivate the radical healing of organized remembering. As white enslavers viewed education as their private property, Black people had to plan elaborate heists to steal schooling for themselves—including a practice called "stealin' the meetin'." In Virginia on January 13, 1937, Elizabeth Sparks was interviewed about her life during the period she was enslaved and recalled, "Once in a while they was free nigguhs fum somewhah. They could come see yer if yer was their folks. Nigguhs used to go way off in quarters an' slip an' have meetins. They called it stealin' the meetin'. The children used to teach me to read."[13]

Some enslaved Black people used "pit schools" as a way to practice fugitive pedagogy. Black people would dig a large hole in the ground out in the woods and conceal it by covering it with branches and vines. Mandy Jones, an enslaved person in Mississippi, recalled that the pits could be used for runaways to hide out or for clandestine schools. Jones said, "[S]laves would slip out of the Quarters at night, and go to dese pits, an some niggah dat had some learning would have school."[14] Jones also knew of a Black man who learned to read and write in a cave.

Some of these fugitive academies provided regular illegal instruction and "[c]landestine schools were in operation in most of the large cities and towns of the South where such enlightenment of the Negroes was prohibited by law."[15] Under the guise of attending sewing classes, free Black children—who were occasionally joined by enslaved children—stole their education in Saint Louis, Missouri. In Virginia, "schools . . . were secretly maintained" and "[c]olored aspirants after knowledge were constrained to keep their books and slates carefully hidden from every prying eye, and to assume the appearance of being upon an errand as they hurried along and watch their chance to slip unnoticed into the sedulously concealed schoolroom."[16]

A Black woman named Deveaux was a fugitive pedagogue who operated one such illicit school in Savannah, Georgia, from 1819 to 1865. She was even able to expand her school during and after the Civil War. Susie King's description of her daily quest for education, also in Savannah, is instructive about the astonishing lengths to which enslaved people would go to subvert the prohibition of literacy: "We went every day about nine o'clock, with our books wrapped in paper to prevent the police or white persons from seeing them. We went in, one at a time, through the gate, into the yard to the kitchen, which was the schoolroom. . . . The Neighbors would see us going in sometime, but they supposed we were there learning trades."[17] This school would enroll around thirty pupils at a time and was run by Mrs. Woodhouse and her daughter Mary Jane.

Another clandestine meeting place for enslaved people was the "hush harbor." These spaces served multiple purposes, primarily providing a refuge for religious worship, cultural preservation, and the nurturing of educational pursuits. Away from the watchful eyes of slaveholders, hush harbors became sites of resilience, community building, and resistance. Hush harbors were much more than physical spaces; they represented a network of solidarity and support. Enslaved individuals from different plantations and regions would gather, forging connections and strengthening bonds.

In this era of harsh truthcrime laws, it is important for educators to consider how they might draw on this history to create new spaces of resistance— contemporary versions of the pit schools and hush harbors—to allow young people to become racially literate.

Collective Healing in the Beloved Classroom

Since collaboration is crucial for achieving the radical healing of organized remembering, it is important to examine methods for developing healthy relationships between students and teachers (and between organizers and the communities from which they emerge). Truth teacher and executive director of Rethinking Schools Cierra Kaler-Jones emphasizes that the restorative power of learning can't be achieved without attending to the social and emotional needs of students: "Healing, for Black and Brown young people, should be centered in SEL [social and emotional learning]. We must not lose the importance of co-constructing spaces with young people to lean into creative expression and joy. . . . Let them dance, sing, laugh, play, scream, organize, and encourage all the brilliant ways they show up."[18] This means that the healing of organized remembering can't be achieved simply by lecturing students or communities on history. Achieving the radical healing of organized remembering requires interactive lessons that encourage play and allow students to learn, not only from the teacher, but from each other. It also requires using restorative and transformative justice practices that support building healthy communities before conflicts arise and can help heal relationships when trust is broken. As Mark R. Warren, Letha Muhammad, and Emma Tynan explain,

> Restorative justice has its roots in a variety of indigenous traditions. It emphasizes community-building and respectful relationships over discipline and control. When conflict occurs, restorative practices seek to uncover the roots of the problem, address the harm it causes, and rebuild relationships. Many know restorative justice circles as one embodiment of restorative practices, where participants share their views, seek to identify responsibility, and rebuild community. It's meant to empower students, not punish them.[19]

Transformative justice practices go even deeper by considering the need for transformation of systems that created the conditions that led to the harm that was caused. The point here is that the radical healing power of historical knowledge is most effectively accessed when the emotional needs of the community are tended to and powerful relationships are developed out of this care. Just as there is no honest education without social and emotional learning, there is no social and emotional learning without honest historical lessons that affirm the lives of BIPOC students. As Kaler-Jones cautions, "SEL devoid of culturally-affirming practices and understandings is not SEL at all. When students are in classrooms, the curriculum and the space is often not culturally affirming, and is psychologically violent to their family, ancestors, and contributions."[20] Culturally affirming social and emotional learning, restorative and transformative justice, and interactive ("dialogic") lessons create the conditions for the beloved classroom community. In turn, the beloved classroom community is a prerequisite to accessing the radical healing of organized remembering. Monique Couvson suggests educators ask themselves four questions to support girls of color in the classroom who are survivors of trauma—recommendations that I believe are an important foundation of any beloved classroom:

1. How might what I'm teaching—or not teaching—participate in the oppression of my students?

2. How does my classroom pedagogy reflect my understanding of intersectionality?

3. How does my classroom culture respond to harm as an exchange that can be remedied or resolved in community?

4. How can I better facilitate conversations, breathing exercises, and quiet moments for meditation/reflection that provide my student community with an opportunity to safely interrogate difficult, potentially triggering, subject matter?[21]

When students (and people engaged in social movements) are part of a beloved community and are supported to develop a robust historical memory, not only can it help the individuals who have learned these lessons heal from trauma they have experienced, but it can create a powerful challenge to uncritical race theorists and the elites who have designed the systemic inequities of our society.

Take the example of veteran truth teacher Adam Sanchez, who taught high school African American history in Philadelphia and serves as the managing editor for *Rethinking Schools*. After engaging his class in several lessons on Reconstruction—many of which he wrote and published in *Rethinking Schools* magazine—Sanchez asked his students what they had learned from the unit and if they thought it was worth studying.[22] Shattering the myth propagated by uncritical race theorists that social justice educators are teaching their students that Black people are only victims, one of Sanchez's students reflected on the Reconstruction unit, writing, "I didn't know how much power Black people had gained in this short period of time and had always just assumed it went immediately from slavery to Jim Crow. It is important for students to learn about this era because it represents a period of mass change that reveals that Black people don't need saving, but have seized and defined freedom on their own." Another of Sanchez's students wrote, "I didn't know that African Americans made significant progress during Reconstruction. . . . It helps us understand why America is currently in the state it is in and the causes of the backlash, both to Reconstruction and Black progress today. But learning about Reconstruction also teaches us that if people come together, they can bring forth major political reforms, even changes to the Constitution."[23]

This is the power of the radical healing of organized remembering: by uncovering the truth about the past that has been purposely excluded from textbooks, students can understand how lessons from advancements for racial justice that were made in the past can be applied in the struggles of today.

I've learned this from my own students. For example, in 2010, during my first year teaching high school at my alma mater, Garfield High School, I was assigned to teach AP US history. Instead of teaching to the AP exam the students would take at the end of the year, I chose to use the interactive, social justice classroom activities produced by Rethinking Schools and the Zinn Education Project. These lessons included engaging students in activities and simulations of the struggles of the abolitionists and women's rights movements in antebellum America, the Freedom Riders of the Civil Rights Movement, the student movements against the Vietnam War, and so many other popular movements. While many of my students ended up doing quite well on the exam, it wasn't until the following year that they actually passed my test.

When Washington State announced in 2011 that it would hold a special legislative session to decide how to further slash the education and health care budgets, I joined a delegation of social justice educators to protest at the Washington State Capitol. I even went so far as to disrupt the House Ways and Means Committee session, where they were voting to cut the education budget, and issued citizen's arrest warrants to legislators for failing to adhere to the Washington State Constitution, which declares education is the state's "paramount duty." Unfortunately, the police in the chamber didn't agree with my interpretation of the state constitution, and as I delivered the arrest warrants to the legislators, an officer arrested me.

While I was in jail, unbeknownst to me, my students at Garfield High School—the ones who had studied the history of social movements with me the year prior—learned of my arrest on the news and set up a Facebook page titled "Free Mr. Hagopian." Hundreds of student Bulldogs joined the page in my support. When I was released that night and appeared for school the next day, the students changed the name of the Facebook page to "Seattle Student Walkout for Education." A multiracial mass of over five hundred students left school in the middle of the day and marched to city hall with a pamphlet they had created to detail how detrimental the budget cuts would be to their education and signs demanding fully funded schools.[24] They wrote an op-ed to *The Seattle Times*, got their photo in *The New York Times*, and formed an organization called Students of Washington for Change (SWaC). "At today's student walkout from Garfield," SWaC wrote, "we demonstrated that this state's students care about their education, and are not afraid to advocate for it."[25]

Educators' unions continued to agitate for more funding. Other high schools soon joined the effort in a mass citywide walkout. Only weeks later, the Washington State Supreme Court ruled that the Washington state legislature was in violation of the constitution and would need to add billions of dollars to the education budget.[26]

Although I didn't have the words for it then, my students had most certainly engaged in the radical healing of organized remembering by collectively applying their knowledge of the social movements we had studied the year before to defend their own education.

This is what uncritical race theorists really fear—not that truth teachers are shaming white students.

The idea that teachers are shaming white kids is useful propaganda to rally the GOP base, but it is not a practice of honest educators and truth teachers. These educators know that "nobody's free until everybody's free," as the great women's rights and civil rights leader Fannie Lou Hamer put it. Hamer's conviction about freedom isn't only an inclusive sentiment, it's also clear-eyed analysis. Although people of color face some of the harshest deprivations in a society replete with structural racism, the elites who horde the wealth at the top of society don't share much with the vast majority of white people either. Honest educators teach about the vast racial wealth gap between BIPOC and white people, but they also teach about the injustice that four million white children live in poverty in the world's wealthiest country. The racial division between white people and BIPOC has been central to the disempowering of the vast majority of the population of all races and a giant obstacle to the attainment of a true multiracial democracy that honest educators strive toward.

This means that empowering white students with the history of white antiracists is central to the task of truth teachers. White students deserve to learn about white people who have joined movements for racial justice and to learn that although there are certainly privileges white people receive from being in a society with racist institutions, there would be more benefits to living in a society that treats everyone equitably and teaches the truth about the history of oppression. In his 1963 "A Talk to Teachers," James Baldwin explained the healing that white people need from learning the truth:

> If . . . one managed to change the curriculum in all the schools so that Negroes learned more about themselves and their real contributions to this culture, you would be liberating not only Negroes, you'd be liberating white people who know nothing about their own history. And the reason is that if you are compelled to lie about one aspect of anybody's history, you must lie about it all. If you have to lie about my real role here, if you have to pretend that I hoed all that cotton just because I loved you, then you have done something to yourself. You are mad.[27]

It is true that teaching about challenging topics like oppression can create discomfort—for both white and BIPOC kids—yet an uncomfortable truth can be the companion of intellectual growth and healing. Learning the truth about structural racism in America, from slavery to mass incarceration today, can no doubt be disquieting. However, discomfort is different than shame—an emotion that some students may feel at times but also one that antiracist educators help guide kids away from and toward the more productive and healing sentiments of solidarity and the determination to create a better society. Ursula Wolfe-Rocca and Christie Nold explained the objectives of antiracist educators in regard to their work with white students:

> Early in their encounters with the history of systemic oppression, white students sometimes express denial, disbelief, anger and yes, guilt. But the right would have you believe that those feelings are the end of the story rather than its beginning. . . . If one were to believe Fox News, a curriculum like ours—one that regularly and explicitly examines white supremacy's manifestations, past and present—is a recipe for demoralized children who hate themselves and their country. But our classrooms are not sites of doom and gloom. Students are hungry for explanations—real explanations—for the world they have inherited, and in our experience, they often feel relieved to gain insight into why

things are the way they are. Moreover, our curriculum emphasizes the varied, powerful and creative ways that people have resisted oppression and built justice. We are careful to offer students models of action, examples of people just like them who have tried to change the world and sometimes succeeded. No, our classrooms are not incubators of cynicism. They are brimming with curiosity, conversation and, yes, joy.[28]

That joy of white students learning how to adopt a white identity in opposition to white supremacy was expressed by a student identified as Terri in an illuminating essay by Beverly Daniel Tatum in the book *Foundations of Critical Race Theory in Education*. Terri reflected on the inspiration she felt from learning about the struggle against racism and white privilege, saying, "Today's class began with a visit from . . . a white woman who has made dismantling white privilege a way of life. . . . Her personal story gave me a feeling of hope in the struggle against racism."[29] In this description you see that healing can also occur for white students when racist curriculum is challenged.

Not only do antiracist truth teachers not engage in shaming white students, but in fact it is the miseducation from those attacking CRT that can harm white children's identity and self-esteem. This point must be underlined. It is actually uncritical race theorists who deny structural racism that end up leading white children to suspect that they are personally responsible for the racial disparities they see all around them—segregated and unequal schools, for example—rather than developing an understanding of the way structural racism functions so that institutions can work to perpetuate inequities, sometimes regardless of the intentions of the individuals who work in them.

I would argue, moreover, that uncritical race theorists' real fear isn't that truth teachers are shaming white kids. Once the studio lighting is powered down, the outcue is delivered, and the cameras are turned off, uncritical race theorist pundits can admit to themselves their real fear: that honest educators are healing white students by teaching them about the tradition of antiracist white people who have abandoned the loneliness and alienation of white supremacy and joined in social movements for racial justice. You can understand why that history scares uncritical race theorists; unlike the delusion that educators who have dedicated their lives to social justice and nurturing everyone in their classroom would want to humiliate their white students, the reality is that truth teachers want to empower white students—not with the false prize of white privilege, but with the power and joy of solidarity. Being denied the history of white people who have organized in movements for racial justice is harmful to white students, who also deserve to heal from this violence of organized forgetting.

I strive for this kind of healing, for example, when I teach about the American Revolution. In this unit, I teach my students about Thomas Paine, the white English American writer whose best-selling book *Common Sense* was one of the most important catalysts for the uprising against the British Crown. In March 1775 Paine published one of the earliest antislavery articles, "African Slavery in America," and asked a question similar to the one Frederick Douglass would later pose in his speech, "What to the Slave Is the Fourth of July?" Paine excoriated the hypocrisy of the American Revolutionaries who fought for freedom yet practiced slavery by inquiring, "With what consistency, or decency, they complain so loudly of attempts to enslave them, while they hold so many hundred thousands in slavery, and annually enslave many thousands more ... ?"[30] When uncritical race theorists charge truth teachers with "presentism," claiming that you can't judge the founding fathers by today's beliefs about slavery and race, I wonder if it would be OK with them if we judged slavery by the beliefs of the truth tellers of their own time, like Thomas Paine? Or in all their unbridled patriotism is there no room for an accurate accounting of one of the leading American Revolutionaries? Although some would want to hide the fact that Paine and his comrades battled wealthy white Americans— as they believed that the country should actually be a democracy and not a slavocracy—honest educators believe in teaching the truth.

Some of the antiracist white organizers, educators, and activists included in my curriculum that students draw inspiration from include Benjamin Lay, John Brown, the Grimke sisters, Eugene Debs, Myles Horton, Anne Braden, and Howard Zinn. We learn about multiracial organizing efforts like the Union Leagues during Reconstruction that united poor white people and Black people in the South to defended Black people's right to vote and organized for economic and racial justice. Or about the SNCC's 1964 Freedom Summer campaign that brought together hundreds of white college students with Black organizers to establish Freedom Schools and register Black people to vote in Mississippi.

Learning about the history of white people in multiracial organizing efforts helps white kids understand that although white antiracist leaders throughout history have not been plentiful enough to end systemic racism, there is an important tradition of multiracial solidarity that white people today have a choice to either join or reject. "I think that some of the legislation being passed disregards young people's ability—especially this generation—to accept new information and process it, without feeling shame or guilt," Texan social studies teacher David Ring told *The New York Times*.[31] Historian, poet, and honest educator Clint Smith has suggested that white students can confront hard truths about things that their families may even have participated in without allowing it to determine their identity. "You are not defined by the decisions that your great-great-grandfather made," he said. "What would it look like to say, 'My great-great-grandfather fought in this [Civil] War for a cause that runs counter to everything that I believe in today. And my family is not defined by that?" I have seen students in my class begin their healing process by asking these very kinds of questions—and continue the healing by organizing and acting to challenge racism.

The Thundering RHOR of Social Movements

Uncritical race theorists especially fear when the radical healing of organized remembering extends beyond one classroom to engage the whole school. In Washington, DC, truth teacher Michele Bollinger works at what was previously known as (Woodrow) Wilson High School, where she participated in the broader efforts to rescind the school's tribute to the aggressively racist twenty-eighth president of the United States. President Wilson is famous for having premiered the film *Birth of a Nation*—a glowing tribute of the KKK—at the White House and for segregating the federal workforce. For years before the 2020 uprising, there were community members, educators, students, and a group called the D.C. History and Justice Collaborative who advocated for changing the name of the school. "There were a lot of kids who really hated the name," Bollinger told me when I interviewed her on December 19, 2022. "And every time they would talk about racism in society or in our school the conversation would always end with, 'what do you expect in a school named after a bigot.'" Yet after years of organizing, Bollinger explained, the movement was "really hitting a wall" and it was unclear if Washington, DC, would ever consider the historical record of Wilson and act appropriately. "Then the George Floyd uprising happened, and the city was basically caught with its pants down. Because nothing looks worse than when you've had years of people asking for justice and then, all of a sudden, the spotlight is on all the forms of racism in your city."[32]

After much organizing and agitation, on December 7, 2021, the DC City Council finally voted to rename the school Jackson-Reed High School, after Edna Jackson, the first Black woman teacher at the then all-white school in 1954, and Vincent Reed, the school's first Black principal in 1968. Bollinger described the victory to me, saying, "People definitely felt that it's hard to change things and people weren't sure that change would ever come. The school's name change created excitement and it raised the possibility that you can make change, that things can be different." Although celebrating the victory, Bollinger also understands that changing the name doesn't create an antiracist school in and of itself:

> When we came back to school the next year, we had a big panel where Edna Jackson's niece came and someone who had worked for Vincent Reed. It was a really great way to start the year because people felt we're aspiring to reflect the values that Jackson and Reed represented. It's a good start but we have a long way to go. You have to look critically at what you're actually doing. Where I am at with all of it now is asking, "How do we truly bring principles of antiracism into our school?"[33]

Although the name change didn't eliminate all the structures of racism that impact the school, it did demonstrate the importance of collective action; and there is healing in organized movements for social change. In addition, it demonstrated that you could win when confronting the violence of organized forgetting. This act of discovering the truth about Woodrow Wilson and renaming the school to honor Black educators is an important example of how the healing process can begin.

Yet it's also important to understand that the radical healing of organized remembering isn't only happening at schools. Sometimes the best lesson plans are written by social movements; sometimes the best classrooms are the streets. On the Fourth of July 2020, Baltimore residents celebrated by toppling a prominent statue of Christopher Columbus, engraved with an inscription that read, "CHRISTOPHER COLUMBUS DISCOVERER OF AMERICA OCTOBER 12 1492." These direct-action truth teachers dumped the statue in the harbor, with one activist group tweeting "Columbus just got deported."[34]

These protest pedagogues understood that Columbus did not discover America. There were, of course, more than fifty million Indigenous people in the Americas before he arrived. Not only that, but he wasn't even the first European to reach the western hemisphere, as the Vikings had a settlement in North America centuries before Christopher Columbus made his journey.[35] But most importantly, what these truth teachers taught the country was that Columbus didn't deserve to be honored with a statue because he was a murderous enslaver. If that statement of fact sounds radical, it is only because the violence of organized forgetting has done so much damage to the American psyche. Columbus personally ordered 1,500 Taíno to be enslaved and implemented a policy that all of the Indigenous people of Ayati (now Haiti) over the age of fourteen were required to produce a large quantity of gold for the Spanish or be killed. Laurence Bergreen's biography *Columbus: The Four Voyages* describes Columbus personally giving one of his men an Indigenous woman to rape. The deranged torture that Columbus oversaw included one of his men who, after capturing a Taíno man, ordered a subordinate to "'cut off his ears' in retribution for the Indians' failing to be helpful to the Spaniards when fording a stream."[36]

"Statues that celebrate European colonialism necessarily celebrate Black slavery, Indigenous genocide, human trafficking and rape," explained Spencer Compton, a white honest educator who filmed the act of organized remembering of protesters dumping the Columbus statue. "These statues traumatize citizens whose ancestors were enslaved in some form or another," he said.[37] The removal of this public celebration of the man who launched a genocide on the Native peoples of the Americas was an important demonstration of the radical healing of organized remembering.

Years earlier, honest educator Bree Newsome's act of civil disobedience that schooled the world about the Confederate States of America was the prescription of organized remembering people needed in the wake of a neo-Confederate gunning down of ten Black people at the Emanuel African Methodist Episcopal Church in Charleston, South Carolina. Newsome and a group of activists decided they would take down the Confederate flag from the South Carolina State House—and that a Black woman should go and a white man should help, "as a sign that our alliance transcended both racial and gender divides."[38]

On the morning of June 27, 2015, Newsome waited until the police turned away from the state house flagpole and began scaling the thirty-foot flagpole.

Before she was able to reach the top, police spotted her and demanded she come down. When Newsome refused to stop her ascension, the police threatened to tase the flagpole—which would have resulted in her electrocution. At that moment, James Tyson, the white man there to help, wrapped his hands around the base of the pole, telling the officers they'd have to electrocute him, too. Newsome cut down the Confederate flag, declaring, "You come against me with hatred, oppression and violence. I come against you in the name of God. This flag comes down today."[39] When she got down, the police arrested both Newsome and Tyson and news of their action went viral. Newsome assessed her achievement, saying, "It just felt triumphant. . . . To have this moment where we demonstrate this agency as Black people . . . the same way that it demonstrated power and agency for the Greensboro Four to go and sit down at the Woolworth's counter. 'You're saying we can't sit here? We're going to sit here.' You're saying we can't lower this flag? We are going to lower this flag today. It was just a feeling of triumph."[40]

This is the radical healing of organized remembering; it happens when people take the lessons of the past with them into the social movements of today. All of these instances of organized remembering—from the classroom to the harbor to the top of a flagpole—are powerful acts of resistance that form a pedagogy of collective truth telling.

And yet it must be stressed that learning the truth about structural racism and teaching it to others is not enough on its own to heal those harmed by oppression. Madeline Morgan, the truth teacher from Chicago who helped organize an important campaign to teach about Black history during the World War II era, explained this when she said, "Knowledge is only power if it is put into action."[41] Truth teaching has to be joined with mass collective organizing that puts the lessons and analyses derived from the history for struggles for justice into sustaining social movements—not merely to make society less oppressive, but to fundamentally transform power relations and uproot oppression. This is about the struggle for a new education system that doesn't perpetuate historical trauma. This is about the struggle for a new economic and political system that isn't designed to educate kids for the purpose of preparing them for a low-wage job or prison.

One of the reasons over the last couple of decades we have seen so many movements against racism and oppression explode into open rebellion, only to then quickly recede, is that too many of the historical lessons from those in the struggles for justice previously have been intentionally stolen. If we go into battle against systemic racism with open wounds inflicted by the violence of organized forgetting, we won't last long. But if we begin to heal the wounds of intellectual violence by collectively studying—in the classroom, in community organizations, in unions, in social movements—the history of systemic racism and oppression and the history of struggles against injustice, we will be much more effective, and our struggles will be much more sustainable.

In addition, it's important to be clear about what the radical healing of organized remembering is not trying to heal. The broken economic, political, and social system we live with doesn't need healing. These oppressive systems are terminally ill and can't be healed. What does need healing are the people who give their labor and lives to a system that allows a handful of billionaires at the top of the capitalist pyramid to profit off of everyone else. When the multiracial masses of students, parents, educators, and working people access the inoculating power of truth, they can be more effective in defeating the disease of racial capitalism that is fundamental to our social ills.

This system isn't going to pull the knife out from the back of antiracist education or dress the wounds inflicted by dishonest schooling on its own. Removing the blade, sterilizing the abrasions, and promoting a full recovery will require healers dedicated to administering this first aid.

Conclusion

Honest Educators and Truth Teachers

Whitfield continued his expert lesson to Congress, saying, "I chose a career in education because of my school experience," a statement drawing on his background of feeling abandoned by the school system but being rescued by deeply caring educators. He went on to say:

> Above all, I want school to be a place where students feel like they belong and they're excited to be each day; where staff are empowered, inspired, and equipped to serve each day; and where families feel connected and have the highest levels of trust as they send their young people into our building each day. I have witnessed what can happen when this environment exists. It's such a beautiful thing.

It is a beautiful thing, and it is deeply healing.

Marcia J. Watson-Vandiver and Greg Wiggan explained the potential healing properties of education: "If we do not heal, we transmit that pain and poison onto others. In this sense, schools have been instrumental in transmitting curriculum violence and miseducation. However, they can also become places of healing and restoration through proper care and support."[42] Honest educators and truth teachers are healers. They understand the harm caused by not teaching the truth and appreciate that "washing one's hands of the conflict between the powerful and the powerless means to side with the powerful, not to be neutral,"[43] as pedagogue of the oppressed Paulo Freire put it. Truth teachers know that in a society with as many inequities as ours, educators decide either to inoculate education against or to succumb to the plague of injustice; they know that they have the power to either withhold or prescribe the medicine that is the history of struggles for liberation. Honest educators are those who defend their students from the violence of organized forgetting by engaging them in the radical healing of organized remembering.

Although it must be underscored that truth teachers aren't infallible.

Honest educators can make honest mistakes—they might get a fact wrong, or even unwittingly reproduce a master narrative. They don't always have the perfect lesson plan that was developed on planet equity. They are, however, willing to learn and grow from dialogue and loving debate with others who are genuinely concerned with struggles against oppression. They are especially open to collaboration and feedback from the students and families with which they interact. Honest educators are willing to admit they don't have all the answers about how to achieve a society free of oppression. But they do know one thing for sure: the subjugation of various peoples is a structural issue in American society and it has always been collective struggle that has made gains against various forms of domination.

Honest educators are courageous enough to teach the truth about the persistent nature of capitalist exploitation, racism, sexism, homophobia, transphobia, ableism, and other forms of oppression in a society that wants them to lie to kids about injustice. Yet truth teaching isn't only about presenting students with accurate information. It isn't even only about ensuring students learn the histories of oppressed people that are often marginalized in traditional textbooks. It is about those things. But truth teachers are more interested in teaching students how to think than what to think. They must refuse to shut down students' questions about injustice, allow them to speak about their experiences, facilitate open dialogue about real-world issues, and provide historical context and honest answers to their questions.

The goal of truth teachers is to develop students who know how to question everything, every message they encounter in the media, as well everything they are learning in class, and develop their own conclusions. The truth teacher's job, then, is to ensure that schooling doesn't get in the way of students' curiosity, to provide context for the issues being investigated, and to ask students questions—especially questions about problems that exist in our communities and our world—that allow their natural inquisitiveness to help them discover how to build a more just society.

Truth teaching isn't only an intellectual endeavor but also an emotional one. Honest educators are guided by love. "Commitment to truth telling lays the groundwork for the openness and honesty that is the heartbeat of love," writes bell hooks.[44] Truth teacher Cornel West has observed, "Justice is what love looks like in public."[45] I would add that truth teaching is what love looks like in public schools. Martin Luther King Jr. centered love in the building of social movements when he imparted, "Our goal is to create a beloved community, and this will require a qualitative change in our souls as well as a quantitative change in our lives."[46] Truth teachers express to their students that they are worthy of being loved. Beyond giving students affirmations and encouragement, truth teachers express their love by being honest with them about history, using culturally sustaining curricula, antiracist pedagogy, and healing circles, granting ample time for rest and play, and using democratic practices that empower students in decision-making. They also express that love by engaging students in reflective practices to help them better understand their own identities and connect their personal experiences with broader social patterns—a process that involves critically evaluating their own beliefs and biases. By centering love, care, and social and emotional learning, truth teachers can help create a beloved classroom community that is transformational in students' lives.

Honest educators also demonstrate their love by collectively organizing and engaging in struggles for the schools children deserve. They know that educators play an important collective role—through their unions and other organizations—in efforts to create a just education system that both empowers educators and meets the needs of their students. They also know that they must become active participants in the social struggles around them if their social justice pedagogy in the classroom is going to be credible with students.

For example, solidarity between students and educators is achieved when a teacher not only teaches about the history of unions struggling to raise families out of poverty, but also joins their union and participates in a strike or a campaign to raise the minimum wage. Educators have a unique position in society as their job connects them with students and parents—a large swath of society—and creates the potential for them to help lead broad social movements, not only to improve education, but to win the resources entire communities need. Honest educators appreciate this position and seek ways to bargain for the common good in their unions and mobilize the vast numbers of people whose lives they impact in a common struggle against racism and all forms of oppression.

Honest educators organize with a social justice union approach—such as the Chicago Teachers Union and the United Teachers Los Angeles—and teach their students as much on the picket line as they do in the classroom by leading struggles for increased school funding, affordable housing, health care, removing police from schools, immigrant rights, and more. At a rally of striking Oakland educators in 2023, parent Linnea Nelson made this point when she said, "We know this is a sacrifice and that you want to be in your classrooms. But you are fighting to go back to better classrooms— Teachers on strike are still teaching."[47] LA truth teacher Gillian Russom told me about her experience on strike in 2019: "It's really hard to overstate the incredible feeling of empowerment, solidarity, and joy that you saw in school site picket lines and at the massive rallies that we held every single day. . . . Loyola Marymount University did a poll of households that have kids in public school, and 82 percent were supportive of us." Russom went on to explain the healing power of collective struggle the LA teachers experienced on the picket line: "The DJ started playing 'Fight the Power' and my coworker turned to me and said, 'This feels like freedom.' Teachers put up with so much, and teachers sacrifice so much for the kids. But if you give teachers the ability to stand up for students in a different kind of way, you will see that same incredible dedication channeled into struggle."[48]

In today's society, to be an honest educator is, paradoxically, to be a "truthcriminal." Yet to be castigated as a truthcriminal in a society that criminalizes teaching truth is no scarlet letter. It is a badge of honor worn by those who refuse to be complicit in the suppression of knowledge and the distortion of history. It's a recognition of the courage to teach truth to power, to challenge the status quo, and to advocate for justice and equity in education.

White educators have both a specific challenge and a specific duty when it comes to becoming honest educators. Talking about race—let alone teaching about race—can be very uncomfortable for white people because they were raised in a school system that taught them uncritical race theory, rather than the realities of BIPOC lives. Educators of color were also raised in a school system that taught uncritical race theory and sometimes can also fail to challenge the structures of racism. Yet because of their experiences facing interpersonal and structural racism, Black people and other people of color have a better vantage point for seeing through the smoke screen of uncritical race theory, and this enables them to locate and sound the truth alarm more quickly when it comes to issues of race in America. White teachers who are interested in becoming truth teachers have specific and demanding work they must engage in to discard the uncritical race theory that has permeated their education. This requires reading the works of Black authors about structural racism and Indigenous authors about settler colonialism. It requires reflecting on how the anti-racist history and analysis they are then learning applies to their own lives and identities. It requires an honest assessment of the ways white supremacy perpetuates harm. It also requires not being paralyzed with guilt for being white in a white supremacist society, but instead being animated by the potential for solidarity. And it requires being willing to take leadership from Black educators and educators of color, while fully engaging in the collective struggles for racial and social justice.

In addition, truth teachers have a commitment to democracy. In the classroom, truth teachers find ways to include students in collective decision making about how the community will function and what will be studied. But the commitment to democracy extends further; it is so deep that honest educators don't believe democracy should be limited to only political affairs or only confined to voting booths that are dusted off every few years. Honest educators believe democracy should be expanded into the entire education system, workplaces, and the broader economy. For all the declarations of politicians who claim to be devoted to democracy, there are few who propose abandoning the transparently autocratic American economy to suggest extending democracy into the workplace. As it is now, working people don't get to vote on their working conditions; workers rarely have a say in how many breaks they get, what the sick leave policy is, or what is done with all the wealth that is produced, for example. The scarcity of democracy in the

American system results in a situation where students, educators, and parents have little control over the funding or policy that govern the schools, and it results in a society where wealth is concentrated in the hands of a few billionaires while approximately forty million people live in poverty in the richest country in the world. "We need education to make schools places where the conditions for democratic consciousness can be established and flourish," hooks reminds us.[49]

Honest educators are blues singers—they tell history like it is and they know how to improvise to bring the class into harmony. As Monique Couvson wrote in *Sing a Rhythm, Dance a Blues*, "More than a conduit for marginalized voices, the blues is a means to stimulate radical possibilities. . . . Millions of people consume the blues as entertainment without acknowledging its most important contributions to the freedom struggle: a platform for truth telling, a forum of resistance, and thus a pathway to healing and learning."[50] Blues music is not just about pain, but about the healing that occurs when you are able to express your feelings. The same is true for blues teaching. Shirley Wade McLoughlin, in her book *A Pedagogy of the Blues*, reinforces blues music as a framework for truth teaching: "A pedagogy of the blues looks and feels different than the type of education so prevalent today. One of the distinguishing characteristics is in the incorporation of testimony in the daily work in the classroom."[51] This means truth teachers are always looking for ways to encourage students to share their stories and uplift their counternarratives to the violence of organized forgetting.

Honest educators are also students. They engage in the dialogical method of teaching championed by Paulo Freire, which acknowledges that teachers are co-learners with students. For example, during the 2020 uprising, honest educators around the country were sure to make space in their classrooms for Black youth to teach about their experiences participating in demonstrations or their experiences with police. As hooks writes, "When students are fully engaged, professors no longer assume the sole leadership role in the classroom. Instead, the classroom functions more like a cooperative where everyone contributes to make sure all resources are being used, to ensure the optimal learning well-being of everyone."[52]

Honest educators are time travelers. They possess the ability to bend the space-time continuum and transport their students to the past to examine an era before race was invented, investigate the origins of where structural racism and oppression came from, and to visit people who helped build social movements to combat these inequities. But they don't get stuck in the past. They are also able to travel to the future to help students imagine a world where the government doesn't spend more money to bomb people than house them and where society doesn't lock human beings in cages. Truth teacher and scholar Barbara Ransby demonstrated the importance of defying the linear progression of time when she described what the world will look like when we win social justice in her "Letter from the Year 2071":

> For our new society, education goes beyond the "schoolhouse" and the "campus." And there are no barriers that exclude anyone from learning. Teaching and learning go on everywhere, with billboards, songs and television commercials that teach, rather than sell. And rather than excluding anyone from education, or labeling some of our precious children "smart" and others "not smart," we recognize all are geniuses. It is the job of learning coaches and co-learners to help them find that genius—and to apply it to the needs of the community and society.[53]

Asking students to travel with you into the future and imagine new possibilities for their education and society is a transformative experience. However, truth teachers don't get stuck in the future either; they are able to then return students to the present to help them understand the social problems we face today and empower them to join collective efforts to address these issues.

Truth teachers and honest educators hail from many traditions of social justice pedagogy. Those in the Teach Truth movement would do well to study these traditions, such as the Citizenship Schools and Freedom Schools that Septima "Mother of the Civil Rights Movement" Clark helped construct by demonstrating that literacy and political empowerment are inextricably linked.

Black studies epistemologies like Carter G. Woodson's concept of "mis-education" and his insistence on teaching the truth about Africa and African American history have played a seminal role in shaping truth teaching throughout the generations. Soviet psychologist Lev Vygotsky's contributions to understanding child and adolescent cognitive development, particularly his concept of the "zone of proximal development" (which highlights the difference between what a learner can do independently and with assistance), have been indispensable to honest education.

The "people's history" tradition, exemplified by Howard Zinn, has provided a crucial framework for honest educators, revealing often suppressed stories of oppressed and exploited people. Ethnic studies approaches, championed by scholars like Ronald Takaki, center the narratives of Black people, Indigenous people, and people of color and analyze colonization and race construction to combat white supremacy.

CRT, developed by scholars like Derrick Bell and applied to education by truth teachers such as Gloria Ladson-Billings, is essential for understanding how racism operates within the law. An intersectional analysis of power and oppression, advanced by Black women like Sojourner Truth, Claudia Jones, Barbara Smith, and Kimberlé Crenshaw, is crucial for countering divide-and-conquer strategies.

The economic analysis by scholars like Samuel Bowles and Herbert Gintis, who developed "correspondence theory," is useful to truth teachers because it sheds light on how changes in the education system often correspond to changes in the economy and explains how capitalism exploits education to increase profits and train obedient workers. Critical pedagogy, rooted in dialogic and interactive principles and developed by educators like Paulo Freire and bell hooks, provides a framework for liberatory learning. Youth development workers such as Shawn Ginwright and Monique Couvson have contributed greatly to developing healing-centered, trauma-informed, social-emotional pedagogy, so vital to truth teaching. Finally, abolitionist principles advocated by Angela Davis, Ruth Wilson Gilmore, Mariame Kaba, and Bettina Love are integral to dismantling the school-to-prison pipeline, fostering Black joy in the classroom, and striving toward liberation.

Every educator must decide if they will become an honest educator or, alternatively, simply read out of a corporate textbook, kowtow to the demands made by uncritical race theorists, and blow the smoke of deception at children. When educators choose to become honest educators and youth are allowed to think for themselves and challenge injustice, it really scares uncritical race theorists; and you can tell a frightened uncritical race theorists because when they can't win a debate, they just try to make it illegal for you to say—or teach—anything that challenges their power. The next, and concluding, chapter of this book examines some of my experiences that shaped what I have written in this volume and makes an argument for what it will take to build a truly just education system.

"Truth for Their Pencils and Pads"

And if we win in the ages to come
We'll have a chapter where the history pages are from
They won't never know our name or face
But feel our soul in free food they taste
Feel our passion when they heat they house
When they got power on the streets
And the police don't beat 'em about
Let's make health care centers on every block
Let's give everybody homes and a garden plot
Let's give all the schools books
Ten kids a class
And give 'em truth for their pencils and pads
              —**Boots Riley,** from his song "Heven Tonite"

I began my teaching career in 2001 at Hendley Elementary School in Southeast Washington, DC—an area cordoned off from the rest of the city both geographically, by the Anacostia River, and socially, by its dearth of everything from jobs to grocery stores. Hendley was full of dedicated educators and brilliant students, but to borrow from the truth teacher and author Jonathan Kozol, it suffered from "savage inequalities."

Hendley was completely segregated, serving 100 percent African

American students. At least until my third year when one white student entered kindergarten. Directly across from the entrance of the school was a decrepit building with vegetation growing through the windows. Around the corner lay a pile of cars that had been stripped and incinerated. Our school didn't provide any such luxuries as a grass field or even a basketball hoop on the playground for kids to use at recess. The library's book collection was more appropriate for an archeological study than a source for topical information. One day when I stepped into the hall, I saw a police officer jack a fifth-grade Black boy up against the wall, his feet dangling in the air as the officer berated him for allegedly throwing paper in class.

I had one hole in the middle of the chalkboard in my classroom—the kids called it the "bullet hole in the lesson"—and another hole in the ceiling. The first time I noticed the opening in the ceiling near the bank of opaque windows was on a Monday morning when I came back to school after a rainy weekend and found standing water on the floor and all of my students' US history poster-board projects waterlogged. After the second flooding of my room, I got smart and put an industrial-sized garbage can underneath the hole, and it stayed there throughout my years in that classroom, as my work order was never filled.

During my first month of teaching, the tragic attacks of 9/11 changed the nation forever and were closely followed by the government's launching of the war on Afghanistan. I received a graduate degree in education theory that year by witnessing the cynicism of our nation's ability to mobilize armies to bomb people on the other side of the world while refusing to find the money to fix the hole in the ceiling of my classroom or properly care for these children in the shadow of the White House. With the fortune spent to invade the Middle East, but not support our schools, it's appropriate—borrowing from Martin Luther King Jr.—to say that the bombs dropped in Afghanistan exploded in my classroom. It's worth noting that none of the injustices my students faced—including a decrepit building, a lack of supplies, police violence, and segregation—prompted uncritical race theorists to launch a parents' rights movement to ensure Black families' children attended schools they deserved.

The contradiction of living and teaching in the capital of the richest country in the world, one that proclaims to be the freest on earth, and seeing my students left to the policies of "organized abandonment"—as the abolitionist and truth teacher Ruth Wilson Gilmore puts it—taught me about the brutal violence of racial capitalism. I want to underscore that I, like most Black people, didn't learn about systemic racism from CRT; the everyday functioning of the system taught us about inequity. One out of every three Black children live in poverty, nearly three times the rate of white children.[1] US police and courts have made Black kids a target of the mass incarceration system, and as Bryan Stevenson explains in *Just Mercy*, "We've sent a quarter million kids to adult jails and prison to serve long prison terms, some under the age of twelve. For years, we've been the only country in the world that condemns children to life imprisonment without parole; nearly three thousand juveniles have been sentenced to die in prison."[2] School districts with the highest enrollments of students of color receive about $1,800 less per student than districts that serve the fewest students of color.[3]

Although critical race theorists didn't teach me about racism, CRT— along with Black studies, cultural studies, and other antiracist methods for analyzing society—have helped me understand how the conditions my students endured were created and maintained; it wasn't a natural disaster that created the conditions of the poverty, racism, and segregation in the southeast neighborhood of Anacostia in Washington, DC. The Smithsonian explains that the disinvestment from Anacostia stemmed from events surrounding the 1954 *Brown v. Board* Supreme Court case:

> To avoid integration, white families fled to the suburbs, and neighborhoods like Anacostia became predominantly Black communities.
>
> The resulting demographic change led to divestment in the community. Residents experienced a withdrawal of public services and the purposeful devaluing of homes. "And then it became the worst place to go," says Styles.
>
> Urban renewal selectively demolished buildings in Black communities, while racist policies like redlining (a practice of denying loans and other economic services to people and areas deemed a racial risk) restricted housing choices.[4]

This is what honest educators mean when they say systemic racism is real. This historical context clears away the smoke of deception created by uncritical race theorists who suggest that Black people's hardships result from a culture of poverty or a lack of personal responsibility and allows one to see the truth: it was the government-sanctioned policies of disinvestment, devaluing of homes, and redlining that resulted in my experience of teaching at a totally segregated school in an impoverished Black neighborhood.

Yet America has a propensity for being dishonest about its dirty conduct, even when its transgressions leave an obvious "go-home" kind of stain on the fabric of society. The nation has had plenty long to outgrow this habit of lying, something it developed in its youth when it claimed that slavery and democracy were both caring friends, and it shouldn't have to pick one over the other. America is so ashamed to admit the truth of its past that it has created harsh punishments for anyone that reads its diary and discover who, over the years, it has loved and who it has hated. Now there is a distant, hollow gaze in the nation's eyes, a country haunted by its violent past and the buried truths it dares not confront. And when it does get an opportunity to take a look at itself, America turns away from the mirror of remembrance, fearful of the reflection it might find staring back. Today, the country clings to a lie about itself; that it can befriend both avarice and benevolence, both mass incarceration and democracy, both history denial and education, both truthcrime and honesty. The root of this deception lies in America's upbringing, raised since its birth by a deceitful, prosperous elite who actively promoted the notion that bullying and abdication of responsibility were virtues. Thus, the nation persists in its cycle of denial, enabled by the powerful few who continue to act as its guardians.

The problem for uncritical race theorists with allowing students to study the history of people of color is that it illuminates so many social struggles that have envisioned what true freedom could look like, and it casts doubt in the minds of students as to whether our current society is the best we can achieve. My students, for example, have been moved to challenge injustices they see in their communities from reading these words from Ella Baker: "Even if segregation is gone, we will still need to be free; we will still have to see that everyone has a job. Even if we can all vote, if people are still hungry, we will not be free. . . . Remember, we are not fighting for the freedom of the Negro alone, but for the freedom of the human spirit, a larger freedom that encompasses all."[5] Uncritical race theorists are right to fear an honest education. If students were allowed to learn the truth about Ella Baker's radical democratic vision for society and compare it to the one we have now—with the largest prison population in the world and unprecedented wealth inequality—it wouldn't be hard for them to choose which society they would prefer. It is that very process of evaluation that began on a mass scale during the 2020 uprising and led uncritical race theorists to criminalize the truth.

To stay in power, uncritical race theorists require a populace that doesn't investigate its flimsy philosophy too deeply. Black students today who are prohibited from learning about systemic racism and the truth about Black history are susceptible to believing that they and their families are responsible for the deplorable conditions they face in this country. It's a lot easier to enact voter suppression laws, as the GOP has kept busy with, if people don't know the history of disenfranchisement of people of color, or women—and the stories of how they won the right to vote. It's a lot easier for politicians on both sides of the aisle to maintain exorbitant expenditures for war or policing Black neighborhoods—while letting the schools crumble—if people are unaware of the history of antiwar movements or don't know about the inspiring examples of organizing for public safety beyond policing.

We now live in an era defined by the rise of truthcrime laws, and a socialization process is occurring that is attempting to train people to accept the ideas not only that historical truths can be banished from consciousness but also that anyone who remembers them should be punished. The educational gag orders placed on teachers are a particularly heinous attack on academic freedom, free speech, and any discourse on antiracism or social justice. The outlawing of an honest education represents a sharp turn toward authoritarianism in the United States—what Barbara Ransby has even called protofascism. Describing Florida governor Ron DeSantis, Ransby explained, "His militant opposition to any teaching of the Black freedom struggle is also reminiscent of the South African apartheid regime's book banning and curricular and speaker censorship, which limited the circulation of ideas that could undermine the legitimacy of an unjust system."[6]

Truthcrime legislation is not the only obstacle to an honest education. The regular process of schooling has long functioned to quell curiosity and impose subordination. Yet now, with almost half of all students in the United States subjected to some form of truthcrime policy, and billionaires using their wealth to mobilize white people behind book bans and attacks on teachers, it's easy to see why many fear the growing influence of fascism.[7] This kind of heightened educational repression is not only a backlash to the 2020 uprising, or just about helping the GOP win elections, or even mainly about privatizing education. It is imperative to place today's truthcrime laws in the historical context of a country that has outlawed literacy for Black people, burned down many hundreds of Black schools, lynched antiracist teachers, segregated education, used the Red Scare to fire and blacklist thousands of educators, forceably removed children from Native families to subject them to abusive boarding schools (until the Indian Child Welfare Act was finally passed in 1978!), diverted billions of dollars away from schools serving students of color, and other such tyrannical acts. When you take stock of this history, today's turthcrime laws are revealed as part of an effort at epistemicide and a drive to annihilate forms of knowledge and analysis that challenge power relations.

Yet as immense as the challenges we face are, we have a key advantage that has led to incredible victories for truth and justice throughout history: We are many; they are few. The richest 1 percent use their wealth to manipulate the education system, no doubt; but the good news is they are only 1 percent of the population. When we are able to overcome the divisions they try to violently impose on us—using racism, sexism, ableism, xenophobia, transphobia, homophobia, and more—we have a power greater than their hoarded gold. Overcoming those divisions has proven to be the most difficult task for social movements throughout US history, yet there are inspiring examples—if only we were allowed to learn them—of times when the divisions in society broke down and true solidarity defeated wealth and power. That's one of the reasons the struggle for honest education is so essential to broader struggles for social justice.

Building the Teach Truth Movement

Seeking truth is essential, yet the truth alone won't set you free—and being alone with the truth certainly can't set you free. Only collective action, with truth as a guide, can lead to liberation. "Sticks in a bundle are unbreakable," goes the African proverb. When people unite in mighty solidarity, they gain the strength to withstand pressure that would snap them like twigs if they were alone. And it is through this collective struggle that people test their theories about how to create a better world and discover what is true in practice.

However, right now, too many of us resemble the lone brittle twig. To be sure, there are important steps that individuals can take to begin to heal from the violence of organized forgetting—like studying the history of social movements. But the medicine is even more potent if you read those books with a study group and then take action to implement the conclusions of your discussions. It has been my experience that the most profound healing from historical trauma and curricular violence—both for myself as an individual and for the communities I have been a part of—has occurred through collaboration: my union going on strike, my educator colleagues unanimously refusing to administer a high-stakes standardized test, my students walking out of class to demand education funding, or my community protesting to replace police with school psychologists and restorative justice counselors.

Forming a study group is often the best place to start for accessing the collective healing power of remembering. The Zinn Education Project offers a free monthly online class called Teach the Black Freedom Struggle and free study groups on the book *Teaching for Black Lives*. There are many other books that will expand your understanding of the struggles for education, social justice, or liberation as well, such as *Teaching to Transgress* (by bell hooks), *The Black Jacobins* (by C. L. R. James), and *How We Get Free* (edited by Keeanga-Yamahtta Taylor).

Taking the lessons of those books into the #TeachTruth National Day of Action and the ongoing #FreedomToLearn campaign will be vital for overcoming truthcrime legislation. Another good place to start in the struggle for educational justice is participating in Black Lives Matter at School's Week of Action and Year of Purpose initiatives and advocating for the movement's four demands:

1. End "zero tolerance" discipline and implement restorative justice.

2. Hire more Black teachers.

3. Mandate Black history and ethnic studies.

4. Fund counselors, not cops.[8]

Winning these demands as part of a larger struggle to achieve education justice will require those of us in the bottom 99 percent of earners forging the political unity needed to take back the wealth we create from the richest 1 percent. Some imagine this kind of unity occurring by people dropping their demands for racial or gender justice and all simply coming together as workers. But what the Black feminist movement has taught us is that all our struggles are deeply intertwined, and we are strongest when everyone's full humanity is respected and defended. Consider the Combahee River

Collective's "A Black Feminist Statement," which contains some of the most important insights for achieving freedom—a document that was removed by the College Board from the reading requirements of their AP African American studies course when the state of Florida protested. They were clearly frightened by the statement's declaration that "we are actively committed to struggling against racial, sexual, heterosexual, and class oppression, and see as our particular task the development of integrated analysis and practice based upon the fact that the major systems of oppression are interlocking."[9] Their idea of "interlocking"—or what many today call "intersectional"— forms of oppression and identity is fundamental to understanding the ways systemic oppressions work and how we can combat them. As they write, "If Black women were free, it would mean that everyone else would have to be free since our freedom would necessitate the destruction of all the systems of oppression."[10] The Combahee River Collective's Black feminist lesbian politics didn't eschew class—to the contrary, they understood the need to build class struggle to challenge capitalists. But they also understood that true unity could not be achieved among diverse groups of working people where racism, sexism, and heterosexism prevailed.

Creating the political unity needed to achieve educational and social justice requires learning about, and organizing against, all forms of oppression that divide us. It also requires building a Teach Truth movement that directly confronts the wealthiest 1 percent and develops a political consciousness that challenges the textbook corporations, the billion-dollar-a-year College Board organization, the uncritical race theorist politicians, the educational arsonists, the PTCAs, and the billionaires who fund it all.

Achieving social movements robust enough to vie for power with the wealthiest 1 percent will require educators, organizers, and unions to take seriously the radical healing of organized remembering—an essential tool for helping people recover from the curricular violence that has erased so many vital lessons of the past necessary for building healthy social movements today. Be assured that an uprising is coming. When this multiracial movement of educators, students, parents, and organizers rises again—this time with more coordination and experience than the 2020 iteration—these rebels won't be satisfied with simply decriminalizing Black history, repealing the antihistory laws, or merely lifting the book bans. There will be little appetite among the legions of BIPOC youth and their white allies for going back to the normal days of schooling when Black history wasn't banned but was omitted or distorted in the textbooks and by the standardized tests. An educational reckoning is approaching, and honest educators are working to hasten the day of its arrival.

Higher Ground

Lifesaving Education and Liberation

"When I sit before you today and tell you that education, specifically, public education, saved my life, I say that from the deepest parts of my soul," James Whitfield told his class of US representatives at the hearing in May 2022. "If not for public school educators filling some deep holes in my life I don't know where I'd be." Whitfield was expressing unbound admiration for educators whose love had rescued him during his tumultuous high school years. He concluded his congressional seminar by saying,

> Far too often, when mentioning "parents" we've left out the vast major-ity of families who are adamantly standing against these hateful efforts, as witnessed in my journey. They stood in the gap for my family and I during such a chaotic time and we are eternally grateful for their love, compassion, encouragement, and support.
> These concerns are real and have a lasting impact on educators, stu-dents, and families. . . .
> Thank you very much for having me.[11]

Whitfield's pedagogical address to Congress drew on many principles of truth teaching. He became the blues singer, sharing his soul and testifying the truth. He became the healer, promoting the radical healing of organized remembering through his advocacy for honest education about the impact of racism and oppression in our society. He fostered the beloved classroom community by advocating for schools that nurture the social and emotional well-being of students, emphasizing the power of love in education, and by sharing his own experience of a loving community that rose up to defend him when uncritical race theorists came to take his job. He sounded the truth alarm on efforts to mandate lying to students, the privatization of pub-lic education, and the media's false narrative of a grassroots parent move-ment forming in opposition to antiracist education.

When I asked Whitfield if he had any regrets about speaking out to his community on the impact of systemic racism, he replied, "Simple answer to the question—absolutely not." He explained, "I'd do it again in a heartbeat, because it's what we're called to do. We stand on the shoulders of giants. And we must become those same shoulders for those who come behind us to stand on."

During his time away from school, Whitfield spent a great deal of time supporting the Teach Truth movement by consulting with grassroots organizers and school board candidates working to challenge truthcrime laws and policies. After a couple of years out of school, Whitfield has returned to education and has been hired to run an international school in Texas. Despite suffering dearly from attacks by uncritical race theorists, he is, once again, using his broad shoulders to give students a boost so they can see over the wall of truthcrime and work to challenge systemic racism and oppression. Whitfield's crucible reveals the emergency facing America and the power we have in joining together in a struggle.

Without honest accounts of history and the truthful transmission of that history from one generation to the next, all the other rights, once secured by people, can be obscured and then erased—enveloped by the smoke of deception created by educational arsonists. That is why the popular slogan of the Black Lives Matter movement, "Legalize being Black," must be coupled with the demand to "Legalize Black history" if Black lives are to ever truly be valued.

To understand how our movement will win, I invite you into my time machine so I can take you on a trip into the future to see how truthcrime laws are finally struck down. Come with me to this time of overreach by uncritical race theorists: Parents are sick of having to sign permission slips to allow their kids to read a book by a Black author. Students are outraged at seeing classes on Black history cancelled. In the face of mounting discontent, a beloved truth teacher is fired for a lesson about Ida B. Wells-Barnett's campaigns against lynching and systemic racism.

Seizing on this widely publicized story of unjust termination, the Teach Truth movement joins with educator unions to launch an unprecedented uprising for honest education. It begins with collective disobedience by coordinating hundreds of teachers in states that have enacted truthcrime laws to participate in the "Light of Truth Day" where they all teach about Wells-Barnett during the same time. Supported by a vast array of civil rights organizations, this action raises consciousness about the incompatibility of truthcrime laws and democracy. Following this event, unions conduct a popular Teach Truth campaign to educate members and school communities about the history of educator unions organizing with community groups in struggles and strikes for educational and social justice. This campaign leads to the healing of organized remembering for many thousands who collectively participate in a "Legalize Black history" tour to learn about successful movements of the past that have forged multiracial unity and to learn ideas and strategies that could help them end truthcrime laws.

After learning this history, students form a national organization—which many call the new SNCC—and lead walkouts from schools around the country to demand Black studies, ethnic studies, and an end to truthcrime legislation. With so many hundreds of students taking the lead, civil rights organizations and parent organizations join the struggle. This emboldens educator unions, which vote to strike in support. They vow to reopen schools when teaching the truth about US history is legalized. Many social justice organizations and political organizations that previously didn't understand the full potential of multiracial organizing with parents and unionized educators begin to prioritize education as one of the most important sites of struggle. Then, in the same way many people couldn't imagine the Red State Revolt strike wave that shut down every school in many states—and before it happened, couldn't conceive of Republican legislators voting to increase taxes for education—the sudden victory of the Teach Truth movement against truthcrime legislation surprises many.

The many thousands of parents, students, educators, and organizers who helped win these victories then organize a national tour to invite people around the country to spread the healing of organized remembering and learn the lessons of how to struggle and win. One of the key lessons they emphasize is the way they resisted the uncritical race theorists, and education closeters' attempts to divide parents, students, and educators by instilling fear of Black, transgender, and immigrant students. Their triumph against truthcrime laws shows people the power of collective action and of fusing social movements with the economic power of going on strike. Soon, a strike wave sweeps the country among workers in many different sectors of the economy—many of them parents and former students who had participated in the Teach Truth movement—demanding a raise to the minimum wage, student debt forgiveness, affordable housing, universal health care, free child care programs, an

expansion of ethnic studies programs, an end to the policies of mass incarceration, and more. As these movements gain confidence, a new era of rebellion
emerges that ushers in proposals and actions for dismantling systemic racism,
organizing systems based on social justice, and creating an economy that is
democratically controlled by the people who do the work.

There have been many names given to the destination of those seeking
relief from racism and oppression. The poet Phillis Wheatley—who had
been enslaved and kidnapped from West Africa before gaining her freedom and becoming the first African American author to publish a book of
poetry—called the destination "Deliverance": "In every human Breast, God
has implanted a Principle, which we call Love of Freedom; it is impatient
of Oppression, and pants for Deliverance."[12] The great gospel/soul band
The Staple Singers simply called it "a place," in their hit single "I'll Take You
There"—and they told us that in this place no one would smile at us while
they lied to our face. Martin Luther King Jr. called it the "beloved community": "The end is reconciliation; the end is redemption; the end is the creation of the Beloved Community. It is this type of spirit and this type of love
that can transform opponents into friends. It is this type of understanding
goodwill that will transform the deep gloom of the old age into the exuber-
ant gladness of the new age."[13] The Black Panther Party called it socialism;
as member Assata Shakur put it, "Capitalism meant that rich business men
owned the wealth, while socialism meant that the people who made the
wealth owned it." Stevie Wonder called it "Higher Ground," and invited us,
in his sonically soaring refrain, to keep on going until we reach it.

This higher ground is not an isthmus with only room for a few; there is
room for everyone, and you are invited to join us there.

I Can ♥ Breathe

Students' Right to the Radical Healing
of Organized Remembering

While I was writing this book, the state of Florida announced it had banned
thirty-five social studies textbooks and pressured numerous other publishers to censor references to racism. One of the textbook passages that was
eliminated would have taught students that the 2020 uprising for Black

lives had, in fact, occurred, and that it was sparked by the murder of George Floyd. A section of the deleted passage read, "In 2020, bystanders captured video footage of a white Minneapolis police officer killing George Floyd, an unarmed Black American accused of using a counterfeit $20 bill. Floyd's brutal killing horrified many Americans, and protests broke out in cities across the country. While many Americans sympathized with the Black Lives Matter movement, others were critical."[14]

We live in a system that not only killed Floyd but also is attempting to murder his memory. As Walter Benjamin told us, "Not even the dead will be safe from the enemy, if he is victorious."[15] Discovering that Florida was so brazenly attempting to apply the violence of organized forgetting to George Floyd's memory by deleting even this basic reference to his life transported my mind back to my September 2021 visit of the intersection at East 38th Street and Chicago Avenue in Minneapolis, Minnesota—the site of George Floyd Square, a celebration of his life created around the place where he was murdered by police. As my wife and I pulled up to the square that day and I got out of the car, a group of preschool students ambled in front of us, hands clasped together, bravely passing through the memorial to Floyd that spills out of the street and onto the sidewalk.

On the pavement that stretched out beside the children were a seemingly endless list of names of people who had been sacrificed on the altar of American white supremacy. These tender children's feet trod on the many frustrations and aspirations of activists who had inscribed their beliefs onto the sidewalk—graffiti that declared "Black Lives Matter," "Viva la Revolución," "Rest in Power George," and, "We march, y'all mad. We sit down, y'all mad. We speak up, y'all mad. We die, y'all silent." And looming in front of these young scholars was the Cup Foods grocery store—the very spot in front of which Floyd had taken his last breath—cordoned off with barricades painted with handprints (the kind you make in preschool) and colorful text that seemed to take on a sacred significance: "Stop the Violence" and "The People United, Will Never Be Divided."

I stood there weeping, in a state of confusion, as I took in the incomprehensible contrast of these vibrant multiracial fledglings passing through a horrific murder scene where a Black man begged for his mother and pleaded for his life before being choked to death by the weight of a system that bore down on white police officer Derek Chauvin's shoulders as he pressed his knee into Floyd's windpipe.

When the children passed, I sat on one of the benches that activists had erected at the memorial and worked on summoning the courage to approach the spot where Floyd had died. After some time, I made my way to the flower boxes that encircled the very spot where his face had been pressed into the concrete. I stood there for a moment, drinking in the colors and fragrances of the flowers activist gardeners had planted. I then looked past the flower boxes to see that, painted where Floyd's body had lain, was a striking image of blue spirit emerging from a radiant yellow light of truth and the words, "I Can 🖤 Breathe, I Can 🖤 Breathe."

When I looked up from the concrete where Floyd had taken his last breath, I saw a magnificent image painted on plywood and resting against a wall: a bird looking backward, perched atop the Adinkra symbol Sankofa. The beauty of Sankofa—looking to the past for historical lessons in service of moving forward into a better future—may never have been so radiant as it was in that moment. I was thunderstruck in that instant with a question: Should the younglings who were walking past this scene to their preschool be allowed to see the memorial, or should society tie a blindfold over their eyes as they walk by?

Uncritical race theorists would prefer the teachers who walked their children through George Floyd Square that day drown out the echoes of his labored breathing—which still seemed to reverberate in the street as I stood there—by raising their voice to demand that their students unquestioningly pledge themselves to America without critique or criticism. These uncritical race theorists envision a world where when children look down at the writing on the sidewalk and inquire of their teacher, "What does 'Rest in Power George' mean?" the teacher replies, "It means the people love the great founding father of our nation George Washington, who could never tell a lie."

On one level, I can understand the impulse to lie about America and to put blinders on the kids as they walk through their neighborhood; the truth, as James Baldwin remarked, is more terrible than anything anyone has ever said about it. I don't delight in recounting to youth the destruction this country has wrought on the dispossessed, and I know that, especially for young children, these discussions must be approached with sensitivity and in age-appropriate ways. Yet Baldwin also reminded us that our history is also more beautiful than anything anyone has said about it, a reality that is lost on students when the truth is hidden in the smoke of lies.

As I stood there wrestling with these questions, my overwhelm and bewilderment were pierced by a few razor-tipped thoughts: these young people deserve to grow up; they deserve to live a full and joyful life; they deserve to be loved and nurtured by their teachers; and they deserve to be told the truth about where they had walked that day. The books that tell Floyd's story shouldn't be censored, banned, or burned. Moreover, the books and lesson plans that explain how Chauvin was socialized to believe Floyd's life didn't matter should not be purged, but rather promoted.

As I watched the young scholars disappear down the street, I knew—at a level much deeper than just the intellect—that as painful as this memorial was, and as painful as American history can be, these students deserve to see it. They deserve to see it—and to grapple with honest accounts of history—because they deserve to know the immense joy and comradeship that comes from struggling against racism and oppression. They deserve this because they have a right to the radical healing of organized remembering that occurs from learning the exhilarating stories of their ancestors whose creativity and ingenuity achieved beauty despite the ugliness of anti-Blackness. They deserve to be part of a beloved classroom community, an unfettered space for inquiry that answers, with veracity, their questions about what they see in their world.

Students deserve the truth because it is a guide to getting free.

ACKNOWLEDGMENTS

In the course of my dad's research on our family, he discovered a document where my great-great-great-grandfather Caleb Ratcliff (Laura Lenoir's father) wrote his name—and another one where Laura wrote her name. As it was illegal for enslaved people to read or write, it is possible that they defied the law and secretly became literate while they were in bondage. Or they might have learned during the incredible literacy campaigns led by Black educators during Reconstruction. Either way, they passed on their belief in education to my great-grandfather, York Alonzo Lenoir. He attended Alcorn State University (the first Black land-grant college in the United States), became a teacher, and then a principal—just one generation removed from slavery. York then married a teacher and poet named Ivy Anita Darensbourg from Louisiana, and the two of them opened up schools and educated youth throughout the South. This is the miraculous tradition that inspired this book.

Had I been born at any time between 1740 and 1865, it would have been illegal for me to write a book as a Black person in many of the colonies or states—and in all the states, it was often perilous for Black people to pursue writing that challenged the entrenched systems of racism. I, therefore, must begin by acknowledging the generations of freedom fighters who struggled and sacrificed to create the conditions that allowed me to write this book. As well, this book is only possible because of my ancestors—those from Africa who were enslaved and those from Armenia who endured genocide—who bequeathed a spirit of resistance that I am doing my best to pass on to the next generation.

In addition, this book is the result of a lifetime of learning from—and struggling alongside—an incredible community of people, too many to name them all, who are dedicated to eradicating exploitation and injustice and to creating a world designed to nurture, uplift, and meet the needs of people. All of you, named and unnamed in this acknowledgment, have contributed to my radical healing through acts of organized remembering and collective struggle.

I am grateful to the unmatched publishing team at Haymarket Books. Anthony Arnove took a chance on me, gave me the opportunity to write my first full-length book (my previous books are edited volumes), gave me invaluable advice, and encouraged me along the way with a warmth and generosity that made this challenging journey a rewarding experience. Katy O'Donnell was a gift to work with; her edits were insightful, and she taught me a lot about how to structure the argument I wanted to make. Rachel Cohen's cover design clearly embodies what Toni Cade Bambara meant when she said, "The role of the artist is to make the revolution irresistible." I am grateful for Jim Plank and Dana Blanchard's collaboration to help me connect this book with educators, parents, caregivers, and students around the country. Additionally, I am indebted to Lynora Williams, who greatly assisted with the editing process during my most difficult days battling long COVID; I couldn't have completed the book without your support.

Dave Zirin and Michele Bollinger have shown me the power of friendship, encouraged me to write this book when it was first percolating in my mind, and helped me envision what it could be; your mentorship and collaboration have been vital to me finding my voice as an educator, organizer, and writer. As well, I'm forever grateful to my friends, the great truth teachers Sarah Knopp and Jeff Bale, for asking me to write a chapter in their book, *Education and Capitalism: Struggles for Learning and Liberation*—an experience that first helped me realize I could write.

I owe the development of my understanding of the Black freedom struggle to many dear friends and comrades, including Aaron Dixon, Brian Jones, Keeanga-Yamahtta Taylor, Barbara Smith, Jeanne Theoharris, Nikkita Oliver, and Khury Petersen-Smith. Their insights and lifelong pursuits have enriched my understanding of how we are all going to get free.

The thousands of students I have taught and organized with over the years have been my greatest teachers. I'm so thankful for the work of all the youth I've had the honor of connecting with through the Black Education Matters Student Activist Award, the Black Student Union at Garfield High School, and the organizers of New Generation. Some of the many students who have educated me about what the struggle for justice could be include Janelle Gary, Chardonnay Bever, Jelani Howard, Bethel Getu, and Obadiah

Terry; your energy and commitment remind me that history is not something we just study but also something we can actively create.

A special thank you to the board members of the Black Education Matters Student Activist Award: Rita Green, Donte Felder, and Ayva Thomas; your friendship, intellectual engagement, creativity, and bold defense of Black students are an inspiration.

Additionally, I want to thank all the educators, organizers, and mentors I've collaborated with over the years in Seattle who work for social justice and to empower youth, especially Toyia Taylor, Indira Bahner, Tanisha Felder, Delbert Richardson, La TaSha Levy, Ben Secord, Jon Greenberg, Alek'zandr Wray, and the members of the Seattle Caucus of Rank-and-File Educators (SCORE). By supporting youth organizations and educating the next generation of changemakers, you are ensuring the continuation of the struggle.

My heart is full thinking about the Black teachers—from K–12 through college—who showed me the true potential of education, including Mahmoud El-Kati, Leola Johnson, Duchess Harris, Paulette Thompson, Faith Davis, Joe Bland, and Wendell "Two Brick Rick" Hicks.

Several education activists have been particularly important to me as I learned how to organize in national struggles. Chicago Teachers Union president, the late Karen Lewis, was a great joy in my life and an important mentor. Truth teacher and CTU past president Jesse Sharkey has been a dear friend and collaborator who I have gone to with countless questions and campaigns. Diane Ravitch has given her time freely to support local education efforts I've been involved in for years; thank you for your kindness and courage.

Special thank you to these educators whose love and teachings will reside in me forever: my preschool teachers, Randy Salinsky, and Susanne Wickert, and my college professor Clay Steinman.

Loving gratitude to all the comrades at Black Lives Matter at School, who have been an inspiration to me and many thousands of educators around the country, including Denisha Jones, Tamara Anderson, Christopher Rogers, Lisa Covington, Sam Carwyn, Klay Weaver, Nkenge Robertson, Awo Okaikor Aryee-Price, Christopher Rogers, Angela Harris, Ismael Jimenez, and Chanel Hurt. Together we are writing a new chapter in the history of the movement for education justice.

Big ups to all the athletes and organizers in Athletes for Impact; agitating with you all to level the playing field has been some of the most joyful work I have done.

The truthcriminals at Rethinking Schools have been the embodiment of lifelong learning, have showed countless thousands of teachers how to educate to liberate, and have been a catalyst for my intellectual growth; this includes Elizabeth Barbian, Bill Bigelow, Grace Cornell Gonzales, Stan Karp, David Levine, Larry Miller, Bob Peterson, Adam Sanchez, Dyan Watson, Moé Yonamine, Missy Zambor, Lindsay Bullock, and Gina Palazzari. Special thanks to Rethinking Schools editors and friends Wayne Au, Ursula Wolfe-Rocca, and Cierra Kaler-Jones for reading and commenting on early drafts of chapters for this book; all your spirits and insights guide my way. I have endless appreciation for the honest historians and educators of the Zinn Education Project, including Deborah Menkart, Mimi Eisen, Josh Davidson, and Julia Salcedo; your work ensures that the freedom struggles of our past are not disremembered.

Thank you to the many people in the movement for a free Palestine I have worked with over the years who have taught me the meaning of solidarity, including Samia Shoman, Suzanna Kassouf, Jen Marlowe, Jody Sokolower, Ari Bloomekatz, and Emily Siegel; your struggle is a reminder to me that the fight for justice knows no borders.

My friends' support and brilliance have been a guiding light in my life, helping me better understand myself and the world. Daniel Rapport is my day one, and we've been running together since before we could walk; thanks for always reminding me of the good things in life, for helping me not take myself too seriously, and for granting me the great joy of music making. Ian Huntington has been my rock since the third grade; your support has meant more than I can express—thanks for keeping me laughing and learning through it all. I'm grateful to Ben Dalbey for his meticulous reading of early drafts of various chapters of this book and giving me his thoughtful feedback based on a lifetime of reading, organizing, and educating for justice; I'm grateful for our conversations on life, music, and liberation. Shane Dillingham has showed me the value of approaching issues with a spirt of inquisitiveness and has helped me, in difficult circumstances, take my cat to the vet. Nihar Bhatt has taught me how to develop analysis, not only of economics and geopolitics but of my own life and identity—and showed me how to challenge my own assumptions. Thanks to Michael Bennett for teaching me about the beauty of resistance, collaboration, and exquisite designs. Mary Saldin and Miguel Saldin are hall-of-famers; together we navigate the innings of life, rooting for each other through every strikeout and every grand slam; I can hear our children laughing together now and it makes my heart cheer. I want to express my gratitude to musician friends whose music has been the soundtrack to my writing, who rap truth to power, and whose artistry makes the world a more beautiful place, including Kevin James, Boots Riley, and Ben Haggerty. Additionally, the classic album *The Blues and the Abstract Truth* powered the writing of this book. Shoutout to the homies that helped me grow up and still have my back: Rahsaan Green, Damon Leichman, Alex Nord, Eddie Espanol, Melissa Ardavany, and Alex Broz.

Without my family, I wouldn't have had the love and support needed to sustain a project of this magnitude. Sadly, my grandma Sue passed away while I was writing this book. I smile thinking of the conversation we had about my research for the book over cups of tea. I wish she were here to read the final product, and I miss her dearly. I'm grateful for the brilliance and support of my siblings, Jamana, Kolya, and Anna; I have learned so much from each of you—about how the world works and about love and courage. Much love to all the LA fam: cousins Erin and Kylie, cousins Vinnie and Zoe, and Uncle John; life is so much more full with you all on my family all-star team.

My parents have made this book possible by teaching me not to accept the world as it is and to question everything; love and gratitude to Amy, Gerald, Dean, and Steve for this supreme gift. Karen's warmth and laughter is a life preserver in a shipwrecked world. Lucia's voice brings harmony not only to music but to the world around her; the music night hoedowns remind us all of the power of family and joy. Without the care for my children by my mother-in-law, Martha, I would not have been able to write this book; your resilience, warmth, and support are truly uplifting. During the writing of this book, we mourned the loss of my brother-in-law David. He was a deeply talented, sensitive, and creative soul—and, while he is gone, I can still hear us beatboxing together now.

My children, Miles and Satchel, are the most loving, creative, and kind people I could ever hope to know; as well, their speaking truth to power is an inspiration, even if sometimes it is in pursuit of a later bedtime or generally shifting the balance of power in our own home. Shoutout to my cat, Paige (who spent more time with me through the writing process than anyone) for warming my feet with her long fur.

My wife, Sarah, is the harvest moon: the source of light in darkness with the strength to move oceans. She taught me to appreciate my gifts before

I knew how, and she believed in me long before I believed in myself. I am profoundly grateful for our loving partnership and our intellectual engagement. Thank you for your vision and execution. Thank you for supporting me through my battle with long COVID and providing emotional and physical labor for our family—this book wouldn't have been possible without you. Our world is deeply troubled, but journeying through it with you feels like dancing at the club on old-school hip-hop night.

Notes

Epigraph

University of Virginia School of Education and Human Development, "Septima Clark," Educating for Democracy, https://educatingfordemocracy. education.virginia.edu/sites/educatingfordemocracy/files/2020-11/Septima_Clark.pdf.

Introduction: Truthcrime and Uncritical Race Theory versus the Beloved Classroom Community

1. "Censored Teachers Speak Out: Stories from the Fight to Teach Truth," hosted by Rethinking Schools, YouTube, video, September 26, 2023, https:// www.youtube.com/watch?v=fsvtbFAW0jI.
2. James Whitfield, "Testimony: In the Crosshairs of Public Education's Enemies," *Facing South*, May 24, 2022, https://www.facingsouth.org/2022/05/ testimony-crosshairs-public-educations-enemies.
3. Brian Lopez, "How a Black High School Principal Was Swept Into a 'Critical Race Theory' Maelstrom in a Mostly White Texas Suburb," *Texas Tribune*, September 18, 2021, https://www.texastribune.org/2021/09/18/colleyville-principal-critical-race-theory/.
4. Andrew Lawrence, "'Our Job Is to Present the Truth': The Texas Principal Caught in a 'Critical Race Theory' Firestorm," *Guardian*, January 13, 2022, https://www.theguardian.com/us-news/2022/jan/13/texas-principal-critical-race-theory.
5. Lawrence, "'Our Job Is to Present the Truth.'"
6. Scott Gordon and Chris Blake, "Grapevine-Colleyville ISD Trustees Vote to Move Forward with Process of Firing Whitfield," NBC DFW, September 21, 2021, https://www.nbcdfw.com/news/local/grapevine-colleyville-isd-school-board-to-vote-on-whitfields-future/2747298/.

7. Hannah Natanson and Moriah Balingit, "Caught in the Culture Wars, Teachers Are Being Forced from Their Jobs," *Washington Post*, June 16, 2022, https://www.washingtonpost.com/education/2022/06/16/teacher-resignations-firings-culture-wars/.

8. Anya Kamenetz, "School Boards Are Asking for Federal Help as They Face Threats and Violence," NPR, September 30, 2021, https://www.npr.org/sections/back-to-school-live-updates/2021/09/30/1041870027/school-boards-federal-help-threats-violence.

9. Daniel Villarreal, "Death Threats and Fights Over Critical Race Theory Have Driven at Least Six Educators to Resign," *Newsweek*, July 14, 2021, https://www.newsweek.com/death-threats-fights-over-critical-race-theory-have-driven-least-six-educators-resign-1609461.

10. Kyle Reinhard, "CRT Forward Releases New Report on Anti-CRT Measures and Trends," *CRT Forward*, April 6, 2023, https://crtforward.law.ucla.edu/new-crt-forward-report-highlights-trends-in-2021-2022-anti-crt-measures/.

11. Beth Hawkins, "Two-Thirds of Teachers Censor Themselves Even When They Don't Have To," The 74, February 15, 2024, https://www.the74million.org/article/new-study-two-thirds-of-teachers-censor-themselves-even-when-they-dont-have-to/.

12. Andrew Albanese, "EveryLibrary Poll Finds Book Bans Are Broadly Unpopular with Voters," *Publishers Weekly*, September 19, 2022, https://www.publishersweekly.com/pw/by-topic/industry-news/libraries/article/90365-everylibrary-poll-finds-book-bans-are-broadly-unpopular-with-voters.html.

13. Sarah D. Sparks, "How These Teachers Build Curriculum 'Beyond Black History,'" *Education Week*, April 15, 2024, https://www.edweek.org/teaching-learning/how-these-teachers-build-curriculum-beyond-black-history/2024/04.

14. Quinnipiac University Poll, "66% Say History Lessons Fell Short on Role of African Americans, Quinnipiac University National Poll Finds; Nearly 4 in 10 Have Family or Friends They Consider Racist," news release, February 17, 2022, https://poll.qu.edu/poll-release?releaseid=3836.

15. Jacey Fortin, "Critical Race Theory: A Brief History," *New York Times*, November 8, 2021, https://www.nytimes.com/article/what-is-critical-race-theory.html.

16. Suggested reading to understand critical race theory: Victor Ray, *On Critical Race Theory: Why It Matters & Why You Should Care* (New York: Random House Publishing Group, 2023); Gloria Ladson-Billings, *Critical Race Theory in Education: A Scholar's Journey* (New York: Teachers College Press, 2021); Gary Peller, Kendall Thomas, Kimberlé Crenshaw, and Neil Gotanda, eds., *Critical Race Theory: The Key Writings That Formed the Movement* (New York: New Press, 1995).

17. Jennifer C. Berkshire and Jack Schneider, *The Education Wars: A Citizen's Guide and Defense Manual* (New York: New Press, 2024), 55.

18. Logan M. Davis, "Davis: American Birthright: A Woodland Park

Investigation," *Colorado Times Recorder,* July 10, 2023, https://coloradotimes-recorder.com/2023/07/davis-american-birthright-a-woodland-park-investi-gation/54661/.

19. Joseph McQuade, "Colonialism Was a Disaster and the Facts Prove It," Con-versation, September 26, 2017, https://theconversation.com/colonialism-was-a-disaster-and-the-facts-prove-it-84496.

20. Georgina Rannard and Eve Webster, "Leopold II: Belgium 'Wakes Up' to Its Bloody Colonial Past," BBC, June 12, 2020, https://www.bbc.com/news/world-europe-53017188.

21. Lauren Kent, "European Colonizers Killed So Many Native Americans That It Changed the Global Climate, Researchers Say," CNN, February 2, 2019, https://www.cnn.com/2019/02/01/world/european-colonization-cli-mate-change-trnd/index.html.

22. Civics Alliance, *American Birthright: The Civics Alliance's Model K–12 Social Studies Standards,* July 2022, https://civicsalliance.org/wp-content/up-loads/2023/01/AmericanBirthright.pdf.

23. James Baldwin, *The Price of the Ticket: Collected Nonfiction: 1948–1985* (Bos-ton: Beacon Press, 2021), 100.

24. David Paul, "The GOP Fiddles as Trump Rips Apart the Fabric of the Nation," *HuffPost,* September 1, 2017, https://www.huffpost.com/entry/gop-fiddles-as-trump-rips-apart-the-fabric-of-the-nation_b_59a99cb8e4b-0bef3378cd836.

25. CBS News, "'I Forgot He Was Black' Fuels Controversy," CBS News, January 29, 2010, https://www.cbsnews.com/news/i-forgot-he-was-black-fuels-con-troversy/.

26. Noelle Swan, "Discussing Race: The Pitfalls of Racial Colorblindness and the Importance of Talk," *Christian Science Monitor,* May 24, 2013, https://www.cs-monitor.com/The-Culture/Family/Modern-Parenthood/2013/0524/Discuss-ing-Race-The-pitfalls-of-racial-colorblindness-and-the-importance-of-talk.

27. Kevin McCarthy, "Critical Race Theory Goes Against Everything Mar-tin Luther King Jr. Taught Us—to Not Judge Others by the Color of Their Skin," X, July 12, 2021, 5:40 p.m., https://x.com/GOPLeader/sta-tus/1414701336520798219?s=20.

28. Michelle Garcia, "3 Often Forgotten Parts from Martin Luther King's 'I Have a Dream' Speech," *Vox,* January 17, 2019, https://www.vox.com/2016/1/18/10785618/martin-luther-king-dream-speech.

29. Kimberlé Williams Crenshaw, "Op-Ed: King Was a Critical Race Theorist Before There Was a Name for It," *Los Angeles Times,* January 17, 2022, https://www.latimes.com/opinion/story/2022-01-17/critical-race-theory-martin-luther-king.

30. Noelle Trent, "...They Had No Rights Which the White Man Was Bound to Respect...," *Black Perspectives,* January 2, 2015, https://www.aaihs.org/they-had-no-rights-which-the-white-man-was-bound-to-respect/.

31. Michelle Alexander, *The New Jim Crow: Mass Incarceration in the Age of*

Colorblindness (New York: New Press, 2010), 31.

32. Alexander, *New Jim Crow*, 24–25.
33. Frederick Douglass, *My Bondage and My Freedom* (London: Partridge and Oakey, 1855), Lit2Go, https://etc.usf.edu/lit2go/45/my-bondage-and-my-freedom/1493/chapter-20-apprenticeship-life/.
34. Gloria Ladson-Billings, *Critical Race Theory in Education: A Scholar's Journey* (New York: Teachers College Press, 2021), 44–45.
35. Stuart Hall, "Race, The Floating Signifier," speech, 1997, Media Education Foundation, https://www.mediaed.org/transcripts/Stuart-Hall-Race-the-Floating-Signifier-Transcript.pdf.
36. Kevin K. Kumashiro, *Surrendered: Why Progressives Are Losing the Biggest Battles in Education* (New York, NY: Teachers College Press, 2020), 32.
37. "Prisoners at Home: Everyday Life in Japanese Internment Camps," Digital Public Library of America, https://dp.la/exhibitions/japanese-internment/education-sports/programs_instructors.
38. Valerie Strauss, "Texas GOP Rejects 'Critical Thinking' Skills. Really," *Washington Post*, July 9, 2012, https://www.washingtonpost.com/blogs/answer-sheet/post/texas-gop-rejects-critical-thinking-skills-really/2012/07/08/gJQAHNpFXW_blog.html.
39. Larry Buchanan, Quoctrung Bui, and Jugal K. Patel, "Black Lives Matter May Be the Largest Movement in U.S. History," *New York Times*, July 3, 2020, https://www.nytimes.com/interactive/2020/07/03/us/george-floyd-protests-crowd-size.html.
40. Hannah Natanson, "High School Students Are Demanding Schools Teach More Black History, Include More Black Authors," *Washington Post*, August 17, 2020, https://www.washingtonpost.com/local/education/high-schoolers-across-the-country-are-banding-together-to-demand-their-schools-teach-more-black-history-and-read-more-black-authors/2020/08/15/a42e6d12-dbef-11ea-809e-b8be57ba616e_story.html.
41. Mark Keierleber, "Federal Data Shows a Drop in Campus Cops, for Now," The 74, January 19, 2024, https://www.the74million.org/article/federal-data-shows-a-drop-in-campus-cops-for-now/.
42. Nikole Hannah-Jones, ed., "The 1619 Project," *New York Times*, August 14, 2019, https://www.nytimes.com/interactive/2019/08/14/magazine/1619-america-slavery.html.
43. Donald J. Trump, "Remarks by President Trump at the White House Conference on American History," September 17, 2020, https://trumpwhitehouse.archives.gov/briefings-statements/remarks-president-trump-white-house-conference-american-history/.
44. Glenn Kessler, Salvador Rizzo, and Meg Kelly, "Trump's False or Misleading Claims Total 30,573 over 4 Years," *Washington Post*, January 24, 2021, https://www.washingtonpost.com/politics/2021/01/24/trumps-false-or-misleading-claims-total-30573-over-four-years/.

45. African American Policy Forum, "From Freedom Riders to Freedom Readers: Books Unbanned," Books Unbanned, http://booksunbanned.org/our-why/.

46. Luona Lin, Juliana Menasce Horowitz, Kiley Hurst, and Dana Braga, "3. What Teens Want to Learn about Race and LGBTQ Issues," Pew Research Center, February 22, 2024, https://www.pewresearch.org/social-trends/2024/02/22/what-teens-want-to-learn-in-school-about-race-and-lgbtq-issues/.

47. Terry Gross, "From Slavery to Socialism, New Legislation Restricts What Teachers Can Discuss," NPR, *Fresh Air*, February 3, 2022, https://www.npr.org/2022/02/03/1077878538/legislation-restricts-what-teachers-can-discuss.

48. "#TeachTruth Syllabus," Zinn Education Project, January 1, 2023, https://www.zinnedproject.org/news/teachtruth-syllabus/.

49. Editors of Rethinking Schools, "Right-Wing Legislators Are Trying to Stop Us from Teaching for Racial Justice. We Refuse," *Rethinking Schools* 35, no. 4, (Summer 2021), https://rethinkingschools.org/articles/right-wing-legislators-are-trying-to-stop-us-from-teaching-for-racial-justice-we-refuse/.

50. Mead Gruver, "Utah Is the Latest State to Ban Diversity, Equity and Inclusion Efforts on Campus and in Government," Associated Press, January 30, 2024, https://apnews.com/article/utah-government-college-university-dei-cox-efdf4862d8a2b96d28606dcb8ce30ca8.

51. Kim Bellware, "Florida Law Blasted After Permission Slip Sent to Hear Black Author's Book," *Washington Post*, February 15, 2024, https://www.washingtonpost.com/education/2024/02/15/florida-book-permission-slip-black-author/.

52. Nadra Nittle, "Florida Education Officials Say These Women Benefited from Slavery. Here's the Truth," *The 19th*, July 26, 2023, https://19thnews.org/2023/07/women-slavery-benefits-florida-department-of-education/.

53. Joan Walsh, "Florida Teachers Hide Their Books to Avoid Felonies," *Nation*, February 1, 2023, https://www.thenation.com/article/politics/book-bans-florida-public-schools/.

54. "Arkansas Tries to Ban Teaching People's History, Again," Zinn Education Project, April 29, 2021, https://www.zinnedproject.org/news/arkansas-ban-peoples-history-again/.

55. Adam Gabbatt, "Outrage as Republican Says That 1921 Tulsa Massacre Not Motivated by Race," *Guardian*, July 8, 2023, https://www.theguardian.com/us-news/2023/jul/08/oklahoma-republican-tulsa-race-massacre.

56. Daniel Villarreal, "Nevada Family Alliance Wants Teachers to Wear Body Cameras to Keep Critical Race Theory Out of Schools," *Newsweek*, June 10, 2021, https://www.newsweek.com/nevada-family-alliance-wants-teachers-wear-body-cameras-keep-critical-race-theory-out-schools-1599233.

57. James Bikales, "Okla. Downgrades School District over Complaint It Shamed White People," *Washington Post*, July 30, 2022, https://www.washingtonpost.com/education/2022/07/30/crt-oklahoma-tulsa-schools-shame-white/.

58. Andrew Atterbury, "Miami-Dade School Board Rejects LGBTQ History Month over Fears It Violates 'Don't Say Gay,'" *Politico*, September 7, 2022,

https://www.politico.com/news/2022/09/07/miami-dade-school-board-spars-over-lgbtq-history-month-recognition-00055368.

59. Movement Advancement Project, "LGBTQ Curricular Laws," July 19, 2024, https://www.lgbtmap.org/equality-maps/curricular_laws.

60. Movement Advancement Project, "Bans on Transgender Youth Participation in Sports," July 19, 2024, https://www.lgbtmap.org/equality-maps/youth/sports_participation_bans.

61. Libby Stanford, "Political Tensions in Schools Are 'Pervasive,' Principals Say," *Education Week*, November 30, 2022, https://www.edweek.org/leadership/political-tensions-in-schools-are-pervasive-say-principals/2022/11.

62. Taifha Alexander, LaToya Baldwin Clark, Kyle Reinhard, and Noah Zatz, "Tracking the Attack on Critical Race Theory," *CRT Forward*, April 6, 2023, https://crtforward.law.ucla.edu/wp-content/uploads/2023/04/UCLA-Law_CRT-Report_Final.pdf

63. Reinhard, "CRT Forward Releases New Report."

64. Jeffrey Sachs, "Steep Rise in Gag Orders, Many Sloppily Drafted," PEN America, January 24, 2022, https://pen.org/steep-rise-gag-orders-many-sloppily-drafted/.

65. Alexander et al., "Tracking the Attack."

66. Zachary Schermele, "Teachers Say in New Survey They're Being Told Not to Talk about Racism and Race," NBC News, August 11, 2022, https://www.nbcnews.com/news/latino/new-survey-teachers-say-re-told-not-talk-racism-race-rcna42457.

67. Gary Burnett, "The Blues, Honesty and Truth," *Down at the Crossroads*, August 5, 2019, https://downatthecrossroads.wordpress.com/2019/08/05/the-blues-honesty-and-truth/.

68. William Randolph Scott, *Upon These Shores: Themes in the African-American Experience, 1600 to the Present* (New York: Routledge, 2000), 262.

69. Bonni McKeown, "Blues for the 99 Percent," *Street Spirit*, August 14, 2015, https://thestreetspirit.org/2015/08/14/blues-for-the-99-percent/.

70. Monique W. Morris, *Sing a Rhythm, Dance a Blues: Education for the Liberation of Black and Brown Girls* (New York: New Press, 2022), 7.

71. Jonathan Sumption, "The Death of Historical Truth," *UnHerd*, March 1, 2023, https://unherd.com/2023/03/the-death-of-historical-truth/.

72. Mildred Lewis Rutherford, *Truths of History: A Fair, Unbiased, Impartial, Unprejudiced and Conscientious Study of History* (Athens, GA: Mildred Lewis Rutherford, 1920), https://archive.org/stream/measuringrodtot00ruth/measuringrodtot00ruth_djvu.txt.

73. Kerry Walters, *Harriet Tubman: A Life in American History* (Santa Barbara, CA: ABC-CLIO, 2019), 92.

74. Wayne Au, *A Marxist Education: Learning to Change the World* (Chicago: Haymarket Books, 2018), 181, 184.

75. Au, *A Marxist Education*, 185.

76. Au, *A Marxist Education*, 186–87.

77. Barsamian, David, "Zinn on Growing Up, Objectivity, Bombing, Media, Genocide, and Propaganda," Zcommunications, November 1, 2002, https://www.howardzinn.org/collection/zinn-on-growing-up-bombing-media-genocide-and-propaganda/.

78. Ira Shor, *Empowering Education: Critical Teaching for Social Change* (Chicago: University of Chicago Press, 1992), 12–13.

79. Doug Davison, "George Carlin: A Master of Whimsical Philosophy," *Houston Herald*, January 23, 2024, https://houstonherald.com/2024/01/george-carlin-a-master-of-whimsical-philosophy/.

80. Bobbi Cieciorka and Frank Cieciorka, *Negroes in American History: A Freedom Primer* (Atlanta, GA: Student Voice, 1965), Civil Rights Movement Archive https://www.crmvet.org/docs/negro_history_primer.pdf.

81. Robin D. G. Kelley, *Freedom Dreams: The Black Radical Imagination* (Boston: Beacon Press, 2002), 157.

82. Robert Gebeloff, Danielle Ivory, Bill Marsh, Allison McCann, and Albert Sun, "Childhood's Greatest Danger: The Data on Kids and Gun Violence," *New York Times*, December 18, 2022, https://www.nytimes.com/interactive/2022/12/14/magazine/gun-violence-children-data-statistics.html.

83. Kayla Jimenez, "Lead in School Water Persists in U.S. Despite Work to Fix the Problem. What Can Be Done?," *USA Today*, February 23, 2023, https://www.usatoday.com/story/news/education/2023/02/23/lead-persists-us-schools-despite-attempts-fix/11316247002/.

84. Mark Lieberman, "America's School Buildings Are Crumbling, and It's a 'National Security Issue,'" *Education Week*, March 28, 2023, https://www.edweek.org/leadership/americas-school-buildings-are-crumbling-and-its-a-national-security-issue/2023/03.

85. James Baldwin, "Nothing Personal," *Contributions in Black Studies* 6, Article 5 (2008), https://scholarworks.umass.edu/cgi/viewcontent.cgi?article=1042&context=cibs.

86. bell hooks, *Teaching Critical Thinking* (New York: Routledge, 2010), 162–63.

87. James Whitfield, "Testimony: In the Crosshairs of Public Education's Enemies," *Facing South*, May 24, 2022, https://www.facingsouth.org/2022/05/testimony-crosshairs-public-educations-enemies.

88. "Teachers Defy GOP Bans on History Lessons," Zinn Education Project, May 15, 2023, https://www.zinnedproject.org/news/teachers-defy-gop-bans-on-history-lessons/.

Chapter 1: Educational Arson, Epistemicide, and Organized Forgetting

"Responses by Freedom Summer School Students to the Burning of Their School, August 10, 1964," Civil Rights Movement Archive, https://www.

crmvet.org/docs/640810_fs_bomb-responses.pdf.

bell hooks, *Teaching Critical Thinking* (New York: Routledge, 2010).

1. Alexandra Hutzler, "Ted Cruz Says Critical Race Theory Is 'Every Bit as Racist as Klansmen in White Sheets,'" *Newsweek*, June 18, 2021, https://www.newsweek.com/ted-cruz-says-critical-race-theory-every-bit-racist-klansmen-white-sheets-1602105.

2. Malcolm X, "Malcolm X's Speech at the OAAU Founding Rally (June 28, 1964)," ICIT Digital Library, https://www.icit-digital.org/articles/malcolm-x-s-speech-at-the-oaau-founding-rally-june-28-1964.

3. Henry A. Giroux, *The Violence of Organized Forgetting: Thinking beyond America's Disimagination Machine* (San Francisco: City Lights Publishers, 2014).

4. Henry A. Giroux, "The Violence of Organized Forgetting," *Truthout*, July 22, 2013, https://truthout.org/articles/the-violence-of-organized-forgetting/.

5. Char Adams, "Here's What Black Students Have to Say about 'Critical Race Theory' Bans," NBC News, September 1, 2021, https://www.nbcnews.com/news/nbcblk/s-black-students-say-critical-race-theory-bans-rcna1862.

6. Clarence Lusane, *Twenty Dollars and Change: Harriet Tubman and the Ongoing Fight for Racial Justice and Democracy* (San Francisco: City Lights Books, 2022), 252.

7. "SPLC Launches Third Edition of Its 'Whose Heritage?' Report Tracking Confederate Memorials and Their Removals across the U.S.," Southern Poverty Law Center, February 1, 2022, https://www.splcenter.org/presscenter/splc-launches-third-edition-its-whose-heritage-report-tracking-confederate-memorials-and; Evie Blad, "More States Push Schools to Drop Native American Mascots," *Education Week*, November 28, 2022, https://www.edweek.org/leadership/more-states-push-schools-to-drop-native-american-mascots/2022/11.

8. Kevin Sullivan and Lori Rozsa, "DeSantis Doubles Down on Claim That Some Blacks Benefited from Slavery," *Washington Post*, July 22, 2023, https://www.washingtonpost.com/politics/2023/07/22/desantis-slavery-curriculum/.

9. Cynthia Greenlee, "How History Textbooks Reflect America's Refusal to Reckon with Slavery," *Vox*, August 26, 2019, https://www.vox.com/identities/2019/8/26/20829771/slavery-textbooks-history.

10. Victoria Bekiempis, "Fourth-grade Textbook Saying Slaves Were 'Like Family' Pulled from Connecticut School District," *New York Daily News*, December 7, 2016, https://www.nydailynews.com/2016/12/07/fourth-grade-textbook-saying-slaves-were-like-family-pulled-from-connecticut-school-district/.

11. Tom Dart, "Textbook Passage Referring to Slaves as 'Workers' Prompts Outcry," *Guardian*, October 5, 2015, https://www.theguardian.com/education/2015/oct/05/mcgraw-hill-textbook-slaves-workers-texas.

12. Daniel Martinez HoSang, *A Wider Type of Freedom: How Struggles for Racial Justice Liberate Everyone* (Berkeley: University of California Press, 2023), 2.

13. Hannah Natanson and Laura Meckler, "Red States Strike Deals to Show Controversial Conservative Videos in Schools," *Washington Post*, June 13, 2024, https://www.washingtonpost.com/education/2024/06/13/prageru-conservative-education-videos/.

14. "Frederick Douglass: The Outspoken Abolitionist," PragerU, September 10, 2021, https://www.prageru.com/video/leo-and-laylas-history-adventures-with-frederick-douglass.

15. Frederick Douglass, "What, to the Slave, Is the Fourth of July," speech, July 5, 1852, Rochester, NY, transcript, Black Past, January 24, 2007, https://www.blackpast.org/african-american-history/speeches-african-american-history/1852-frederick-douglass-what-slave-fourth-july/.

16. Mike Hixenbaugh, *They Came for the Schools: One Town's Fight Over Race and Identity, and the New War for America's Classrooms* (New York: Mariner, 2024), 98.

17. House Bill 2988, 58th Leg., 2nd Sess. (Okla. 2022), https://legiscan.com/OK/text/HB2988/2022.

18. American History Association, "AHA Sends Letter Opposing Oklahoma Bill That Would Limit Teaching of Race and Slavery in America (December 2021)," American Historical Association, December 22, 2021, https://www.historians.org/news/aha-letter-opposing-oklahoma-bill-that-would-limit-teaching-of-race-and-slavery-in-america/.

19. Kate Shuster, *Teaching Hard History: American Slavery* (Southern Poverty Law Center, 2018), 14, https://www.splcenter.org/sites/default/files/tt_hard_history_american_slavery.pdf.

20. Cory Collins, "Queer People Have Always Existed—Teach Like It," *Learning for Justice*, March 15, 2021, https://www.learningforjustice.org/magazine/queer-people-have-always-existed-teach-like-it.

21. Annika Butler-Wall, Kim Cosier, Rachel L. S. Harper, Jeff Sapp, Jody Sokolower, and Melissa Bollow Tempel, eds., *Rethinking Sexism, Gender, and Sexuality* (Milwaukee: Rethinking Schools, 2016), 20.

22. Micaela Wells, "In My Advanced High School History Textbook, It's as If Women Didn't Exist," *Washington Post*, January 1, 2022, https://www.washingtonpost.com/opinions/2022/01/01/advanced-placement-history-textbook-women/.

23. Andrew C. Holcom, "Misrepresentation as Complicity: The Genocide Against Indigenous Americans in High School History Textbooks" (master's thesis, Western Washington University, 2010), https://doi.org/10.25710/hwvw-6t38.

24. Philip Lee-Shanok, "GTA Book Publisher Accused of Whitewashing Indigenous History," CBC News, October 5, 2017, https://www.cbc.ca/news/canada/toronto/childrens-textbook-includes-inaccurate-account-of-indigenous-history-1.4315945.

25. Deepa Shivaram, "Textbook That Asked If Treatment of Native Americans Was 'Exaggerated' Is Recalled," NPR, October 26, 2021, https://www.

npr.org/2021/10/26/1049264026/textbook-treatment-native-ameri-
cans-exaggerated-recalled-hodder.

26. Ileana Najarro, "Is a Comprehensive U.S. History Course Still Possible?
Scholars Weigh In," *Education Week*, November 16, 2022, https://www.
edweek.org/teaching-learning/is-a-comprehensive-u-s-history-course-still-
possible-scholars-weigh-in/2022/11.

27. Sarah Schwartz, "Latino History Is U.S. History. High School Textbooks
Neglect It," *Education Week*, May 16, 2023, https://www.edweek.org/teach-
ing-learning/latino-history-is-u-s-history-high-school-textbooks-neglect-
it/2023/05.

28. Elizabeth Martínez, "How California Texts Portray Latinos: When Slavery
Is a 'Life-style,' What Happens to Mexicans?," *Rethinking Schools* 7, no. 2
(Winter 1992/1993), https://rethinkingschools.org/articles/how-califor-
nia-texts-portray-latinos/.

29. Aliza Chasan, "NAACP Issues Travel Advisory in Florida, Says State 'Hostile'
to Black Americans," CBS News, May 20, 2023, https://www.cbsnews.com/
news/naacp-travel-advisory-florida-says-state-hostile-to-black-americans/.

30. Steve Peoples and Brendan Farrington, "DeSantis Booed at Vigil for Jacksonville Shooting Victims," PBS *NewsHour*, August 29, 2023, https://www.pbs.org/
newshour/politics/desantis-booed-at-vigil-for-jacksonville-shooting-victims.

31. Peoples and Farrington, "DeSantis Booed at Vigil."

32. "Jacksonville Shootings: Historically Black Colleges Address Security
Concerns," NBC News, August 28, 2023, https://www.nbcnews.com/news/
nbcblk/jacksonville-shootings-historically-black-colleges-address-securi-
ty-co-rcna102769.

33. "The Burning of Books," The History Place, 2001, https://www.historyplace.
com/worldwar2/triumph/tr-bookburn.htm.

34. "Those Who Burn Books Will in the End Burn People,' Warn Jewish, Muslim
Communities in Sweden," *Middle East Monitor*, January 26, 2023, https://
www.middleeastmonitor.com/20230126-those-who-burn-books-will-in-
the-end-burn-people-warn-jewish-muslim-communities-in-sweden/.

35. Octavia Butler, *Parable of the Sower* (New York: Grand Central Publishing,
2023).

36. Steve Russell, "Early Indigenous Peoples and Written Language," *ICT*, September 13, 2018, https://ictnews.org/archive/early-indigenous-peoples-writ-
ten-language.

37. Boaventura de Sousa Santos, *Epistemologies of the South: Justice Against Epistemicide* (New York: Routledge, 2014), 92.

38. Gillian Brockell, "Burning Books: Six Outrageous, Tragic and Weird Examples in History," *Washington Post*, November 13, 2021, https://www.washing-
tonpost.com/history/2021/11/13/book-burning-history/.

39. "November 26, 1935: NYC Burns 'Tons' of Books," Today in Civil Liberties
History, http://todayinclh.com/?event=nyc-burns-tons-of-books.

40. "March 31, 1950: US Seizes, Burns 3,000 Copies of 'Scientific American,'" Today in Civil Liberties History, http://todayinclh.com/?event=u-s-seizes-burns-3000-copies-of-scientific-american.

41. "Responses by Freedom Summer School Students."

42. Interview with Charles Cobb conducted by Jesse Hagopian on July 27, 2002.

43. Meagan Day, "This Violent 1974 Clash over Textbooks in West Virginia Prepped the Nation for a New Right Movement," *Medium*, January 24, 2017, https://medium.com/timeline/this-violent-1974-clash-over-textbooks-in-west-virginia-prepped-the-nation-for-a-new-right-movement-a94a2245743f.

44. Trey Kay, Deborah George, and Stan Bumgardner, *The Great Textbook War*, "Books and Beliefs: The Kanawha County Textbook Wars," American Radio-Works, June 1, 2010, http://americanradioworks.publicradio.org/features/textbooks/books_and_beliefs.html.

45. Zack Budryk, "Kanawha County Textbook War: The History of a 1970s Fight Over Books in Schools," *Teen Vogue*, October 5, 2023, https://www.teen-vogue.com/story/kanawha-county-textbook-war-history.

46. Brenna Daldorph, "'Two Thousand Black Churches Burned Between 1995-2005, but No One Paid Attention,'" *The Observers*, July 21, 2015, https://observers.france24.com/en/20150702-usa-church-burning-arson-black-emanuel.

47. PBS, "Black Church Burnings," PBS, *This Far by Faith*, n.d., https://www.pbs.org/thisfarbyfaith/journey_5/p_4.html.

48. Eric Harrison, "216 Church Attacks Investigated Since '90," *Los Angeles Times*, June 20, 1996, https://www.latimes.com/archives/la-xpm-1996-06-20-mn-16721-story.html.

49. Bess Levin, "Conservatives Are Just Openly Endorsing Book Burning Now," *Vanity Fair*, November 11, 2021, https://www.vanityfair.com/news/2021/11/virginia-school-board-book-burning.

50. Joe Hernandez and Bill Chappell, "New Bomb Threats Disrupt Campus Activities at Several HBCUs," NPR, February 1, 2022, https://www.npr.org/2022/01/31/1077000576/hbcu-howard-bomb-threat-lockdown.

51. Gerrard Kaonga, "Tennessee Rep. Jerry Sexton Vows to Burn Banned Books," *Newsweek*, April 29, 2022, https://www.newsweek.com/jerry-sexton-tennessee-representative-banned-book-book-burning-library-1702072.

52. Kacen Bayless, "Republican Candidate for Missouri Governor Vows to Burn Books After Viral Flamethrower Video," *Kansas City Star*, September 18, 2023, https://news.yahoo.com/republican-candidate-missouri-governor-vows-174700455.html.

53. Kelly Jensen, "Another Round of Public Library Bomb Threats," Book Riot, January 11, 2024, https://bookriot.com/minnesota-library-bomb-threats/.

54. Diane Ravitch, "David C. Berliner on Censorship," *Diane Ravitch's Blog*, November 30, 2022, https://dianeravitch.net/2022/11/30/david-c-berliner-on-censorship/.

55. Cornel West, *Race Matters* (Boston: Beacon Press, 2001), vii.

56. Adams, "What Black Students Have to Say."

57. C. L. R. James, *Black Jacobins: Toussaint L'Ouverture and the San Domingo Revolution* (New York: Vintage Books), 17.

58. Peter H. Wood, *The Black Majority: Negroes in Colonial South Carolina from 1670 through the Stono Rebellion* (New York: W. W. Norton & Company, 1974), 324.

59. Jarvis R. Givens, *Fugitive Pedagogy: Carty G. Woodson and the Art of Black Teaching* (Cambridge, MA: Harvard University Press, 2021), 11.

60. Matthew Desmond, "In Order to Understand the Brutality of American Capitalism, You Have to Start on the Plantation," *New York Times*, August 14, 2019, https://www.nytimes.com/interactive/2019/08/14/magazine/slavery-capitalism.html.

61. David Walker, *David Walker's Appeal* (Boston: Printed by David Walker, 1829), accessed July 28, 2024, https://docsouth.unc.edu/nc/walker/walker.html.

62. Heather Andrea Williams, *Self-Taught: African American Education in Slavery and Freedom* (Chapel Hill, NC: University of North Carolina Press, 2005), 14.

63. Quoted in editors of Rethinking Schools, "Right-Wing Legislators Are Trying to Stop Us from Teaching for Racial Justice. We Refuse," *Rethinking Schools*, https://rethinkingschools.org/articles/right-wing-legislators-are-trying-to-stop-us-from-teaching-for-racial-justice-we-refuse/.

64. Brian Jones, "The Struggle for Black Education," in *Education and Capitalism: Struggles for Learning and Liberation*, ed. Jeff Bale and Sarah Knopp (Chicago: Haymarket Books, 2012), 45.

65. Jones, "The Struggle for Black Education," 7.

66. Jones, "The Struggle for Black Education," 7.

67. Givens, *Fugitive Pedagogy*, 12.

68. James D. Anderson, *The Education of Blacks in the South* (Chapel Hill, NC: University of North Carolina Press, 1988), 17.

69. Anderson, *The Education of Blacks*, 16.

70. Adam Fairclough, *Better Day Coming: Blacks and Equality, 1890–2000* (New York: Viking, 2001), https://books.google.com/books.

71. NAACP, *Anti-Negro Propaganda in School Textbooks* (New York: National Association for the Advancement of Colored People, 1939), 15.

72. Donna Jean Murch, *Living for the City* (Chapel Hill, NC: University of North Carolina Press, 2010), 55.

73. Francesca López and Christine E. Sleeter, *Critical Race Theory and Its Critics: Implications for Research and Teaching* (New York: Teachers College Press, 2023), 40.

74. Editors of Rethinking Schools, "Outlawing Solidarity in Tucson," *Rethinking Schools*, February 23, 2012, https://rethinkingschools.org/2012/02/23/outlawing-solidarity-in-tucson/.

75. Roque Planas, "Arizona Education Officials Say It's Illegal to Recite This Poem in School," *Huffpost*, January 13, 2015, https://www.huffpost.com/

entry/in-laketch_n_6464604.

76. Roque Planas, "Arizona Education Officials Say It's Illegal To Recite This Poem In School," *HuffPost*, January 13, 2015, https://www.huffpost.com/ entry/in-laketch_n_6464604.

77. Curtis Acosta, "Behind the Curtain in Tucson: A Letter from Curtis Acosta," *Rethinking Schools*, January 28, 2012, https://rethinkingschools. org/2012/01/28/behind-the-curtain-in-tucson-a-letter-from-curtis-acosta/.

78. Maggie Astor, "Tucson's Mexican Studies Program Was a Victim of 'Racial Animus,' Judge Says," *New York Times*, August 23, 2017, https://www.ny-times.com/2017/08/23/us/arizona-mexican-american-ruling.html.

79. "Arkansas Tries to Ban Teaching People's History, Again," Zinn Educa-tion Project, April 29, 2021, https://www.zinnedproject.org/news/arkan-sas-ban-peoples-history-again/.

80. Andrea Salcedo, "A Lawmaker Wanted to Ban 'Divisive' Teaching on Race. Then He Mentioned 'the Good' of Slavery," *Washington Post*, April 28, 2021, https://www.washingtonpost.com/nation/2021/04/28/ray-garofalo-louisi-ana-good-slavery/.

81. "Iowa's Backlash Against Teaching Truth," *Iowa Informer*, June 2021, accessed July 29, 2024, https://iowainformer.com/politics/2021/06/iowas-backlash-against-teaching-truth/.

82. Sofia DeMartino, "Partisan Battles Loom Over Iowa School Board Elec-tions," *Gazette*, October 23, 2021, https://www.thegazette.com/staff-colum-nists/partisan-battles-loom-over-iowa-school-board-elections/.

83. DeMartino, "Partisan Battles Loom."

84. "Superintendent Unsure If Teachers Can Teach Slavery Was Wrong," You-Tube video, 3:23, posted by Indisputable with Dr. Rashad Richey, June 17, 2021, https://www.youtube.com/watch?v=BvUaBQm7b0M.

85. Hannah Natanson, "Slavery Was Wrong and 5 Other Things Educators Won't Teach Anymore," *Washington Post*, updated March 6, 2023, https://www. washingtonpost.com/education/2023/03/06/slavery-was-wrong-5-other-things-educators-wont-teach-anymore/.

86. Natanson, "Slavery Was Wrong."

87. Auguste Meyrat, "In Bemoaning What They 'Won't Teach Anymore,' Educa-tors Reveal 6 Ways They Indoctrinate Students," *Federalist*, March 17, 2023, https://thefederalist.com/2023/03/17/in-bemoaning-what-they-wont-teach-anymore-educators-reveal-6-ways-they-indoctrinate-students/.

88. James Whitfield, "Testimony: In the Crosshairs of Public Education's Ene-mies," *Facing South*, May 24, 2022, https://www.facingsouth.org/2022/05/ testimony-crosshairs-public-educations-enemies.

89. Reagan Reese, "Parents Say School 'Totally Duped' Son into Taking 'An-ti-American Socialist' History Class," *Daily Caller*, September 21, 2022, https://dailycaller.com/2022/09/21/parents-school-duped-son-anti-ameri-can-socialist-history/.

90. Erin Blakemore, "Did George Washington Really Free Mount Vernon's Enslaved Workers?" History, February 18, 2020, https://www.history.com/news/did-george-washington-really-free-mount-vernons-slaves.
91. W. E. B. Du Bois, *Black Reconstruction in America, 1860–1880* (New York: Free Press, 1998), 722.
92. Keeanga-Yamahtta Taylor, "The Enduring Power of 'Scenes of Subjection,'" *New Yorker*, October 17, 2022, https://www.newyorker.com/books/second-read/the-enduring-power-of-scenes-of-subjection-saidiya-hartman.
93. Williams, *Self-Taught*, 14.
94. Jonathan Butcher and Mike Gonzalez, "Critical Race Theory, the New Intolerance, and Its Grip on America," Heritage Foundation, https://www.heritage.org/civil-rights/report/critical-race-theory-the-new-intolerance-and-its-grip-america.

Chapter 2: "We're Going to Hunt You Down": The Attack on Students, Educators, and Books

Rich Donnelly, "Teacher Frustrated by Book Policy: 'The State of Florida Definitely Put Duval Public Schools in a Hole,'" *First Coast News*, February 17, 2023, https://www.firstcoastnews.com/article/news/local/teacher-says-florida-book-policy-too-restrictive/77-d1c1f329-db72-4156-9b16-862920cb60c5.
1. James Whitfield, "Testimony: In the Crosshairs of Public Education's Enemies," *Facing South*, May 24, 2022, https://www.facingsouth.org/2022/05/testimony-crosshairs-public-educations-enemies.
2. "Hate at School," Southern Poverty Law Center, May 2, 2019, https://www.splcenter.org/20190502/hate-school.
3. Dana Goldstein, "Hate Crimes Reported in Schools Nearly Doubled Between 2018 and 2022," *New York Times*, January 29, 2024, https://www.nytimes.com/2024/01/29/us/hate-crimes-schools-universities.html.
4. "Investigation: No Adults Involved in Mock Slave Auction at North Carolina School," Associated Press, March 22, 2022, https://www.yahoo.com/news/investigation-no-adults-involved-mock-193651955.html.
5. Alexandra E. Petri, "California High School Football Team Forfeits Season After Players Staged 'Slave Auction'," *Los Angeles Times*, October 3, 2022, https://www.latimes.com/california/story/2022-10-03/slave-auction-high-school-football-team-forfeits-season-yuba-city-river-valley.
6. Kalyn Womack, "Cali Middle Schoolers Handed Out Cotton Balls to Celebrate Black History Month," *Root*, February 13, 2023, https://www.theroot.com/cali-middle-schoolers-handed-out-cotton-balls-to-celeb-1850108428.
7. Christopher F. Rufo, "Don't Be Evil," September 8, 2021, https://christopher-rufo.com/p/dont-be-evil.

8. Zack Linly, "White Parents Oppose Michigan School Board's Anti-Racism Resolution Prompted by White Student's Snapchat Slave Auction," *Root*, July 26, 2021, https://www.theroot.com/white-parents-in-oppose-michigan-school-board-s-anti-ra-1847361854.

9. Hannah Natanson, "It Started with a Mock 'Slave Trade' and a School Resolution Against Racism. Now a War over Critical Race Theory Is Tearing This Small Town Apart," *Washington Post*, July 24, 2021, https://www.washingtonpost.com/local/education/mock-slave-trade-critical-race-theory/2021/07/23/b4372c36-e9a8-11eb-ba5d-55d3b5ffcaf1_story.html.

10. Andrew Jeong, "White Teacher in Texas Tells Students His Race Is 'Superior,'" *Washington Post*, November 15, 2022, https://www.washingtonpost.com/nation/2022/11/15/texas-teacher-pflugerville-racist/.

11. Laura Meckler and Hannah Natanson, "New Critical Race Theory Laws Have Teachers Scared, Confused and Self-Censoring," *Washington Post*, February 14, 2022, https://www.washingtonpost.com/education/2022/02/14/critical-race-theory-teachers-fear-laws/.

12. Jalen Brown and Justin Gamble, "Illinois School Board Fires High School Teacher Caught on Video Yelling Racial Slur at Black Student," CNN, October 28, 2022, https://www.cnn.com/2022/10/28/us/illinois-teacher-fired-racial-slur/index.html.

13. Brian Planalp, "Cincinnati Police Officer Fired After Using Racial Slur Outside CPS School," Fox19, August 29, 2022, https://www.fox19.com/2022/08/29/cincinnati-police-officer-terminated-after-n-word-during-incident-outside-cps-school/.

14. Eesha Pendharker, "Students of Color Disproportionately Suffer from Police Assaults at School, Says Report," *Education Week*, January 13, 2023, https://www.edweek.org/leadership/students-of-color-disproportionately-suffer-from-police-assaults-at-school-says-report/2023/01.

15. West Resendes, "Police in Schools Continue to Target Black, Brown and Indigenous Students with Disabilities. The Trump Administration Has Data That's Likely to Prove It," ACLU, July 9, 2020, https://www.aclu.org/news/criminal-law-reform/police-in-schools-continue-to-target-black-brown-and-indigenous-students-with-disabilities-the-trump-administration-has-data-thats-likely-to-prove-it.

16. Aaron Brenner, Robert Brenner, and Cal Winslow, *Rebel Rank and File: Labor Militancy and the Revolt from Below During the Long 1970s* (New York: Verso, 2010), 177.

17. "February 28, 1997: Teachers Suspended for Chicano Studies Lessons," Zinn Education Project, n.d., https://www.zinnedproject.org/news/tdih/cordova-sisters-suspended-for-teaching-chicano-studies/.

18. Eugenia Kaledin, *Daily Life in the United States, 1940–1959: Shifting Worlds* (Westport, CT: Greenwood Press, 2000), 78.

19. Kaledin, *Daily Life,* 10.

20. Kaledin, *Daily Life*, 126.

21. Stephen Francoeur, "McCarthyism and Libraries: Intellectual Freedom under Fire, 1947–1954" (master's thesis, Hunter College, CUNY, 2006), 33, https://academicworks.cuny.edu/cgi/viewcontent.cgi?article=2218&context=bb_pubs.

22. Robert Justin Goldstein, *Political Repression in Modern America from 1870 to 1976* (Urbana: University of Illinois Press, 2001), 359.

23. Clarence Taylor, *Reds at The Blackboard* (New York: Columbia University Press, 2013).

24. Taylor, *Reds at The Blackboard*, 241.

25. Taylor, *Reds at The Blackboard*, 242.

26. Taylor, *Reds at The Blackboard*, 254.

27. David Caute, *The Great Fear: The Anticommunist Purge under Truman and Eisenhower* (New York: Touchstone, 1978), 441.

28. Robert L. Dahlgren and Piotr Mikiewicz (Reviewing Editor), "Red Scare in the Sunshine State: Anti-Communism and Academic Freedom in Florida Public Schools, 1945–1960," *Cogent Education* 3, no. 1, https://www.tandfon-line.com/doi/full/10.1080/2331186X.2016.1262307.

29. Quoted in Manning Marable, *Race, Reform, and Rebellion: The Second Reconstruction and Beyond in Black America, 1945–2006*, 3rd ed. (Jackson: University Press of Mississippi, 2009), 16.

30. Marable, *Race, Reform, and Rebellion*, 31.

31. Michael Hines, *A Worthy Piece of Work: The Untold Story of Madeline Morgan and the Fight for Black History in Schools* (Boston: Beacon Press, 2022), 151.

32. "Caught in the Culture Wars, Teachers Are Being Forced from Their Jobs," *Washington Post*, June 16, 2022, https://www.washingtonpost.com/education/2022/06/16/teacher-resignations-firings-culture-wars/.

33. Anthony Conwright, "The Lethal Logic of White Supremacist Violence," *Forum*, May 19, 1922, https://www.aapf.org/theforum-lethal-logic-white-supremacist-violence.

34. Gabriella Borter, Joseph Ax, and Joseph Tanfani, "U.S. School Districts Face Threats of Violence and Protests over Race, Curriculum," Reuters, February 15, 2022, https://www.reuters.com/investigates/special-report/usa-education-threats/.

35. Anya Kamenetz, "School Boards Are Asking for Federal Help as They Face Threats and Violence," NPR, September 30, 2021, https://www.npr.org/sections/back-to-school-live-updates/2021/09/30/1041870027/school-boards-federal-help-threats-violence.

36. "Teaching in Dangerous Times," Zinn Education Project, November 21, 2022, https://www.zinnedproject.org/news/teaching-dangerous-times/.

37. Phillip Smith, "Community, Alumni Voice Their Opinions in Changing Name of Robert E. Lee High School," *First Coast News*, March 17, 2021, https://www.firstcoastnews.com/article/news/education/community-alumni-voice-their-opinions-in-changing-name-of-robert-e-lee-high-school-

dcps/77-7d5f92d8-8aee-44a2-bdaf-425ff3aaa37b.

38. Sydney Boles, "Can a Teacher Fly a Black Lives Matter Flag at School? A Florida Court Will Consider," NPR, *All Things Considered*, April 30, 2021, https://www.npr.org/2021/04/30/992038052/blm-and-teacher-s-free-speech.

39. Emily Bloch, "EVAC Movement Leader Amy Donofrio Removed from Classroom for 'Several Matters,'" *Florida Times-Union*, March 25, 2021, https://www.jacksonville.com/story/news/education/2021/03/25/evac-movement-teacher-removed-jacksonvilles-lee-high-after-refusing-remove-black-lives-matters-flag/6999517002/.

40. Emily Bloch, "Florida Education Commissioner Says He Made Sure Amy Donofrio Was Fired; Now Her Legal Team's Responding," *Florida Times-Union*, May 18, 2021, https://www.jacksonville.com/story/news/education/2021/05/17/florida-education-commissioner-richard-corcoran-says-fired-duval-county-teacher-supporting-blm/5134544001/.

41. Tyler Kingkade, "Critical Race Theory Battles Are Driving Frustrated, Exhausted Educators Out of Their Jobs," NBC News, July 12, 2021, https://www.nbcnews.com/news/us-news/critical-race-theory-battles-are-driving-frustrated-exhausted-educators-out-n1273595.

42. Cameron Probert, "Tri-Cities Teacher Threatened After She Signs onto Controversial Pledge," *Tri-City Herald*, July 19, 2021, https://www.tri-cityherald.com/news/local/education/article252793703.html

43. Probert, "Tri-Cities Teacher."

44. Matthew Ablon and Shamarria Morrison, "Charlotte Charter School Teacher Fired over Claims He Taught Critical Race Theory in Classroom, Attorneys Claim," WCNC Charlotte, June 14, 2023, https://www.wcnc.com/article/news/education/charlotte-secondary-critical-race-theory-firing-book-education-local/275-6a7f24e2-11d1-45e9-b825-3bd8d4e27031.

45. Jon Skolnik, "Oklahoma Middle School Teacher Says He Was Fired for Pride Flags in Classroom," *Salon*, April 20, 2022, https://www.salon.com/2022/04/20/oklahoma-middle-school-teacher-says-he-was-fired-for-pride-flags-in-classroom/.

46. Tamron Hall Show, "This Teacher Was Fired After Reading a 'White Privilege' Poem in Class," YouTube video, September 24, 2021. https://www.youtube.com/watch?v=orWuSouQ2Zg.

47. Pilar Melendez, "Oklahoma Teacher Quits After Directing Kids to Banned Books," *Daily Beast*, August 23, 2022, https://www.thedailybeast.com/summer-boismier-of-norman-high-school-in-oklahoma-gave-kids-qr-code-to-brooklyn-library-list-of-banned-books.

48. Pilar Melendez, "How a Harmless Teacher Got Branded a 'Pedophile' by Extremists," *Daily Beast*, September 4, 2022, https://www.thedailybeast.com/summer-boismier-exiled-norman-oklahoma-teacher-faces-cloudy-future.

49. Shannon Power, "Parent Outrage over 'Rainbowland' Song Ban at Wisconsin School," *Newsweek*, March 29, 2023, https://www.newsweek.com/

miley-cyrus-dolly-parton-rainbowland-wisconsin-school-ban-1791051.

50. Power, "Parent Outrage."

51. Associated Press, "Wisconsin School Bans Miley Cyrus-Dolly Parton Duet from Class Concert," NPR, March 29, 2023, https://www.npr.org/2023/03/29/1166718124/wisconsin-school-bans-miley-cyrus-dolly-parton-duet-from-class-concert.

52. "Alliance Statement in Support of Melissa Tempel," Alliance for Education in Waukesha, April 11, 2023, https://www.alliancewaukesha.org/index.php/2023/04/11/alliance-statement-in-support-of-melissa-tempel/.

53. "Defender of Truth," *We2.0* 59, no. 4 (Fall 2021), https://www.washingtonea.org/file_viewer.php?id=50565.

54. Kahleb Richwine, "Inside the Mind of My High School English Teacher," *Medium*, October 22, 2019, https://medium.com/@richwik/inside-the-mind-of-my-high-school-english-teacher-9cca0031700c.

55. Paulo Freire and Donaldo Macedo, *Literacy: Reading the Word and the World* (New York: Routledge, 1987), https://www.routledge.com/Literacy-Reading-the-Word-and-the-World/Freire-Macedo/p/book/9780710214171.

56. Kingkade, "Critical Race Theory."

57. Michael Cavna, "He Was Fired for Reading a 'Butt' Book. Will His Life Return to Normal?" *Washington Post*, May 11, 2022, https://www.washingtonpost.com/comics/2022/05/11/toby-price-butt-book-school/.

58. Nassim Benchaabane and Blythe Bernhard, "Rockwood Leader Resigns as Parents Speak Out Against Cuts to Black Student Programs, Racism in Schools," *St. Louis Post-Dispatch*, December 17, 2022, https://www.stltoday.com/news/local/education/rockwood-leader-resigns-as-parents-speak-out-against-cuts-to-black-student-programs-racism-in/article_e2d417fb-d19e-5112-be12-bb721f011257.html.

59. Nicole Carr, "White Parents Rallied to Chase a Black Educator Out of Town. Then They Followed Her to the Next One," *ProPublica*, June 16, 2022, https://www.propublica.org/article/georgia-dei-crt-schools-parents.

60. Kalyn Womack, "White Parents Drive Out Black Educator in Anti-CRT Rage," *Root*, June 16, 2022, https://www.theroot.com/white-parents-drive-out-black-educator-in-anti-crt-rage-1849070798.

61. Carr, "White Parents."

62. Carr, "White Parents."

63. Carr, "White Parents."

64. Carr, "White Parents."

65. Jonee Lewis, "Critics Plan Rallies After DeSantis Administration Rejects AP African American Studies Course," Fox 13 Tampa Bay, January 23, 2023, https://www.fox13news.com/news/desantis-gives-reasons-ap-african-american-studies-course-was-rejected-critics-plan-rallies.

66. Jesse Hagopian, "Legalize Black History," *Progressive*, February 21, 2023, https://progressive.org/public-schools-advocate/

legalize-black-history-hagopian-21223/.

67. Fabiola Cineas, "The Controversy over AP African American Studies, Explained," *Vox*, February 9, 2023, https://www.vox.com/policy-and-politics/23583240/ap-african-american-studies-college-board-florida-ron-desantis.

68. "Keeanga-Yamahtta Taylor, Khalil Gibran Muhammad, and E. Patrick Johnson on the Fight over Black History," *Democracy Now!*, February 3, 2023, https://www.democracynow.org/2023/2/3/crt_black_studies_roundtable.

69. Dominique Hazzard, "Queering Black History and Getting Free," *Rethinking Schools* 3, no. 2 (Winter 2018–2019), https://rethinkingschools.org/articles/queering-black-history-and-getting-free/.

70. Abbie E. Goldberg, "IMPACT OF HB 1557 (FLORIDA'S DON'T SAY GAY BILL) on LGBTQ+ Parents in Florida," January 2023, UCLA School of Law and Clark University, https://williamsinstitute.law.ucla.edu/wp-content/uploads/Dont-Say-Gay-Impact-Jan-2023.pdf.

71. Christina Pushaw, "If You're Against the Anti-Grooming Bill, You Are Probably a Groomer or at Least You Don't Denounce the Grooming of 4–8 Year Old Children," X, March 4, 2022, 6:33 p.m. https://x.com/ChristinaPushaw/status/1499886619259777029.

72. Patrick Wall, "'Unsafe, Unwelcoming': LGBTQ Students Report Facing Hostility at School," *Chalkbeat*, October 25, 2022, https://www.chalkbeat.org/2022/10/25/23421548/lgbtq-students-mental-health-school-safety-survey.

73. Karen Graves, *And They Were Wonderful Teachers: Florida's Purge of Gay and Lesbian Teachers* (Urbana: University of Illinois Press, 2009), 16–18.

74. Jeff R. Woods, *Black Struggle, Red Scare: Segregation and Anti-Communism in the South, 1948–1968* (Baton Rouge: LSU Press, 2004), 2.

75. Graves, *Wonderful Teachers*, 1.

76. Graves, *Wonderful Teachers*, 10.

77. "Vigils Held for Late Gender-Nonconforming Teenager Nex Benedict," *Democracy Now!*, February 26, 2024, https://www.democracynow.org/2024/2/26/headlines/vigils_held_for_late_gender_nonconforming_teenager_nex_benedict.

78. Veban Hurley, "Oklahoma Banned Trans Students from Bathrooms. Now Nex Benedict Is Dead After a Fight at School," *Independent*, February 20, 2024, https://www.independent.co.uk/news/world/americas/nex-benedict-dead-oklahoma-b2501844.html

79. Movement Advancement Project, "LGBTQ Curricular Laws," https://www.lgbtmap.org/equality-maps/curricular_laws.

80. Sharon Lurye, "First They Tried Protests of Anti-Gay Bills. Then Students Put on a Play at Louisiana's Capitol," *AP News*, March 30, 2024, https://apnews.com/article/transgender-visibility-lgbtq-student-play-a30468fff-90127c379eba7b8eccdaa56.

81. Wall, "'Unsafe, Unwelcoming.'"

82. "Teach Truth Day of Action," Zinn Education Project, accessed July 24,

2024, https://www.zinnedproject.org/news/teach-truth-day-of-action/.

83. Alex Kane, "A 'McCarthyite Backlash' Against Pro-Palestine Speech," *Jewish Currents*, October 20, 2023, https://jewishcurrents.org/a-mccarthyite-back-lash-against-pro-palestine-speech.

84. Tesfaye Negussie and Nadine El-Bawab, "Doxxing Campaign Against Pro-Palestinian College Students Ramps Up," ABC News, October 20, 2023, https://abcnews.go.com/International/doxxing-campaign-pro-palestin-ian-college-students-ramps/story?id=104141630.

85. Michael Arria, "Crackdown on Palestine in Education Goes Far Beyond Universities," *Mondoweiss*, January 5, 2024, https://mondoweiss.net/2024/01/crackdown-on-palestine-in-education-goes-far-beyond-universities/.

86. Editors of Rethinking Schools, "Gaza and the Growing Attack on Social Justice Teaching," *Rethinking Schools*, 38, no. 3 (Spring 2024), https://rethinking-schools.org/articles/gaza-and-the-growing-attack-on-social-justice-teaching/.

87. Alaa Elassar, "A Palestinian Student Was Expelled from a Florida High School After His Mother Made Pro-Palestinian Posts on Social Media," CNN, December 15, 2023, https://www.cnn.com/2023/12/15/us/palestin-ian-student-expelled-pine-crest-florida/index.html.

88. Vimal Patel and Anna Betts, "Campus Crackdowns Have Chilling Effect on Pro-Palestinian Speech," *New York Times*, December 17, 2023, https://www.nytimes.com/2023/12/17/us/campus-crackdowns-have-chilling-effect-on-pro-palestinian-speech.html.

89. Mark Gaurino, "Professor Fired for Israel Criticism Urges University of Illinois to Reinstate Him," *Guardian*, September 9, 2014, https://www.theguardian.com/education/2014/sep/09/professor-israel-criticism-twit-ter-university-illinois.

90. Jacey Fortin, "She Won't Promise Not to Boycott Israel, So a Texas School District Stopped Paying Her," *New York Times*, December 19, 2018, https://www.nytimes.com/2018/12/19/us/speech-pathologist-texas-israel-oath.html.

91. Jody Sokolower, "Save Arab American Studies," *Rethinking Schools* 35, no. 2 (Winter 2020–2021), https://rethinkingschools.org/articles/save-ar-ab-american-studies/.

92. Sokolower, "Save Arab American Studies."

93. Sokolower, "Save Arab American Studies."

94. Inae Oh, "Trump Defends Claim That There Were 'Very Fine People on Both Sides,' of White Supremacist Rally," *Mother Jones*, April 26, 2019, https://www.motherjones.com/politics/2019/04/trump-defends-claim-that-there-were-very-fine-people-on-both-sides-of-white-supremacist-rally/.

95. Meryl Kornfield and Timothy Bella, "Texas School Official Tells Teachers That Holocaust Books Should Be Countered with 'Opposing' Views," *Washington Post*, October 15, 2021, https://www.washingtonpost.com/educa-tion/2021/10/15/holocaust-texas-school-books-opposing/.

96. Mike Schneider, "Illustrated Anne Frank Book Removed by Florida

School," *AP News*, April 10, 2023, https://apnews.com/article/censor-ship-books-school-libraries-holocaust-anne-frank-bb65349704ab2dae1a-c90a0f9856d7b9.

97. Sky Palma, "Holocaust Text Books Rejected in Florida's Crack Down on 'Woke Indoctrination': Report," *Raw Story*, May 12, 2023, https://www.rawstory.com/holocaust/.

98. Adriana Gomez Licon, "DeSantis Says Florida Helped Send Weapons to Isra-el—a Move That Could Boost Him in the GOP Primary," *AP News*, October 26, 2023, https://apnews.com/article/desantis-drones-weapons-shipment-is-rael-gaza-3fedd0b434552bad313f9109379df071.

99. Summer Concepcion, "Ron DeSantis Defends Banning Pro-Palestinian Groups From Florida Colleges: 'Not Cancel Culture,'" NBC News, October 29, 2023, https://www.nbcnews.com/politics/2024-election/ron-desan-tis-defends-banning-palestinian-groups-florida-colleges-not-c-rcna122663.

100. Alberto Toscano, "The War on Education—in Gaza and at Home," *In These Times*, February 15, 2024, https://inthesetimes.com/article/campus-wars-gaza-higher-ed-christopher-rufo.

101. Phyllis Bennis, "Human Rights Groups Agreee: Israel Is Practicing Apart-heid," Institute for Policy Studies, February 10, 2022, https://ips-dc.org/human-rights-groups-agree-israel-is-practicing-apartheid/.

102. Loay Ayyoub, Miriam Berger, and Hajar Harb, "Gaza Becomes 'a Graveyard for Children' As Israel Intensifies Airstrikes," *Washington Post*, November 2, 2023, https://www.washingtonpost.com/world/2023/11/02/isra-el-stikes-gaza-children-victims/.

103. "Jewish Voice for Peace Calls on All People of Conscience to Stop Immi-nent Genocide," Jewish Voice for Peace, https://www.jewishvoiceforpeace.org/2023/10/11/statement23-10-11/.

104. Editors of Rethinking Schools, "Gaza and the Growing Attack on Social Jus-tice Teaching," *Rethinking Schools* 38, no. 3 (Spring 2024), https://rethinking-schools.org/articles/gaza-and-the-growing-attack-on-social-justice-teaching/.

105. Matthew Arrojas, "New State Laws Target Critical Race Theory in High-er Ed," Best Colleges, April 15, 2022, https://www.bestcolleges.com/news/2022/04/15/state-laws-critical-race-theory-higher-education/.

106. Ben Unglesbee, "AAUP Calls Out Think Tanks for 'Culture War Against Higher Education,'" *Higher Ed Dive*, May 30, 2024, https://www.highered-dive.com/news/aaup-culture-war-higher-ed-report-DEI-critical-race-theory-bills/717559/.

107. "PEN America Index of Educational Gag Orders," PEN America, November 1, 2023, https://docs.google.com/spreadsheets/d/1Tj5WQVBmB6SQg-zP_M8uZsQQGH09TxmBY73v23zpyr0/edit#gid=267763711.

108. Arrojas, "New State Laws."

109. Unglesbee, "AAUP Calls Out Think Tanks."

110. Keeanga Yamahtta-Taylor, "The Campaign Against DEI," *New Yorker*, January

22, 2024, https://www.newyorker.com/news/our-columnists/the-campaign-against-dei.

111. Yamahtta-Taylor, "Campaign Against DEI."

112. Stella Rouse and Shibley Telhami, "Poll Reveals White Americans See an Increase in Discrimination Against Other White People and Less Against Other Racial Groups," *Conversation*, July 1, 2022, https://theconversation.com/poll-reveals-white-americans-see-an-increase-in-discrimination-against-other-white-people-and-less-against-other-racial-groups-185278.

113. Gloria Oladipo, "FBI Report Shows Stark Increase in US Hate Crimes and Drop in Violent Crime," *Guardian*, October 16, 2023, https://www.theguardian.com/us-news/2023/oct/16/hate-crimes-increasing-fbi-report.

114. Catherine Thorbecke, "US Economy 'Has Never Worked Fairly for Black Americans,' Treasury Chief Says," ABC News, January 17, 2022, https://abcnews.go.com/Business/treasury-secretary-us-economy-worked-fairly-black-americans/story?id=82308011.

115. Jessica Guynn and Jayme Fraser, "How Diverse Is Corporate America? There Are More Black Leaders but White Men Still Run It," *USA Today*, February 16, 2023, https://www.usatoday.com/in-depth/money/2023/02/16/white-men-corporate-america-diversity/11114830002/.

116. Yamahtta-Taylor, "Campaign Against DEI."

117. Benjamin D. Reese, "Diversity and Inclusion Are Not Enough," *Inside Higher Ed*, June 17, 2020, https://www.insidehighered.com/views/2020/06/18/colleges-shouldnt-simply-focus-diversity-and-inclusion-also-attack-systemic-racism.

118. Debarati Biswas and Erik Wallenberg, "New College of Florida: The Conservative Christian Takeover by Ron DeSantis, Chris Rufo," *Teen Vogue*, March 6, 2023, https://www.teenvogue.com/story/new-college-of-florida-ron-desantis.

119. Ryan Dailey, "New College Ousts Its President and Names Richard Corcoran as an Interim Replacement," WUSF, February 1, 2023, https://wusfnews.wusf.usf.edu/education/2023-02-01/new-college-ousts-president-names-richard-corcoran-interim-replacement.

120. Biswas and Wallenberg, "New College of Florida."

121. Nathan M. Greenfield, "Professors Are Victims as DeSantis' Culture War Heats Up," *University World News*, May 6, 2023, https://www.universityworldnews.com/post.php?story=20230506085146565.

122. Greenfield, "Professors Are Victims."

123. Debarati Biswas and Erik Wallenberg, "New College."

124. Florida College System Presidents, "Florida College System Presidents Statement on Diversity, Equity, Inclusion and Critical Race Theory," Florida Department of Education, January 18, 2023, https://www.fldoe.org/core/fileparse.php/5673/urlt/FCSDEIstatement.pdf.

125. S.B. 2113, Reg. Sess. (Miss. 2022), http://billstatus.ls.state.ms.us/documents/2022/pdf/SB/2100-2199/SB2113SG.pdf.

126. Violet Jira, "ASB Senate Votes to Condemn MS State Senate's Passage of SB 2113," *Daily Mississippian*, February 22, 2022, https://thedmonline.com/asb-senate-votes-to-condemn-ms-state-senates-passage-of-senate-bill-2113/.

127. House Bill 377, 66th Leg., 1st Sess. (Idaho 2021), https://legislature.idaho.gov/wp-content/uploads/sessioninfo/2021/legislation/H0377.pdf.

128. Beth Hawkins, "New Study: Two-Thirds of Teachers Censor Themselves Even When They Don't Have To," The 74, February 15, 2024, https://www.the74million.org/article/new-study-two-thirds-of-teachers-censor-them-selves-even-when-they-dont-have-to/.

129. Daniel Bergner, "Daring to Speak Up About Race in a Divided School District," *New York Times*, September 6, 2022, https://www.nytimes.com/2022/09/06/magazine/leland-michigan-race-school.html.

130. Laura Beth Kelly, Laura Taylor, Cara Djonko-Moore, and Aixa D. Marchand, "The Chilling Effects of So-Called Critical Race Theory Bans," *Rethinking Schools* 37, no. 2 (Winter 2022–2023), https://rethinkingschools.org/articles/the-chilling-effects-of-so-called-critical-race-theory-bans/.

131. Aina Marzia, "Teachers and Students Respond to Black History Bans," *Yes!*, February 15, 2023, https://www.yesmagazine.org/social-justice/2023/02/15/black-history-bans-students-teachers.

132. "In Their Own Words: Youth Voices on Books Unbanned," p. 35, Brooklyn Public Library and Seattle Public Library, https://booksunbanned.com/documents/Books%20Unbanned%20Teen%20Testimonials.pdf.

133. Anna Caplan, "Southlake Carroll ISD Votes to Reprimand Teacher After Parents Complain About Anti-Racist Book," *Dallas Morning News*, October 6, 2021, https://www.dallasnews.com/news/2021/10/06/southlake-pac-backed-carroll-trustees-did-not-recuse-themselves-from-teacher-discipline-vote/.

134. American Library Association, "The American Library Association Opposes Widespread Efforts to Censor Books in US Schools and Libraries," American Library Association, November 29, 2021, https://www.ala.org/news/press-releases/2021/11/american-library-association-opposes-widespread-efforts-censor-books-us.

135. American Library Association, "Top 10 Most Challenged Books and Frequently Challenged Books Archive," 2002, https://www.ala.org/bbooks/frequentlychallengedbooks/top10/archive.

136. Alexandra Alter, "Attempts to Ban Books Accelerated Last Year," *New York Times*, March 14, 2024, https://www.nytimes.com/2024/03/14/books/book-bans.html.

137. On *Maus*, see Dan Mangan, "Tennessee School Board Bans Holocaust Graphic Novel 'Maus'—Author Art Spiegelman Condemns the Move as 'Orwellian,'" CNBC, January 28, 2022, https://www.cnbc.com/2022/01/26/tennessee-school-board-bans-holocaust-comic-maus-by-art-spiegelman.html. On the book about Martin Luther King Jr., see Igor Derysh, "Right-Wing Moms Group Wants to Use Tennessee's 'Critical Race Theory' Law

to Ban MLK Jr. Book," *Salon*, November 30, 2021, https://www.salon.com/2021/11/30/right-wing-moms-group-wants-to-use-tennessees-critical-race-theory-law-to-ban-mlk-jr-book/. On book burning, see WZTV Staff, "Tennessee Pastor Holds Burning of Books, Other Material Deemed 'Demonic,'" *Fox 17 WZTV Nashville*, February 4, 2022, https://fox17.com/news/local/tennessee-pastor-holds-burning-of-books-other-materials-deemed-demonic-nashville-mt-juliet-religion-church-state-politics-twitter.

138. Ariana Figueroa, "LGBTQ Community, People of Color in the Crosshairs of the Banned Book Movement," *Ohio Capital Journal*, April 18, 2022, https://ohiocapitaljournal.com/briefs/lgbtq-community-people-of-color-in-the-crosshairs-of-banned-book-movement/.

139. Nate Wegehaupt and WORT News Department, "Following National Trend, Wisconsin Lawmakers Introduce Book Ban," WORT-FM, February 6, 2023, https://www.wortfm.org/following-national-trend-wisconsin-lawmakers-introduce-book-ban/.

140. Nathalie Baptiste, "A Wyoming Public Library Board Fired Its Head Librarian After She Refused to Remove Books," *Huffpost*, August 15, 2023, https://www.huffpost.com/entry/librarian-fired-wyoming-books_n_64da5ab9e-4b08e55c4cd8325.

141. Figueroa, "LGBTQ Community."

142. Hannah Natanson, Clara Ence Morse, Anu Narayanswamy, and Christine Brause, "An Explosion of Culture War Laws Is Changing Schools. Here's How," *Washington Post*, October 18, 2022, https://www.washingtonpost.com/education/2022/10/18/education-laws-culture-war/.

143. Eesha Pendharkar, "Nearly 300 Books Removed from Schools Under Missouri's 'Sexually Explicit Materials' Law," *Education Week*, November 18, 2022, https://www.edweek.org/teaching-learning/nearly-300-books-removed-from-schools-under-missouris-sexually-explicit-materials-law/2022/11.

144. Kate Grumke, "School Librarian Recalls 'Surreal' Police Visits over Books Months Before New Missouri Law," St. Louis Public Radio, September 22, 2022, https://news.stlpublicradio.org/education/2022-09-22/school-librarian-recalls-surreal-police-visits-over-books-months-before-new-missouri-law.

145. Valerie Nava, "'Access Equals Equity': Anti-Censorship Advocates Fear New Book Ban's Impact," *Columbia Missourian*, September 25, 2022, https://www.columbiamissourian.com/news/k12_education/access-equals-equity-anti-censorship-advocates-fear-new-book-bans-impact/article_81c334b0-3610-11ed-8eef-2f65fd6ac929.html.

146. Joan Walsh, "Florida Teachers Hide Their Books to Avoid Felonies," *Nation*, February 1, 2023, https://www.thenation.com/article/politics/book-bans-florida-public-schools/.

147. Joan Walsh, "Florida Teachers Hide Their Books to Avoid Felonies," *Nation*, February 1, 2023, https://www.thenation.com/article/politics/book-bans-florida-public-schools/.

148. Zinn Education Project, "Best Defense Against Anti-CRT Chilling Effect: *Teaching for Black Lives* Study Groups," Zinn Education Project, March 14, 2023.

149. Li Cohen, "Florida School District Pulls Dictionaries and Encyclopedias as Part of 'Inappropriate' Content Review," CBS News, January 12, 2024, https://www.cbsnews.com/news/florida-school-district-pulls-dictionaries-and-encyclopedias-as-part-of-sexual-or-inappropriate-content-review/.

150. Colin Kaepernick, Robin D. G. Kelley, and Keeanga-Yamahtta Taylor, eds., *Our History Has Always Been Contraband: In Defense of Black Studies* (Chicago: Haymarket Books, 2023), 14.

151. Moira Marquis and Juliana Luna, "Reading Between the Bars," PEN America, Freewrite Project, October 25, 2023, https://pen.org/report/reading-between-the-bars/.

152. Nicquel Terry Ellis, "A Texas Teacher Can't Afford Health Insurance or Buy a Home. Here's Why Black Leaders Say the Student Loan Crisis Is a Civil Rights Issue," CNN, October 6, 2021, https://www.cnn.com/2021/10/06/us/black-student-loan-crisis/index.html.

153. Wall, "'Unsafe and Unwelcome.'"

154. Laura Beth Kelly, Laura Taylor, Cara Djonko-Moore, and Aixa D. Marchand, "The Chilling Effects of So-Called Critical Race Theory Bans," *Rethinking Schools* (Winter 2022–23), https://rethinkingschools.org/articles/the-chilling-effects-of-so-called-critical-race-theory-bans/.

155. "New CDC Data Illuminate Youth Mental Health Threats During the COVID-19 Pandemic," Centers for Disease Control and Prevention, March 31, 2022, https://www.cdc.gov/media/releases/2022/p0331-youth-mental-health-covid-19.html; Mary Ellen Flannery, "Mental Health in Schools: The Kids Are Not All Right," *NEA Today*, July 20, 2022, https://www.nea.org/advocating-for-change/new-from-nea/mental-health-schools-kids-are-not-all-right.

156. Zinn Education Project, "Best Defense Against Anti-CRT Chilling Effect: Teaching for Black Lives Study Groups," March 14, 2023, https://www.zinnedproject.org/news/defense-against-anti-crt-chilling-effect-t4bl-study-groups/.

Chapter 3: The Political Economy of Truthcrime: Billionaires, Parent Truthcrime Associations, and the Origins of the Attack on CRT

Zack Beauchamp, "Chris Rufo's Dangerous Fictions: The Right's Leading Culture Warrior Has Invented a Leftist Takeover of America to Justify His Very Real Power Grabs," *Vox*, September 10, 2023, https://www.vox.com/23811277/christopher-rufo-culture-wars-ron-desantis-florida-critical-race-theory-anti-wokeness.

Jasmine Banks, "The Radical Capitalist Behind the Critical Race Theory Furor: How a Dark-Money Mogul Bankrolled an Astroturf Backlash," *The Nation*, August 13, 2021, https://www.thenation.com/article/politics/

charles-koch-crt-backlash/.

1. James Whitfield, "Testimony: In the Crosshairs of Public Education's Enemies," *Facing South*, May 24, 2022, https://www.facingsouth.org/2022/05/testimony-crosshairs-public-educations-enemies.

2. Jason Wilson, "Activist Who Led Ouster of Harvard President Linked to 'Scientific Racism' Journal," *Guardian*, January 31, 2024, https://www.theguardian.com/world/2024/jan/31/rightwing-activist-christopher-rufo-ties-scientific-racism-journal.

3. Christopher F. Rufo, "Homelessness," Discovery Institute, https://www.youtube.com/watch?v=TbybniI38gU.

4. Benjamin Wallace-Wells, "How a Conservative Activist Invented the Conflict over Critical Race Theory," *New Yorker*, June 18, 2021, https://www.newyorker.com/news/annals-of-inquiry/how-a-conservative-activist-invented-the-conflict-over-critical-race-theory.

5. Wallace-Wells, "How a Conservative Activist."

6. Russell Vought, "Memorandum on Training in the Federal Government," Executive Office of the President Office of Management and Budget, September 4, 2020, https://www.whitehouse.gov/wp-content/uploads/2020/09/M-20-34.pdf.

7. Joyce Chen, "Donald Trump's Golf Course Plaque Honors Fake Civil War Battle," *Rolling Stone*, August 17, 2017, https://www.rollingstone.com/politics/politics-news/donald-trumps-golf-course-plaque-honors-fake-civil-war-battle-253119/.

8. Donald J. Trump, "Remarks by President Trump at the White House Conference on American History," September 17, 2020, https://trumpwhitehouse.archives.gov/briefings-statements/remarks-president-trump-white-house-conference-american-history/.

9. Zinn Education Project, "Trump Attacks Howard Zinn and the Zinn Education Project—Defend Teaching People's History Today!," Zinn Education Project, December 15, 2020, https://www.zinnedproject.org/news/trump-attacks-zinn-and-zep/.

10. Johnston, Nicholas, "How 9 'Art of the Deal' Quotes Explain the Trump Presidency," *Axios*, January 26, 2017, https://www.axios.com/2017/12/15/how-9-art-of-the-deal-quotes-explain-the-trump-presidency-1513300122.

11. American Historical Association, "AHA Condemns Report of Advisory 1776 Commission (January 2021)," American Historical Association, January 20, 2021, https://www.historians.org/news/aha-statement-condemning-report-of-advisory-1776-commission/.

12. American Historical Association, "AHA Condemns."

13. Jake Lahut, "Fox News Has Mentioned 'Critical Race Theory' Nearly 1300 Times Since March, According to Watchdog Study," *Business Insider*, June 15, 2021, https://www.businessinsider.com/fox-news-critical-race-theory-mentions-thousand-study-2021-6.

14. Laura Meckler and Josh Dawsey, "Republicans, Spurred by an Unlikely Figure, See Political Promise in Targeting Critical Race Theory," *Washington Post*, June 21, 2021, https://www.washingtonpost.com/education/2021/06/19/critical-race-theory-rufo-republicans/.
15. Lis Power, "Fox News' Obsession with Critical Race Theory, by the Numbers," Media Matters for America, June 15, 2021, https://www.mediamatters.org/fox-news/fox-news-obsession-critical-race-theory-numbers.
16. Joy Resmovits, "Your Kids Take 112 Tests Between Pre-K and High School," *Los Angeles Times*, October 28, 2015, https://www.latimes.com/local/education/standardized-testing/la-me-edu-how-much-standardized-testing-report-obama-20151023-story.html.
17. Adam Fairclough, *A Class of Their Own: Black Teachers in the Segregated South* (Cambridge, MA: Harvard University Press, 2007), 148.
18. Susan Rayburn, ed., *Rosa Parks: In Her Own Words* (Athens, GA: University of Georgia Press, 2020), 17.
19. James D. Anderson, *The Education of Blacks in the South, 1860–1935* (Chapel Hill, NC: University of North Carolina Press, 2010), 82.
20. Noliwe Rooks, *Cutting School: The Segrenomics of American Education* (New York: New Press, 2020), 60.
21. Rooks, *Cutting School*, 61.
22. Rooks, *Cutting School*, 61.
23. Jarvis R. Givens, *Fugitive Pedagogy: Carty G. Woodson and the Art of Black Teaching* (Cambridge, MA: Harvard University Press, 2021), 105.
24. Adam Sanchez, "What the Koch Brothers Want Students to Learn About Slavery," Zinn Education Project, March 7, 2018, https://www.zinnedproject.org/if-we-knew-our-history/koch-brothers-want-students-learn-slavery/.
25. Hannah Natanson, Lauren Tierney, and Clara Ence Morse, "America Has Legislated Itself into Competing Red, Blue Versions of Education," *Washington Post*, April 4, 2024, https://www.washingtonpost.com/education/2024/04/04/education-laws-red-blue-divide/.
26. Lisa Graves and Alyssa Bowen, "Tax Docs Link Right-Wing 'Parents Group' to Leonard Leo's Dark Money Network," *Truthout*, February 9, 2023, https://truthout.org/articles/tax-docs-link-right-wing-parents-group-to-leonard-leos-dark-money-network/.
27. James Oliphant, "ABCs Not LGBTs: Battles over Race, Gender Inflame Texas School Board Vote," Reuters, October 24, 2022, https://www.reuters.com/world/us/abcs-not-lgbts-battles-over-race-gender-inflame-texas-school-board-vote-2022-10-22/.
28. Libby Stanford, "Why National Advocates Are Getting More Involved in School Board Elections," *Education Week*, October 31, 2022, https://www.edweek.org/leadership/why-national-advocates-are-getting-more-involved-in-school-board-elections/2022/10.
29. Stanford, "Why National Advocates."

30. Libby Stanford, "Conservative Advocates Vow Continued Push for School Board Seats Despite Middling Midterms," *Education Week*, November 16, 2022, https://www.edweek.org/leadership/conservative-advocates-vow-continued-push-for-school-board-seats-despite-middling-midterms/2022/11.

31. Roger Sollenberger, "The Aristocrats Funding the Critical Race Theory 'Backlash,'" *Daily Beast*, November 8, 2021, https://www.thedailybeast.com/right-wing-aristocrats-fund-critical-race-theory-backlash.

32. Jasmine Banks, "The Radical Capitalist Behind the Critical Race Theory Furor," *Nation*, August 13, 2021, https://www.thenation.com/article/politics/charles-koch-crt-backlash/.

33. Kevin D. Brown, "NEPC Review: How to Regulate Critical Race Theory in Schools: A Primer and Model Legislation (Manhattan Institute, August 2021)," National Education Policy Center (NEPC) Review, December 14, 2021, https://nepc.colorado.edu/thinktank/crt-regulation.

34. Sarah Schwartz, "Who's Really Driving Critical Race Theory Legislation? An Investigation," *Education Week*, July 19, 2021, https://www.edweek.org/policy-politics/whos-really-driving-critical-race-theory-legislation-an-investigation/2021/07.

35. Anya Kamenetz, "A Look at the Groups Supporting School Board Protesters Nationwide," NPR, October 26, 2021, https://www.npr.org/2021/10/26/1049078199/a-look-at-the-groups-supporting-school-board-protesters-nationwide.

36. Paul Blumenthal, "The GOP's New Culture War Is Ripped Right from the 1970s," *HuffPost*, March 25, 2023, https://www.huffpost.com/entry/gop-culture-war-1970s_n_641dcb8ae4b0fef1524a2ab0.

37. Edited by Paul Dans and Steven Groves, *Mandate for Leadership 2025: The Conservative Promise (Project 2025)* (Washington, DC: The Heritage Foundation, 2023), https://static.project2025.org/2025_MandateForLeadership_FULL.pdf, 343.

38. David Theo Goldberg, *The War on Critical Race Theory* (Cambridge, UK: Polity Press, 2023), 15.

39. Khanyi Mlaba, "The Richest 1% Own Almost Half the World's Wealth & 9 Other Mind-Blowing Facts on Wealth Inequality," Global Citizen, January 19, 2023, https://www.globalcitizen.org/en/content/wealth-inequality-oxfam-billionaires-elon-musk/.

40. Alyssa Bowen, Ansev Demirhan, Julia Peck, and Evan Vorpahl, "Many 'Parent' Groups Opposing Masks and CRT Are Actually Driven by Dark Money," *Truthout*, January 29, 2022, https://truthout.org/articles/many-parent-groups-opposing-masks-and-crt-are-actually-driven-by-dark-money/.

41. Graves and Bowen, "Tax Docs."

42. Center for Media and Democracy, "Parents Defending Education," SourceWatch, February 24, 2023, https://www.sourcewatch.org/index.php/Parents_Defending_Education.

43. Bowen, Demirhan, Peck, and Vorpahl, "Many 'Parent' Groups."

44. "The Money Behind the Critical Race Theory Outrage Machine," Progress Michigan, December 14, 2021, https://progressmichigan.org/wp-content/uploads/2021/12/PM-CRT-Report.pdf.

45. Lisa Lerer and Patricia Mazzei, "Florida Sex Scandal Shakes Moms for Liberty, as Group's Influence Wanes," *New York Times*, December 18, 2023, https://www.nytimes.com/2023/12/16/us/politics/moms-for-liberty-sex-scandal.html.

46. Mark Frauenfelder, "Homophobic Bridget Ziegler Should Be Fired for Being Bad at Her Job, Not for Having Sex with a Woman, Says Former Student (Video)," *Boing Boing*, December 18, 2023, https://boingboing.net/2023/12/18/homophobic-bridget-ziegler-should-not-be-fired-for-being-bad-at-at-her-jab-not-for-having-sex-with-a-woman-says-former-student-video.html.

47. Olivia Little, "Unmasking Moms for Liberty," Media Matters for America, November 12, 2021, https://www.mediamatters.org/critical-race-theory/unmasking-moms-liberty.

48. Andrew Atterbury, "Publix Heiress Gives $50K to Conservative Education Group Moms for Liberty PAC," *Politico*, July 20, 2022, https://www.politico.com/news/2022/07/20/moms-liberty-pac-publix-heiress-00046921.

49. Maurice T. Cunningham, "Just Who Is Behind Moms for Liberty? | Column," *Tampa Bay Times*, July 9, 2022, https://www.tampabay.com/opinion/2022/07/09/just-who-is-behind-moms-for-liberty-column/.

50. Olivia Little, "Moms for Liberty Is Hiding behind These Front Groups as They Gut Public School Libraries," *Media Matters for America*, September 20, 2022, https://www.mediamatters.org/moms-liberty/moms-liberty-hiding-behind-these-front-groups-they-gut-public-school-libraries.

51. Olivia Little, "Banning Books About Martin Luther King Jr. and Opposing School District Desegregation Efforts: Inside Moms for Liberty's Deep Ties to the Anti-Civil Rights Movement," *Media Matters for America*, November 15, 2021, https://www.mediamatters.org/critical-race-theory/banning-books-about-martin-luther-king-jr-and-opposing-school-district.

52. Moms for Liberty NH, "We've Got $500 for the First Person That Successfully Catches a Public School Teacher Breaking This Law," X, November 12, 2021, 9:28 am, https://x.com/Moms4LibertyNH/status/1459166253084467205.

53. Jennifer D. Jenkins, "I'm a Florida School Board Member. This Is How Protesters Come after Me," *Washington Post*, October 20, 2021, https://www.washingtonpost.com/outlook/2021/10/20/jennifer-jenkins-brevard-school-board-masks-threats/.

54. Jeff Bryant, "The Proud Boys Are Coming for Public Schools," *Progressive*, October 19, 2021, https://progressive.org/public-schools-advocate/proud-boys-coming-public-schools-bryant-211019/.

55. Lauren Camera, "School Board Recalls at All-Time High as GOP Puts K-12

Issues in Spotlight," *U.S. News & World Report*, November 1, 2021, https://www.usnews.com/news/education-news/articles/2021-11-01/school-board-recalls-at-all-time-high-as-gop-puts-k-12-issues-in-spotlight.

56. Alex Woodward, "Moms for Liberty and the 'Parental Rights' Agenda Flopped in This Week's Elections," *Independent*, November 9, 2023, https://www.independent.co.uk/news/world/americas/us-politics/moms-for-liberty-election-results-b2444882.html.

57. Nora De La Cour, "School Privatizers Are Leaning Hard into the Culture Wars," *Jacobin*, May 24, 2022, https://jacobin.com/2022/05/right-school-privatization-choice-crt-capitalism.

58. Christopher Bedford, "Masks and CRT Are Just the Start: It's Time to Break the Public Schools (and Here's How), *Federalist*, August 3, 2021, https://thefederalist.com/2021/08/03/masks-and-crt-are-just-the-start-its-time-to-break-the-public-schools-heres-how/.

59. Stephanie Mencimer, "Fox in the Schoolhouse: Rupert Murdoch Wants to Teach Your Kids!" *Mother Jones*, September 23, 2011, https://www.motherjones.com/politics/2011/09/rupert-murdoch-news-corp-wireless-generation-education/.

60. Nancy MacLean, *Democracy in Chains: The Deep History of the Radical Right's Stealth Plan for America* (New York: Viking, 2017).

61. Nancy MacLean, "'School Choice' Developed as a Way to Protect Segregation and Abolish Public Schools," *Washington Post*, September 27, 2021, https://www.washingtonpost.com/outlook/2021/09/27/school-choice-developed-way-protect-segregation-abolish-public-schools/.

62. Raymond Pierce, "The Racist History of 'School Choice,'" *Forbes*, May 6, 2021, https://www.forbes.com/sites/raymondpierce/2021/05/06/the-racist-history-of-school-choice/?sh=2b84ac8a6795.

63. Nancy MacLean, *Democracy in Chains: The Deep History of the Radical Right's Stealth Plan for America* (New York: Viking, 2017), 72.

64. Lauren Camera, "Biden to Face Teachers Union After Toxic Relationship During the Obama Years," *U.S. News & World Report*, May 28, 2019, https://www.usnews.com/news/education-news/articles/2019-05-28/biden-to-face-teachers-union-after-toxic-relationship-during-the-obama-years.

65. Kevin Kumashiro, "Understanding the Attacks on Teaching: A Background Brief for Educators and Leaders," *Kevin Kumashiro*, August 5, 2021, https://static1.squarespace.com/static/58db0f5d3a0411bcea5da678/t/610c72876a-f845307997a642/1628205703605/BackgroundBriefAttacksOnTeaching8.5.2021.pdf.

66. "US: Arizona Teachers Vote for First-Ever Statewide Strike," Al Jazeera, April 20, 2018, https://www.aljazeera.com/news/2018/4/20/us-arizona-teachers-vote-for-first-ever-statewide-strike.

67. Paul Schwartzman, "In Tight Governor's Race, Virgina GOP Targeting Critical Race Theory to Draw Votes," *Washington Post*, October 2, 2021,

https://www.washingtonpost.com/local/virginia-politics/critical-race-the-ory-virginia-governor-youngkin/2021/10/01/17ad45f0-1cc8-11ec-8380-5f
badbc43ef8_story.html.

68. Matthew Impelli, "McAuliffe Saying Parents Shouldn't Tell Schools What to Teach Big Factor in Election: Poll," *Newsweek*, November 15, 2021, https://www.newsweek.com/mcauliffe-saying-parents-shouldnt-tell-schools-what-teach-big-factor-election-poll-1649488.

69. Impelli, "McAuliffe Saying Parents Shouldn't Tell."

70. Gustavo Solis, "Report Reveals Migrant Family Separations Continue Under Biden," KPBS, July 29, 2024, https://www.kpbs.org/news/border-immigra-tion/2024/07/29/report-reveals-migrant-family-separations-continue-un-der-biden.

71. Paul Waldman and Greg Sargent, "Why Democrats Must Figure Out Their Message on Schools and Race," *Washington Post*, March 31, 2022, https://www.washingtonpost.com/opinions/2022/03/31/democrats-message-schools-race-crt/.

72. Annie Gowen, "'Blue' Suburban Moms Are Mobilizing to Counter Con-servatives in Fights over Masks, Book Bans and Diversity Education," *Washington Post*, February 9, 2022, https://www.washingtonpost.com/na-tion/2022/02/09/suburban-women-voters-organize/.

73. Daniel Kreiss, Alice Marwick, and Francesca Bolla Tripodi, "The Anti-Crit-ical Race Theory Movement Will Profoundly Affect Public Education," *Sci-entific American*, November 10, 2021, https://www.scientificamerican.com/article/the-anti-critical-race-theory-movement-will-profoundly-affect-pub-lic-education/.

74. Jamelle Bouie, "Democrats, You Can't Ignore the Culture Wars Any Longer," *Washington Post*, April 22, 2022, https://www.nytimes.com/2022/04/22/opinion/red-scare-culture-wars.html.

75. Waldman and Sargent, "Why Democrats."

76. Diana Ravitch, "Who Has Been AWOL in Defending the Schools Against the Attacks on CRT?," *Diana Ravitch's Blog*, January 17, 2022, https://dianerav-itch.net/2022/01/17/who-has-been-awol-in-defending-the-schools-against-the-attacks-on-crt/.

77. Dave Murray, "Bill Gates: Poverty Is an Obstacle, But Not an Excuse for Poor Education," MLive Media Group, July 29, 2011, https://www.mlive.com/news/grand-rapids/2011/07/bill_gates_poverty_is_an_obsta.html.

78. Bryan Metzger, "These 9 House Democrats Voted to Block 'Race-Based The-ories' from Being Taught in Military-Run Schools," *Business Insider*, August 3, 2023, https://www.businessinsider.com/which-house-democrats-vot-ed-chip-roy-critical-race-theory-military-2023-7.

79. E. J. Dionne Jr., "Democrats Have Only Themselves to Blame," *Washing-ton Post*, November 3, 2021, https://www.washingtonpost.com/opin-ions/2021/11/03/ej-dionne-youngkin-win-in-virginia-is-no-fluke/.

80. Natalie Wexler, "Democrats Can't Keep Dismissing Complaints About Critical Race Theory," *Forbes*, November 4, 2021, https://www.forbes.com/sites/nataliewexler/2021/11/04/democrats-cant-keep-dismissing-complaints-about-critical-race-theory/.

81. "One-On-One with Bill Maher," CNN, *Cuomo Prime Time*, aired November 24, 2021, https://transcripts.cnn.com/show/CPT/date/2021-11-24/segment/02.

82. Nicole Guadino, "Democrats Plan to Swing Back Aggressively at Republicans on Critical Race Theory," *Business Insider*, November 16, 2021, https://www.businessinsider.com/democrats-critical-race-theory-strategy-should-be-aggressive-against-republicans-2021-11.

83. Sarah D. Sparks, "How These Teachers Build Curriculum 'Beyond Black History,'" *Education Week*, April 15, 2024, https://www.edweek.org/teaching-learning/how-these-teachers-build-curriculum-beyond-black-history/2024/04.

84. James Whitfield, "Testimony: In the Crosshairs of Public Education's Enemies," *Facing South*, May 24, 2022, https://www.facingsouth.org/2022/05/testimony-crosshairs-public-educations-enemies.

85. Khanyi Mlaba, "The Richest 1%."

Chapter 4: "We Will Teach This Truth!": The Teach Truth Movement

1. James Whitfield, "Testimony: In the Crosshairs of Public Education's Enemies," *Facing South*, May 24, 2022, https://www.facingsouth.org/2022/05/testimony-crosshairs-public-educations-enemies.

2. Amanda Andrews, "Students Protest Critical Race Theory Legislation at State Capitol," GPB News, February 25, 2022, https://www.gpb.org/news/2022/02/25/students-protest-critical-race-theory-legislation-at-state-capitol.

3. Hannah Brandt, "Central York School District Reverses Book Ban after Growing Protests," ABC27 News, September 20, 2021, https://www.abc27.com/local-news/york/students-parents-teachers-and-community-members-protest-central-york-book-ban/.

4. Beth Greenfield, "High School Students Get Controversial Book Ban Reversed in Pennsylvania: 'They Are Heroes,'" Yahoo! Life, September 21, 2021, https://www.yahoo.com/lifestyle/high-school-activists-reverse-controversial-book-ban-pennsylvania-205916534.html.

5. Greenfield, "High School Students."

6. Bill Bigelow, "Reconstructing the South: A Role Play," Zinn Education Project, accessed July 28, 2024, https://www.zinnedproject.org/materials/reconstructing-south-role-play/.

7. Bigelow, "Reconstructing the South."

8. "The People's History They Don't Want Our Students to Know," Zinn Education Project, April 3, 2022, https://www.zinnedproject.org/news/

peoples-history-dont-want-students-know/.

9.   Claudia Tate, ed., *Black Women Writers at Work* (Chicago: Haymarket Books, 2023), 140.

10. National Association of Scholars, *American Birthright: The Civics Alliance's Model K–12 Social Studies Standards*, Civics Alliance, July 2022, https://civicsalliance.org/wp-content/uploads/2023/01/AmericanBirthright.pdf.

11. Adam Sanchez, "Teaching SNCC," Zinn Education Project, https://www.zinnedproject.org/materials/teaching-sncc.

12. Ruth Terry, "Critical Race Theory Opens Up New Opportunities for Student Learning," *Yes!*, March 8, 2022, https://www.yesmagazine.org/social-justice/2022/03/08/critical-race-theory-student-learning.

13. "Pledge to Teach the Truth," Zinn Education Project, January 15, 2022, https://www.zinnedproject.org/news/pledge-to-teach-truth?signature_page=13.

14. "Teachers Refuse to Lie to Students," Zinn Education Project, May 15, 2023, https://www.zinnedproject.org/news/teachers-defy-gop-bans-on-history-lessons/.

15. Rachel Cohen, "As States Build Barriers to Racial Justice Teaching, Educators Fight Back," *Rethinking Schools* 36, no. 2 (Winter 2021–2022), https://rethinkingschools.org/articles/as-states-build-barriers-to-racial-justice-teaching-educators-fight-back/.

16. Cohen, "As States Build Barriers."

17. House Bill 322, 134th Gen. Assembly, Reg. Sess. (Ohio 2021-2022), https://search-prod.lis.state.oh.us/solarapi/v1/general_assembly_134/bills/hb322/IN/00/hb322_00_IN?format=pdf.

18. Cohen, "As States Build Barriers."

19. "Waterloo, Iowa Educators Pledge to Teach Truth at Historic Sites," Zinn Education Project, June 14, 2021, https://www.zinnedproject.org/news/waterloo-june12-pledge.

20. "Black Lives Matter Week of Action—Philly," Facebook, June 12, 2021, https://www.facebook.com/watch/live/?ref=watch_permalink&v=322106496177804.

21. David Waters, "Surrounded by History, Teachers Pledge to 'Teach Truth,' about Racism," *Institute for Public Service Reporting Memphis*, June 14, 2021, https://www.psrmemphis.org/surrounded-by-history-teachers-pledge-to-teach-truth-about-racism/.

22. Mackenzie Lanum, "Memphis Riot, 1866," Black Past, November 20, 2011, https://www.blackpast.org/african-american-history/memphis-riot-1866/.

23. "From Freedom Riders to Freedom Readers: Books Unbanned Bus Tour," Books Unbanned, n.d., http://booksunbanned.org/.

24. Rich Donnelly, "Teacher Frustrated by Book Policy: 'The State of Florida Definitely Put Duval Public Schools in a Hole,'" *First Coast News*, February 17, 2023, https://www.firstcoastnews.com/article/news/local/teacher-says-florida-book-policy-too-restrictive/77-d1c1f329-db72-4156-9b16-862920cb60c5.

25. Zinn Education Project, "'If the Truth Will Set You Free,' Then Lies Will Lock You Up,'" Instagram, May 4, 2023, https://www.instagram.com/p/Cr1KuX-LAI8N/.
26. Thomas Cunningham, "Message to College Board Leadership: Stand Up to DeSantis or Step Down," National Black Justice Coalition, February 21, 2023, https://nbjc.org/nbjc-calls-for-college-board-coleman-to-stand-up-to-desantis-or-stand-down/.
27. National Black Justice Coalition, letter to College Board trustees, February 2023, https://files.constantcontact.com/3b708663201/866545fc-bbd5-4c57-81d2-a3d5223b89d6.pdf.
28. "Open Letter on Fighting 'Anti-Woke' Censorship of Intersectionality and Black Feminism," African American Policy Forum, accessed July 28, 2024, https://www.aapf.org/freedomtolearn.
29. Zinn Education Project, "National Teach Truth Day of Action Press Call Highlights," June 6, 2024, https://www.zinnedproject.org/news/day-of-action-press-call-highlights-2024/.
30. "Study Group: Florida Online," Teaching for Black Lives, https://www.teachingforblacklives.org/study-group-florida-online/.
31. Teaching for Black Lives, "Meet 2022–2023 Study Groups," Teaching for Black Lives, https://www.teachingforblacklives.org/meet-2022-2023-study-groups/.
32. Jack Schneider and Jennifer Berkshire, "Parents Claim They Have the Right to Shape Their Kids' School Curriculum. They Don't." *Washington Post*, October 21, 2021, https://www.washingtonpost.com/outlook/parents-rights-protests-kids/2021/10/21/5cf4920a-31d4-11ec-9241-aad8e48f01ff_story.html.
33. Valerie Strauss, "Imagine a Class with 25 kids—and All of Their Parents Insist on Telling the Teacher What to Teach," *Washington Post*, October 28, 2021, https://www.washingtonpost.com/education/2021/10/28/parental-rights-in-schools-untenable/.
34. Hilary Beaumont, "How Teachers and Librarians Are Subverting Book Bans in the US," Al Jazeera, April 7, 2023, https://www.aljazeera.com/news/2023/4/7/how-teachers-and-librarians-are-subverting-book-bans-in-the-us.
35. Lori Rozsa, "A Black Professor Defies DeSantis Law Restricting Lessons on Race," *Washington Post*, January 21, 2023, https://www.washingtonpost.com/nation/2023/01/21/florida-black-history-ron-desantis/.
36. Rozsa, "A Black Professor."
37. "Jan. 1, 1923: Rosewood Massacre," Zinn Education Project, n.d., https://www.zinnedproject.org/news/tdih/rosewood-massacre/.
38. Rozsa, "A Black Professor."
39. "Teach No Lies: Historian Marvin Dunn Takes on Ron DeSantis & Florida's Attack on Black History," *Democracy Now!*, August 18, 2023, https://www.democracynow.org/2023/8/18/florida_desantis_schools.
40. "The Rebellious Life of Mrs. Rosa Parks in Classrooms Nationwide," Zinn

Education Project, June 15, 2023, https://www.zinnedproject.org/news/rebellious-life-rosa-parks-teaching-stories/#:~:text=The%20town%20where%20I%20teach,I%20helped%20start%20Foundation%20451.

41. Beaumont, "How Teachers."

42. Kiara Alfonseca, "Florida Students Walk Out to Protest DeSantis Race Education Policies," ABC News, February 23, 2023, https://abcnews.go.com/US/florida-students-walkout-protest-desantis-race-education-policies/story?id=97417150.

43. Shira Moolten, "Threatened with Suspension, Plantation High School Student Leads Classmates on Walkout to Protest DeSantis," *South Florida Sun Sentinel*, February 25, 2023, https://www.sun-sentinel.com/2023/02/25/threatened-with-suspension-plantation-high-school-student-leads-classmates-on-walkout-to-protest-desantis.

44. Moolten, "Threatened with Suspension."

45. Asher Lehrer-Small, "ACLU Lawsuit Looks to Take Down Oklahoma's CRT Teaching Ban as Free Speech Violation," The 74, October 25, 2021, https://www.the74million.org/article/aclu-lawsuit-looks-to-take-down-oklahomas-crt-teaching-ban-as-free-speech-violation/.

46. Asher Lehrer-Small, "The ACLU's Fight against Classroom Censorship, State by State," The 74, https://www.the74million.org/article/the-aclus-fight-against-classroom-censorship-state-by-state/.

47. American Civil Liberties Union, "Virginia Obscenity Proceedings against Two Books," ACLU, June 22, 2022, https://www.aclu.org/cases/virginia-obscenity-proceedings-against-two-books.

48. ACLU, "Breaking: A Virginia Court Just Dismissed an Attempt to Use Baseless Obscenity Claims to Ban Two Books from Being Sold and Distributed in Bookstores and Libraries in State," X, August 30, 2022, 3:39 pm., https://X.com/ACLU/status/1564699395962142723.

49. Andrew Atterbury, "'Positively Dystopian': Florida Judge Blocks DeSantis' Anti-Woke Law for Colleges," *Politico*, November 17, 2022, https://www.politico.com/news/2022/11/17/florida-anti-woke-law-block-colleges-education-00069252.

50. Becky Sullivan, "With a Nod to '1984,' a Federal Judge Blocks Florida's Anti-'Woke' Law in Colleges," NPR, November 18, 2022, https://www.npr.org/2022/11/18/1137836712/college-university-florida-woke-desantis-1984.

51. Atterbury, "'Positively Dystopian.'"

52. "Black Studies in SPS," Seattle Public Schools, May 12, 2021, https://www.seattleschools.org/news/black-studies-in-sps/.

53. Eleanor J. Bader, "Amid Attacks from Right, Racial Justice Curricula Gain Momentum in Blue States," *Truthout*, April 29, 2023, https://truthout.org/articles/amid-attacks-from-right-racial-justice-curricula-gain-momentum-in-blue-states/.

54. Matt Dixon and Gary Fineout, "DeSantis Prepares for 2024 with

Second-Term Focus," *Politico*, January 3, 2023, https://www.politico.com/news/2023/01/03/desantis-2024-second-term-00076160.

55. Peter Greene, "Florida Wanted to Take Her Teaching License over a Black Lives Matter Flag. A Judge Just Said No," *Forbes*, June 13, 2024, https://www.forbes.com/sites/petergreene/2024/06/13/florida-wanted-to-take-her-teaching-license-over-a-black-lives-matter-flag-a-judge-just-said-no/.

56. "On the Anniversary of Brown v. Board, How Can We Defend Our Freedom to Learn?," Schott Foundation for Public Education, https://schottfoundation.org/the-latest/on-the-anniversary-of-brown-v-board-how-can-we-defend-our-freedom-to-learn/.

Chapter 5: The Radical Healing of Organized Remembering

Malcolm X, "If You Stick a Knife in My Back," YouTube, https://www.youtube.com/watch?v=XiSiHRNQlQo.

Judith Herman, *Trauma and Recovery: The Aftermath of Violence—from Domestic Abuse to Political Terror* (New York: Basic Books, 1997), 1.

1. Char Adams, "Here's What Black Students Have to Say about 'Critical Race Theory' Bans," NBC News, September 1, 2021, https://www.nbcnews.com/news/nbcblk/s-black-students-say-critical-race-theory-bans-rcna1862.

2. Shawn Ginwright, "The Future of Healing: Shifting from Trauma Informed Care to Healing Centered Engagement," *Medium*, May 31, 2018, https://ginwright.medium.com/the-future-of-healing-shifting-from-trauma-informed-care-to-healing-centered-engagement-634f557ce69c.

3. Resmaa Menakem, *My Grandmother's Hands: Racialized Trauma and the Pathway to Mending Our Hearts and Bodies* (Las Vegas, NV: Central Recovery Press, 2017), 258.

4. Herman, *Trauma and Recovery*, 1.

5. Jasmin Joseph, "Healing Generational Trauma," *Yes!*, February 16, 2022, https://www.yesmagazine.org/issue/personal-journeys/2022/02/16/black-indigenous-healing-generational-trauma.

6. "Hitler and the Armenian Genocide," Genocide Education Project, n.d., https://genocideeducation.org/background/hitler-and-the-armenian-genocide/.

7. Herman, *Trauma and Recovery*, 8.

8. Joyce King and Ellen E. Swartz, *Heritage Knowledge in the Curriculum: Retrieving an African Episteme* (New York: Routledge, 2018), xiv.

9. Eddie S. Glaude Jr., *Democracy in Black: How Race Still Enslaves the American Soul* (New York: Broadway Books, 2017), 47.

10. Jack Saul, *Collective Trauma, Collective Healing: Promoting Community Resilience in the Aftermath of Disaster* (New York: Routledge, 2022), 105.

11. Herman, *Trauma and Recovery*, 133.

12. Cynthia B. Dillard, *The Spirit of Our Work: Black Women Teachers (Re)member*

(Boston: Beacon Press, 2022), 16.

13. "'Autobiography of Elizabeth Sparks' (1937)." n.d. *Encyclopedia Virginia*, https://encyclopediavirginia.org/entries/autobiography-of-elizabeth-sparks-1937/.

14. Heather Andrea Williams, *Self-Taught: African American Education in Slavery and Freedom* (Chapel Hill, NC: The University of North Carolina Press, 2005), 20.

15. Meyer Weinberg, *A Chance to Learn: The History of Race and Education in the United States* (Long Beach, CA: The University Press California State University, Long Beach, 1995), 13.

16. Brian Jones, "The Struggle for Black Education," in *Education and Capitalism: Struggles for Learning and Liberation*, ed. Jeff Bale and Sarah Knopp (Chicago: Haymarket Books, 2012), 43.

17. William Loren Katz, *Breaking the Chains: African American Slave Resistance* (New York: Seven Stories Press, 2024).

18. Cierra Kaler-Jones, "When SEL Is Used as Another Form of Policing," *Medium*, accessed July 28, 2024, https://medium.com/@justschools/when-sel-is-used-as-another-form-of-policing-fa53cf85dce4.

19. Mark R. Warren, Letha Muhammad, and Emma Tynan, "Restorative Justice: Authentic Responses to the 'Pandemic-to-Prison Pipeline,'" Dignity in Schools Campaign, March 16, 2022, https://dignityinschools.org/restorative-justice-authentic-responses-to-the-pandemic-to-prison-pipeline/.

20. Communities for Just Schools Fund, "When SEL Is Used as Another Form of Policing," *Medium*, May 7, 2020, https://medium.com/@justschools/when-sel-is-used-as-another-form-of-policing-fa53cf85dce4.

21. Monique W. Morris, *Sing a Rhythm, Dance a Blues* (New York: New Press, 2022), 81.

22. "Teach Reconstruction Campaign," Zinn Education Project, n.d., https://www.zinnedproject.org/campaigns/teach-reconstruction/#lesson.

23. "The People's History They Don't Want Our Students to Know," Zinn Education Project, April 3, 2022, https://www.zinnedproject.org/news/peoples-history-dont-want-students-know/.

24. Laura Hibbard, "Garfield High School Students Walk Out of Class, Protest Statewide Budget Cuts to Education," *HuffPost*, December 1, 2011, https://www.huffpost.com/entry/garfield-high-school-students-walk-out-of-class_n_1123820; William Yardley, "Washington State Democrats Hope Voters Have New Attitude on Taxes," *New York Times*, December 2, 2011, https://www.nytimes.com/2011/12/03/us/washington-state-looks-at-tax-increases-to-fill-budget-gap.html.

25. "An Open Letter to the People of Washington State," *Students of Washington for Change*, November 30, 2011, https://studentsofwashington.blogspot.com/2011/11/to-whom-it-may-concern_30.html.

26. Washington State Supreme Court, *McCleary v. State of Washington*, No.

84362-7, October 6, 2017, Right to Education Project, https://www.right-to-education.org/sites/right-to-education.org/files/resource-attachments/RTE_McCleary_v_State_Supreme_Court_of_Washington_2017_E.

27. Dyan Watson, Jesse Hagopian, and Wayne Au, eds., *Teaching for Black Lives* (Milwaukee, WI: Rethinking Schools, 2018), 291.

28. Ursula Wolfe-Rocca and Christie Nold, "Opinion: Why the Narrative That Critical Race Theory 'Makes White Kids Feel Guilty' Is a Lie," *Hechinger Report*, August 2, 2022, https://hechingerreport.org/opinion-why-the-narrative-that-critical-race-theory-makes-white-kids-feel-guilty-is-a-lie/.

29. David Gillborn, Edward Taylor, and Gloria Ladson-Billings, eds., *Foundations of Critical Race Theory in Education* (New York: Taylor & Francis, 2009), 285.

30. Alan Hart, "Tom Paine and the 4th of July: The Worker Who Helped Make a Revolution," UE, June 29, 2012, https://www.ueunion.org/es/ue-news-feature/2012/tom-paine-and-the-4th-of-july-the-worker-who-helped-make-a-revolution.

31. Jacey Fortin and Giulia Heyward, "Teachers Tackle Black History Month, under New Restrictions," *New York Times*, February 12, 2022, https://www.nytimes.com/2022/02/12/us/black-history-month-schools-teachers.html.

32. Michele Bollinger (educator, DC Public Schools), interview with the author, December 19, 2022.

33. Bollinger, interview.

34. Erin Cox and Martin Weil, "Columbus Statue in Baltimore Toppled, Thrown in Inner Harbor," *Washington Post*, July 5, 2020, https://www.washingtonpost.com/local/columbus-statue-in-baltimore-apparently-toppled-thrown-in-inner-harbor/2020/07/04/c1a99de0-be66-11ea-bdaf-a129f921026f_story.html.

35. "Vikings Settled in North America in 1021AD, Study Says," BBC, October 21, 2021, https://www.bbc.com/news/world-us-canada-58996186.

36. Dylan Matthews, "Nine Reasons Christopher Columbus Was a Murderer, Tyrant, and Scoundrel," *Vox*, October 12, 2015, https://www.vox.com/2014/10/13/6957875/christopher-columbus-murderer-tyrant-scoundrel.

37. Erin Cox and Martin Weil, "Columbus Statue in Baltimore Toppled, Thrown in Inner Harbor," *Washington Post*, July 5, 2020, https://www.washingtonpost.com/local/columbus-statue-in-baltimore-apparently-toppled-thrown-in-inner-harbor/2020/07/04/c1a99de0-be66-11ea-bdaf-a129f921026f_story.html.

38. Abby Phillip, "Why Bree Newsome Took Down the Confederate Flag in S.C.: 'I Refuse to Be Ruled by Fear,'" *Washington Post*, June 29, 2015, https://www.washingtonpost.com/news/post-nation/wp/2015/06/29/why-bree-newsome-took-down-the-confederate-flag-in-s-c-i-refuse-to-be-ruled-by-fear/.

39. Clarence Lusane, *Twenty Dollars and Change: Harriet Tubman and the Ongoing Fight for Racial Justice and Democracy* (San Francisco: City Lights Books, 2022), 247.

40. Lottie Joiner, "Bree Newsome Reflects on Taking Down South Carolina's Confederate Flag Two Years Ago," *Vox*, June 27, 2017, https://www.vox.com/identities/2017/6/27/15880052/bree-newsome-south-carolinas-confederate-flag.

41. Michael Hines, *A Worthy Piece of Work: The Untold Story of Madeline Morgan and the Fight for Black History in Schools* (Boston, MA: Beacon Press, 2022), 163.

42. Marcia J. Watson-Vandiver and Greg Wiggan, *The Healing Power of Education: Afrocentric Pedagogy as a Tool for Restoration and Liberation* (New York: Teachers College Press, 2021), x.

43. Paulo Freire, *The Politics of Education: Culture, Power, and Liberation* (South Hadley, MA: Bergin & Garvey Publishers, 1985), 122.

44. bell hooks, *All about Love: New Visions* (New York: William Morrow, 2018).

45. "Justice Is What Love Looks Like in Public," Pride Foundation, February 28, 2017, https://pridefoundation.org/2017/02/justice-is-what-love-looks-like-in-public/.

46. Martin Luther King Jr., "Nonviolence: The Only Road to Freedom," *Ebony*, October 1966, 30.

47. Allyson Aleksey, "No End in Sight to Oakland Teachers' Strike," *San Francisco Examiner*, May 12, 2023, https://www.sfexaminer.com/news/no-agreement-on-table-as-oakland-teachers-continue-strike/article_6132327e-f0fe-11ed-aff9-b35c9fd6b042.html.

48. Jesse Hagopian, "Jesse Hagopian Talks with Gillian Russom: How Los Angeles Teachers Organized and What They Won," *Rethinking Schools* 34, no. 1 (Fall 2019), https://rethinkingschools.org/articles/jesse-hagopian-talks-with-gillian-russom-how-los-angeles-teachers-organized-and-what-they-won/.

49. bell hooks, *Teaching Critical Thinking* (New York: Routledge, 2010), 22.

50. Monique W. Morris, *Sing a Rhythm, Dance a Blues: Liberatory Education for Black and Brown Girls* (New York: New Press, 2022), 6–7.

51. Shirley Wade McLoughlin, *A Pedagogy of the Blues* (Leiden, Netherlands: Brill, 2019), 88–89.

52. hooks, *Teaching Critical Thinking*, 22.

53. Barbara Ransby, "Letter trom the Year 2071," *In These Times*, July 2021, https://inthesetimes.com/article/letter-from-ancestors-revolutionary-future.

Conclusion: Truth for Their Pencils and Pads

1.   Annie E. Casey Foundation, "Children in Poverty by Race and Ethnicity in United States," Kids Count Data Center, September 2023, https://datacenter.aecf.org/data/tables/44-children-in-poverty-by-race-and-ethnicity#detailed/1/any/false/2048,1729,37,871,870,573,869,36,868,867/10,11,9,12,1,185,13/324,323.

2.   Bryan Stevenson, *Just Mercy: A Story of Justice and Redemption* (New York:

One World, 2015), 15.

3. Derek W. Black and Axton Crolley, "Legacy of Jim Crow Still Affects Funding for Public Schools," University of South Carolina, April 19, 2022, https://www.sc.edu/uofsc/posts/2022/04/conversation-jim-crow.php.

4. "Desegregation and DC's Anacostia Neighborhood: Stories from the Community," Smithsonian, Our Shared Future: Reckoning with Our Racial Past, https://oursharedfuture.si.edu/stories/desegregation-and-dc-anacostia-neighborhood-stories-from-the-community.

5. Daniel Martinez HoSang, *A Wider Type of Freedom: How Struggles for Racial Justice Liberate Everyone* (Berkeley, CA: University of California Press, 2023), xiv.

6. Barbara Ransby, "Ron DeSantis's Attack on Black Studies Is Textbook Proto-Fascism," *Truthout*, January 28, 2023, https://truthout.org/articles/ron-desantiss-attack-on-black-studies-is-textbook-proto-fascism/.

7. Taifha Alexander, LaToya Baldwin Clark, Kyle Reinhard, and Noah Zatz, "Tracking the Attack on Critical Race Theory," *CRT Forward*, April 6, 2023, https://crtforward.law.ucla.edu/wp-content/uploads/2023/04/UCLA-Law_CRT-Report_Final.pdf.

8. "The 4 Demands," Black Lives Matter at School, accessed August 1, 2024, https://www.blacklivesmatteratschool.com/the-4-demands.html.

9. Keeanga-Yamahtta Taylor, ed., *How We Get Free: Black Feminism and the Combahee River Collective* (Chicago: Haymarket Books, 2017), 15.

10. Taylor, *How We Get Free*, 23.

11. James Whitfield, "Testimony: In the Crosshairs of Public Education's Enemies," *Facing South*, May 24, 2022, https://www.facingsouth.org/2022/05/testimony-crosshairs-public-educations-enemies.

12. Robin Santos Doak, *Phillis Wheatley: Slave and Poet* (Minneapolis: Compass Point Books, 2006), 66.

13. Chuck Reece, "Dr. Martin Luther King Jr.'s 'Beloved Community,'" GBP News, January 13, 2023, https://www.gpb.org/blogs/salvation-south/2023/01/13/dr-martin-luther-king-jrs-beloved-community.

14. "2022–2023 K–12 Social Studies Examples of Rejected Materials," Florida Department of Education, n.d., https://www.fldoe.org/academics/standards/instructional-materials/2223-k12-ss-examples.stml.

15. Walter Benjamin, "On the Concept of History," trans. Dennis Redmond, Marxists Internet Archive, 2005 [1940], https://www.marxists.org/reference/archive/benjamin/1940/history.htm.

INDEX

ABOUT THE AUTHOR

Jesse Hagopian has taught in public elementary, middle, and high schools for over twenty years. He is an editor for Rethinking Schools, serves on the Black Lives Matter at School steering committee, and is on the leadership team of the Zinn Education Project.

Jesse is the editor or coeditor of four books, including *More Than a Score: The New Uprising Against High Stakes Testing*, *Teaching for Black Lives*, *Black Lives Matter at School*, and *Teachers Unions and Social Justice*. Jesse's writing on education, politics, and social movements has appeared in *The Seattle Times*, *The Nation*, *The Progressive*, PBS News, *Word In Black*, *Truthout*, and *The Washington Post*. His website is www.IAmAnEducator.com, and you can follow him on X, @JesseDHagopian, or on Instagram, @JesseHagopian.